Disciplining Terror

How Experts Invented "Terrorism"

LISA STAMPNITZKY

CAMBRIDGE
UNIVERSITY PRESS

CAMBRIDGE
UNIVERSITY PRESS

University Printing House, Cambridge CB2 8BS, United Kingdom

Cambridge University Press is part of the University of Cambridge.

It furthers the University's mission by disseminating knowledge in the pursuit of
education, learning and research at the highest international levels of excellence.

www.cambridge.org
Information on this title: www.cambridge.org/9781107697348

© Lisa Stampnitzky 2013

First published 2013
First paperback edition 2014

A catalogue record for this publication is available from the British Library

Library of Congress Cataloguing in Publication data

Stampnitzky, Lisa.
    Disciplining terror : how experts invented "terrorism" / Lisa Stampnitzky.
        pages   cm.
    Includes bibliographical references.
    ISBN 978-1-107-02663-6 (Hardback)
    1. Terrorism.   2. Terrorism–Study and teaching–History.
3. Terrorism–Research–History.   I. Title.
    HV6431.S69 2013
    363.325–dc23

                                                        2012044908

ISBN 978-1-107-02663-6 Hardback
ISBN 978-1-107-69734-8 Paperback

*This book is dedicated to the memory of my father,
Michael Stampnitzky.*

Contents

Figures

Tables

Acknowledgments

As sociologists, and particularly as sociologists of knowledge, we know that intellectual work is not produced by the author alone but through connections with others. This book began as a PhD dissertation at Berkeley, where I was blessed with an extraordinary set of advisors. Ann Swidler had faith in this project from the very beginning, and her influence is present at every level, from the theoretical to the grammatical. Raka Ray has been a supportive and challenging advisor, and a model as both scholar and teacher. Jonathan Simon was a sharp reader and provided insightful commentary. Gil Eyal first steered me towards the study of experts as I was searching for a sociological entry point to the events of 9/11, and his generosity in remaining actively engaged with this project, even after leaving Berkeley, and his incisive comments have left an indelible imprint upon the manuscript. In addition, I had four excellent research assistants in Marisa Broudy, Christina Dawber, Evan Denerstein, and Shabnam Tai, who provided invaluable assistance with data entry and other tasks. As I completed the dissertation, from 2006 to 2008, I was welcomed as a visiting fellow at the Stanford University Center for International Security and Cooperation, where the faculty and fellows not only provided a crash course in security studies and international relations but were unfailingly interested in my work and willing to share their own research. Lynn Eden in particular has been a true mentor, providing incisive commentary, challenging questions, and secure faith in my work.

I am particularly indebted to the other institutions that have supported me and provided temporary intellectual and physical homes as this project took shape in its transition from dissertation to book, including the Robert Schuman Centre at the European University Institute, the Mershon Center for International Security Studies at The Ohio State University, the Institute for Science Innovation and Society at the University of Oxford, and the Charles Warren Center for Studies in American History at Harvard University. Colleagues at all these institutions, particularly Idalina Baptista, Will Davies, Sarah DeLange, Nadia Fadil, Stephanie Hofmann, Andy Jewett, Javier Lezaun, Gail McElroy, Linsey McGoey, John Mueller, Steve Rayner, Julie Reuben, Mark Solovey, Pascal Vennesson, and Jessica Wang, provided friendship, support, and advice; and staff people at each of these institutions, particularly Elsa Tranter, Linda Flory, Carmen Privat-Gilman, and Belinda White at Berkeley and Larissa Kennedy and Arthur Patton-Hock at Harvard, helped smooth the process.

Parts of this project were presented, and helpful commentary was received, at workshops and conferences at the University of Copenhagen, Kings College London, the University of Cambridge, the American Sociological Association, the International Sociological Association, and the Society for Social Studies of Science. This project also benefited from discussion with many others along the way, including Tarak Barkawi, Rina Bliss, Christian Bueger, Stephen Collier, John R. Hall, Richard Jackson, Jerry Karabel, Monika Krause, Richard Lachmann, Andrew Lakoff, Luis Lobo-Guerrero, Jon Norman, Charles Perrow, Rebecca Slayton, Meg Stalcup, and Trine Villumsen. I am also indebted to Carrie Parkinson and John Haslam at Cambridge University Press, as well as to several anonymous reviewers, who provided insightful feedback and advice. My lovely and amazing dissertation group – Elizabeth Popp Berman, Hwa-Jen Liu, Teresa Sharpe, and Youyenn Teo – provided support both personal and intellectual, and Gretchen Purser and Greggor Mattson provided encouragement and timely feedback on the entire manuscript.

A number of organizations graciously allowed me to attend events and speak to their staff and researchers, and otherwise assisted with this project. I attended conferences at the START Center at the University of Maryland, at the John Jay College Center on Terrorism, and at the Institute on Global Conflict and Cooperation at the University of California, San Diego. Lt. Colonel Joe Felter and colleagues from the Combating Terrorism Center at West Point spoke with me on several occasions about their ongoing projects. Karen Colvard shared the history of the Harry Frank Guggenheim Foundation's work on terrorism, and provided a number of reports from their library. The staff at the University of California, Berkeley, interlibrary loan office reliably sought out my often peculiar requests. Archivists at the Library of Congress and the Hoover Institution archives provided assistance on my visits there. At RAND, Vivian Arterbery and Ann Horn guided me through the archives, while Karen Treverton shared insights into the history of the RAND terrorism database. Financial support was provided by the National Science Foundation (Doctoral Dissertation Improvement Grant no. SES-0526144), the University of California Institute on Global Conflict and Cooperation, the Charlotte W. Newcombe Foundation, and the University of California, Berkeley, Graduate Division and Department of Sociology.

Most of all, I am indebted to the many experts who generously shared their time and thoughts about the field of terrorism studies, including Daniel Benjamin, Nora Bensahel, Peter Bergen, Dan Byman, Joseph Cirincione, Martha Crenshaw, Sara Daly, Bruce Hoffman, Brian Jenkins, Arie Kruglanski, Walter Laqueur, Gary LaFree, David Kilcullen, Michael Kraft, Clark McCauley, Brigitte Nacos, Timothy Naftali, Robert Pape, Ami Pedahzur, Jerrold Post, William Rosenau, Marc Sageman, Jake Shapiro, Jessica Stern, Charles Strozier, and Karen Von Hippel, along with a number of others who spoke off the record. While I do not expect that they will agree with all my conclusions, I hope they will find that I have faithfully represented their views.

I   Introduction

The aide said that guys like me were "in what we call the reality-based community... That's not the way the world really works anymore," he continued. "We're an empire now, and when we act, we create our own reality. And while you're studying that reality – judiciously, as you will – we'll act again, creating other new realities, which you can study too, and that's how things will sort out. We're history's actors...and you, all of you, will be left to just study what we do."[1]

Men make their own history, but they do not make it as they please; they do not make it under self-selected circumstances, but under circumstances existing already, given and transmitted from the past.[2]

On August 3, 1961, Leon Bearden and his sixteen-year-old son hijacked a Continental Airlines Boeing 707 (*New York Times* 1961a). During the nine-hour standoff, Bearden, a former convict, demanded that the pilot fly to Cuba, later reporting that he had hoped to sell the plane to Fidel Castro (*New York Times* 1961d). The plot, which *The New York Times* would subsequently describe as a "wild adventure" (*New York Times* 1961b), was foiled when the pilot told Bearden he would need to stop in El Paso to refuel, where Federal Bureau of Investigation (FBI) and border agents shot out the tires of the plane and one of its engines (*New York Times* 1961c). The Beardens were tried and convicted of federal charges of kidnapping and of transporting a stolen aircraft across a state line – charges for which Bearden the elder was sentenced to life in prison, while his son was sentenced to a correctional facility until the age of twenty-one (*New York Times* 1961d). The convictions were later reversed, however, leaving the Beardens liable only for a charge of "obstruction of international commerce" (*New York Times* 1963). Congress subsequently acted to make hijacking a crime subject to life imprisonment if "deadly or dangerous" weapons

---

[1] Ron Suskind (2004).
[2] Karl Marx (1994 [1852]).

were used, and security measures at airports and on airplanes were increased. The overall response was moderated, though, due to antici-pated resistance from passengers, and to a desire "to avoid over-dramatizing hijacking" (*New York Times* 1961b). As Federal Aviation Administration (FAA) director Najeeb A. Halaby argued at the time, "There are in every country many discontented, maladjusted people who may get the wrong idea" (*New York Times* 1961b).

The limited extent and relatively subdued nature of the res-ponse to the Bearden hijackings, "the most dramatic" of a series of such events according to *The New York Times* (1964), pale when compared to more recent incidents. Airline hijackings were not uncommon in the late 1950s and early 1960s,[3] many committed by Americans hoping to defect to Cuba, or, conversely, Cubans trying to make their way to the United States (see, for example, *New York Times* (1965a, 1965b)). According to FAA statistics, there were seventy-nine hijackings worldwide between 1930 and 1967 (Guelke 1995: 49), with *Penthouse* magazine reporting eighty-five US planes hijacked to Cuba between 1961 and 1973.[4] Yet these were not con-sidered to be acts of terrorism. As one account of this period put it, "These attacks were not generally or consistently called terrorism; nor were those who committed them generally or consistently called terrorists"; rather, "they were bandits, rebels, guerrillas, or, later, urban guerrillas, revolutionaries, or insurgents" (Tucker 1997: 2). As late as 1968 the United States generally treated hijacking, or "air piracy," as it was sometimes called, as a routine domestic criminal matter (Naftali 2005: 21).

---

[3] According to a 1973 report from the President's Science Advisory Committee's (PSAC's) subpanel on hijacking, the "earliest generally recognized hijacking of an aircraft occurred in 1930 in Peru," but "this event, however, was generally unheralded in the world's press at the time of its occurrence." National Archives and Records Administration (NARA), Nixon papers, Nixon presidential materials project (NPMP), White House special files (WHSF), staff member and office files, Richard C. Tufaro, box 2, folder "Terrorism 3," "Report of the PSAC's subpanel on hijacking," March 1973.

[4] Photocopy of article from *Penthouse* magazine, April 1973, "Unhappy landings," Martin Schram and John Wallach, NARA, Nixon papers.

By the middle of the 1970s, however, this relatively complacent approach had been displaced by a new and urgent problem: "terrorism."[5] By the end of the decade bombings, hijackings, kidnappings, and hostage-takings were melded together, conceptualized not simply as tactics but as identifying activities, and joined to a new and highly threatening sort of actor: the "terrorist." As the Beardens' story illustrates, neither hostage-taking nor hijacking were new, but the hijackings of the 1950s and 1960s had not caused the sort of panicked response that "terrorism" would call forth. Yet only a few years later, hijackings would come to be seen as *the* archetypal terrorist event. This book tells the story of how the phenomenon of political violence was transformed into "terrorism," and the effects this would have for the creation of expert knowledge, public understanding, and policy in the United States.[6]

Since 9/11 Americans have been told that terrorists are pathological evildoers, beyond our comprehension, and that our response, in the form of the "war on terror," will be (in the words of George W. Bush) "a very long struggle against evil." Yet, before the 1970s, the acts we now understand as "terrorism" were generally considered the work of rational, sometimes even honorable, actors. The ways in which we create knowledge about and respond to terrorism are neither post-9/11 inventions nor ahistorical constants. Rather, terrorism is a problem with a history, and this history matters for the ways we think about it, the questions we ask, and the possible remedies we apply, as well as the questions that we don't ask – those silences that may even go unobserved.

---

[5] As Joseba Zulaika and William Douglass put it, "The year 1972 marked a major transition in the framing of the media's treatment of political violence. Events that previously were covered under the rubrics of assassination, bombing, torture, repression, massacre, etc., were now classified as 'terrorism'" (Zulaika and Douglass 1996).

[6] Although I examine the production of expertise through international networks, the reader should keep in mind that my goal was to trace how the meanings of terrorism took shape in the particular US context, and that my conclusions are not necessarily applicable elsewhere.

"Terrorism" has become the dominant framework for understanding illegitimate political violence. But despite its centrality in contemporary political discourse, terrorism is not a stable or fixed category. Rather, it is through constant conflicts over what is or is not "terrorism" that we determine which sorts of violence are, and are not, illegitimate. This book traces the creation of "terrorism" as a problem, and the corresponding emergence of a new set of "terrorism experts" who aimed to shape this seemingly uncontrollable problem into an object of rational knowledge. By "rational," I am referring to what Max Weber called formal, or instrumental, rationality: the establishment of routines of action that increase predictability, and that connect actions to desired goals. The problem of "rationality" in the discourse on terrorism is tied up with the dual meaning of "reason": to think through, and to provide accounts for. The refusal to consider terrorist attacks, and terrorists themselves, as rational is the refusal to consider that those we label "terrorist" might have reasons, or rational explanations, for their actions (whether we judge these to be worthy or not). Rather than simply judge terrorists' reasons as unworthy, the terrorism discourse places such actions outside the realm of moral consideration entirely.[7] In other words, the terrorism discourse refuses to grant terrorism and terrorists the consideration of whether or not such actions may be justifiable – for, if they are justifiable, they are no longer "terrorism."

As illustrated by the familiar cliché that "one man's terrorist is another man's freedom fighter," terrorism is a highly contested concept. And this "problem of definition" is not just something that afflicts popular or political discourse. Terrorism experts themselves have been unable to settle upon a definition. As Brian Jenkins, head of terrorism research at the think tank RAND, told me in an interview,

---

[7] As Judith Butler has written of one prominent analyst: "For [Michael] Walzer, 'terrorist violence' falls outside the parameters of both justified and unjustified violence [and] so-called 'terrorist' violence, as he conceives it, falls outside of the purview of this debate... The form of violence his scheme puts outside of reflection and debate is patently unreasonable and non-debatable" (Butler 2010: 153–4).

"Definitional debates are the great Bermuda Triangle of terrorism research. I've seen entire conferences go off into definitional debates, never to be heard from again." A 1988 survey of the literature found over 100 different definitions in use among terrorism researchers (Schmid and Jongman 1988). Similarly, an observer at a mid-1980s Department of Defense symposium reported that there were "almost as many definitions as there were speakers" (Slater and Stohl 1988: 3), and a 2001 article described a "perverse situation where a great number of scholars are studying a phenomenon, the essence of which they have [by now] simply agreed to disagree upon" (Brannan, Esler, and Strindberg 2001: 11).

Rather than trying to determine the one true meaning of "terrorism," this book investigates how the concept of "terrorism" is used empirically in the world. In other words, it analyzes how the concept of terrorism is socially constructed. It is often assumed that demonstrating that some phenomenon is socially constructed is akin to an unveiling, pulling back the mask to show the true face underneath, and thus causing it to lose its power over us. But to show that something is constructed is not to negate its reality. As W. I. Thomas wrote in 1929, "If men define situations as real, they are real in their consequences" (Thomas and Thomas 1929: 572). And, as Bruno Latour has written, buildings are also constructed – and to analyze their structure is not to make them fall down but, rather, the opposite: to investigate how they were put together, and ask what the elements are that make for a strong and lasting construction, as opposed to a weak and flimsy one (Latour 2005). In the social world, this means asking how problems, concepts, and institutions came to be, and what makes them powerful. And it is this question that drives this study: how an object of knowledge such as "terrorism" is able to hold together and remain meaningful despite its contradictions and instability. I show not just that terrorism is socially constructed, but *how* the problem came to take shape as it did (as suggested by Tilly 2004 and Zelizer 2006: 531).

I analyze the emergence of "terrorism" as the outcome of a confluence of new events, new experts, and new practices of knowledge and governance. In so doing, I draw upon William Sewell's (1996: 844) characterization of "events" as not just happenings but processes through which incidents transform structures of meaning. Likewise, I use Michel Foucault's (2003) notion of "eventalization," in which incidents are most likely to take on historical significance as "events" when they disrupt and destabilize prior modes of understanding the world. "Eventalization" is, in turn, linked to Foucault's concept of problematization, described as an historical process resulting in the diagnosis of a new problem subject to certain forms of knowledge. This is not simply the relabeling of a prior phenomenon but a concrete historical development that makes a problem "subject to thought," and requiring action (Foucault 1987, 1991).

Foucault's focus on the actions required by experts has been fruitfully explored by Latour, a sociologist of science, who describes the role of "actor-networks" that include both expert-actors and the objects that are being made knowable (Latour 1987, 1993 [1991]). Latour speaks of the ways that experts "enroll" problems into particular knowledge projects. This metaphor highlights the ways in which experts actively work to bring a problem under their purview. Previous ways of describing this process often used the metaphor of frames that experts could lay over a pre-existing and passive problem. But the problem with the framing metaphor is that it can't account for why one frame succeeds while others fail. The answer to this question, according to Latour, is that the problem itself must be attributed explanatory power and is not simply a function of the interests, resources, and power of the human actors involved. In other words, the thing to be known is not merely an inert object but an active participant in this process, which may accept some ways of knowledge about it and reject others. Expert knowledge works only when two moving targets – the definition of the problem and the solution – can be aligned and held in place long enough to make sense to others. Enrollment is a process in which the "problem" itself and the techniques of knowledge must fit together in order to produce a new object (Callon 1986; Latour 1987).

The book proceeds by analyzing how the problem of "terrorism" first emerged, and how it subsequently took shape via conflicts over the production of knowledge about it. "Terrorism" first took shape in the 1970s, when it emerged out of, and differentiated from, the discourse on insurgency. In that decade both the concept of "terrorism" and a community of terrorism experts coalesced. But neither the problem of "terrorism" nor the field of terrorism expertise has been fully "disciplined." This manifests itself in the persistent "problem of definition," an ongoing series of conflicts over what terrorism is, and is not. In the 1980s a new set of actors promoted the idea that terrorism was organized by the Soviet Union, rendering legal and criminal approaches irrelevant, and bringing about a new framing of counterterrorism as war. And in the 1990s a new framework emerged that solidified the terrorism discourse around the notion that terrorists were becoming ever more dangerous and irrational, raising the specter of terrorist "weapons of mass destruction" (WMDs). This new framework, I argue, set the stage for the pre-emptive war on terror that would emerge in 2001.

The study of terrorism has been cursed by an ongoing inability to settle upon a stable meaning, and this problem of definition has come to hinge around three core axes: politicization, rationality, and morality.[8] Throughout the entire period I examine, experts and policymakers have been unable to "rationalize" management of the terrorism problem. And terrorism experts' "failure" to develop into a profession or a discipline has manifested itself in the continual presence of "self-proclaimed" experts in arenas ranging from congressional hearings and the nightly news to the scholarly realm of conferences and publications.

---

[8] Struggles over the shifting terrain of the political and the apolitical, and the rational and the irrational, and the relation of morality to epistemology are not a phenomenon unique to the problem of terrorism and terrorism expertise. Claims to politicization and neutrality are a common feature of expertise and public discourse. One need think only of recent public debates on such topics as global warming, genetically modified crops, sex education, and reproductive rights to realize the widespread role of claims and counterclaims to neutrality, bias, and the politicization of knowledge in public controversies (Mooney 2005).

An ongoing conflict has centered on the question of whether terrorism experts are politically biased. Rather than seeking to answer this question, this book asks what these debates over politicization can themselves tell us about the field of terrorism studies and the production of expertise. I argue that this discourse of politicization does not merely reflect the fact that terrorism is a controversial subject, but is also part of an ongoing process in which struggles over the nature of "politicized" and "apolitical" knowledge themselves structure the production of terrorism experts and expertise. In arguing over whether particular analyses of terrorism are biased (or not), analysts not only aim to establish their own positions as experts but also construct "terrorism" as one of the "domains of objects about which true or false statements can be made" (Foucault 1987: 97). When terrorism experts level charges of politicized knowledge against each other, they are attempting to manage both the field of expertise and the proper definition of terrorism itself.

These struggles over politicization, morality, and rationality are similar to Bourdieusian classification struggles, in which claims to establish certain types of knowledge as "political" and "apolitical" are part of an ongoing battle for credibility among different actors in and about the field of terrorism expertise (Bourdieu 1988 [1984], 1996 [1992]). This is particularly true insofar as this opposition of "politicization" and "neutrality" is not just an attempt to *describe* the field of terrorism expertise but also constitutes part of an active process through which claims to authority, and credible positions from which to speak, are established. In other words, it is partly through these conflicts over politicization that spaces and positions of knowledge production are produced.

Discourse about the inherent immorality of terrorism has centrally shaped the possibilities for the creation of both knowledge about terrorism and terrorism experts themselves. I show that, as it took shape, the concept of terrorism became inherently associated with a moral judgment about the acts that we place in that category: terrorism *is* unacceptable violence. And, while experts have repeatedly attempted to "purify" the concept of this moral character, aiming to create a morally neutral concept that can be used to analyze violence scientifically in a neutral manner, these projects have been continually forestalled. This vacillating process, through which the concept of terrorism is alternately "purified" of, and then reinvested with, political and moral content, has been central to the construction of the concept and of expertise about it.

Although the terms "terror" and "terrorism" were in use before the 1970s, earlier uses of these terms were just as, if not more, likely to refer to *institutional* or *state* violence as to the sort of oppositional activity we associate it with today. Writers on political violence during the 1960s classified "terror/terrorism" as largely an attribute of states and political systems, and only secondarily of revolutionary groups (Walter 1964). The state itself was seen to engage in "enforcement terror," which was differentiated from insurgent violence (Thornton 1964). The new framework of "terrorism" that emerged over the course of the 1970s, 1980s, and 1990s, however, would recast such incidents as the acts of pathological, irrational actors, precluding its application to the actions of states or legitimate institutions. "Terrorism" emerged from this transformation as an inherently problematic concept – undefinable, infused with moral absolutism, and deeply politicized – leading to persistent difficulties for those who would create rational knowledge about it.

PREVIOUS WORK ON TERRORISM AND TERRORISM EXPERTISE

Despite the centrality of terrorism in contemporary political discourse, there have been few empirical studies of terrorism experts. A number of studies have analyzed popular and expert discourses on terrorism, but these works have generally failed to link discursive analysis to an empirical analysis of the production of expertise.[9]

---

[9] See Burnett and Whyte (2005), Lustick (2006), Mueller (2006), and Ross (2004) for some moves in this direction, however, while Wagner-Pacifici (1986,1995) has written extensively on the functioning of terrorism discourse in particular contexts.

A few recent authors have presented more nuanced views of terrorism expertise that analyze the role of experts and their specific interests as differentiated from the state. John Mueller (2006) focuses on the interests of experts and politicians to account for the persistence of a "terrorism industry," and Ian Lustick (2006) suggests that the "war on terror" may have become a self-perpetuating phenomenon, generating incentives for its own continuation. And more recently a "critical terrorism studies" movement has emerged to critique existing research on terrorism and its political effects. Richard Jackson, founding editor of the new journal *Critical Studies on Terrorism*, asserts that terrorism discourse "is at the same time a highly complex and intertwined set of narratives and rhetorical strategies that aims to reinforce the authority of the state and reify its disciplinary practices" (Jackson 2005: 178).

It would be easy, but misleading, to see the rise of terrorism expertise as simply a response to an increase in political violence. This simplistic empirical approach neglects the reflexive relationship between experts and their objects of knowledge. Others have suggested that we view terrorism expertise as a product of political propaganda by governments seeking to demonize their enemies and draw attention away from their own use of violence. But this "critical" approach (see, for example, Chomsky 2001; Herman and O'Sullivan 1989), which argues that terrorism experts constitute an "industry," funded and organized by the state and other elite interests, neglects the agency and interests of the experts themselves, and the ways in which these interests may either harmonize or clash with those of the state, the media, and the "terrorists" themselves. Terrorism experts have been more independent of the state and more divided among themselves than these theories can explain. Furthermore, these approaches cannot account for shifts in the ways that terrorism has been constituted as an object of knowledge, nor for why particular sorts of experts have been highly influential, while others have lost credibility and other specialists with seemingly relevant knowledge have stayed absent from the fray. Perhaps most crucially, to the extent that the state does influence the production of terrorism expertise, this approach is unable to explain adequately how or why it is able to exert such influence.

TERRORISM EXPERTISE AS A LIMINAL FIELD

As an empirical study of the production of terrorism expertise, this book draws upon a long tradition in the sociology of culture that aims to connect the conditions of cultural production with the form and content of cultural products (Becker 1982; Bourdieu 1993 [1983]; Crane 1976; Peterson 1976; Peterson and Anand 2004). This project also speaks to a key question at the intersection of culture and politics, that of how we identify and understand social and political problems, and how such problems are socially constructed, such as when they arise, command attention, or lose salience (see, for example, Edelman 1988; Gusfield 1981; Jacobs 1996; Nelson 1984). Most centrally, however, this book engages with the sociological literature on the production of science and expert knowledge, and its central concepts of discipline, profession, and "field."

A "field" may be understood as "a field of forces within which the agents occupy positions that statistically determine the positions they take with respect to the field, these position-takings being aimed either at conserving or transforming the structure of relations that is constitutive of that field" (Bourdieu 2005: 30).[10] The field concept has proved immensely useful for understanding social action as a set of strategic relations; and particularly useful for analyzing arenas in which we would like to understand both social actors and their products.

This book is not a simple application of Bourdieusian field theory, however, which is primarily useful for understanding relations within a particular field. Sites of action that cross multiple institutional fields, or that operate on the boundaries of fields, are apt to

---

[10] See also Bourdieu (1993 [1983]), Fligstein (2001), Fligstein and McAdam (2012), Martin (2003), and Ringer (1990).

appear puzzling or hard to understand within this framework.[11] The production of terrorism expertise actually occupies a space that straddles several "fields." It is not a bounded space of its own with established boundaries and forms of "capital." Indeed, one of the key "classificatory struggles" under contention is that of whether the production of objective knowledge about terrorism is possible at all.

Similarly, the literature on expertise stresses the importance of institutionalization, the process by which disciplines coalesce into recognizable forms such as academic departments and professional organizations in order to establish control over both the definition of their particular problem and the production and certification of legitimate experts (Abbott 1988; Bourdieu 1996 [1992], 2005; Gieryn 1983; Larson 1977). The archetypal case here is medicine, with its highly structured training and certification processes, collective ethical self-regulation, and monopolistic control over who may practice, backed by the power of the state. This focus on institutionalization is illustrated perhaps most starkly by Scott Frickel and Neil Gross (2005), who argue that "intellectual movements" are driven to institutionalize by carving out a settled space within the structure of disciplines, and predict that intellectual movements that fail to do so will fade away and die. Much of this work draws on a Bourdieusian conception of the field of cultural production, in which mature cultural fields are characterized by highly regulated boundaries (similar to the notion of "closure" in the study of professions), and sufficient relative autonomy that they have a distinct logic shaping relations of production and among producers (Bourdieu 2005: 33).

Yet terrorism experts have never consolidated control over the production of either experts or knowledge. New "self-proclaimed" experts constantly emerge, no licensing body exists to certify "proper" expertise, and there is no agreement among terrorism experts

---

[11] While many scholars have tended to apply the concept of "field" to almost everything, I retain Bourdieu's original meaning that the concept indicates particularly structured social space, with features such as defined boundaries and a distinct form of value, or "capital," over which actors in the field struggle.

about what constitutes useful knowledge. In sociological terms, the boundaries of the field are weak and permeable. There is little regulation of who may become an expert, and the key audience for terrorism expertise is not an ideal-typical scientific community of other terrorism experts but, rather, the public and the state.

If sociological work on professions and intellectuals has tended to conceptualize the world in terms of separate, bounded spheres, where might we turn for an understanding of intellectual production as a more intersectional arena? I suggest that the case of terrorism expertise may, in fact, be only one of many examples of the organized production of expertise in liminal spaces, a set of cases that have largely been neglected in favor of a focus on more strictly institutionalized sites of knowledge production. While sociological work on social and symbolic boundaries has begun to conceptualize boundary spaces as potential sites of hybridization and creativity, sociological studies of science and the professions have mostly persisted in focusing on processes of boundary construction and defense, rather than viewing the boundary itself as a potentially productive site (Lamont and Molnar 2002). I situate my conceptualization of terrorism studies in relation to recent work that focuses on irregular or interstitial fields (Bliss 2012; Eyal 2002, 2006; Eyal and Bucholtz 2010; Frickel 2004; Medvetz 2012; Panofsky 2006).

Rather than a purely political or analytical concept, expert discourse on "terrorism" must be understood as operating at the contested boundary between politics and science, between academic expertise and the state. And this has had significant consequences for the sorts of expert discourses that tend to be produced and disseminated. Those who would address terrorism as a rational object, subject to scientific analysis and manipulation, produce a discourse that they are unable to control, and such attempts at scientific discourse are continually hybridized by the moral discourse of the public sphere, in which terrorism is conceived as a problem of evil and pathology.

STUDYING TERRORISM EXPERTS

Studying a phenomenon such as terrorism expertise presents a number of methodological challenges. My research does not aim to be the arbiter of what constitutes legitimate terrorism expertise, or to define terrorism a priori, but, rather, to follow empirically how questions such as "Who is an expert?" are resolved. In other words, I do not begin by drawing boundaries around the field I study; rather, I observe the very construction of that field and its boundaries.

This means that collecting suitable data for my research has been tricky. There were few prior studies of terrorism expertise, and terrorism expertise has not been organized as a typical academic discipline but, rather, as an interstitial arena that crosses multiple institutional and organizational boundaries, making it difficult to know when I had mapped all corners of the field.[12] Additionally, because "terrorism" and terrorism expertise are relatively new, and constantly changing, phenomena, an approach sensitive to change over time was required. I dealt with these challenges by triangulating multiple types and sources of data, including archival research; an original database of sponsors, participants, and major themes at 150 major terrorism conferences; archival and published textual sources; and interviews with university-, think-tank-, and government-based experts.

I used reports from conferences on terrorism to trace the development of the field. Conferences were, and still are, one of the primary modes of communication among those who consider themselves terrorism experts, and many of these conferences were attended not just by terrorism experts but also by representatives from government and other counterterrorism practitioners, making these events forums for the transmission of knowledge between different sectors (Reid 1983: 24–5). Conference records also provide a time-sensitive window into changing approaches and participants in the study of terrorism, and

---

[12] Note, however, that the delineation of the boundaries of a field is a methodological problem even in the study of more normative "fields" (Bourdieu and Wacquant 1992).

are thus a useful source for identifying changes over time, as opposed to more formal modes of publication, which are often subject to delays in production.

I also analyzed published conference proceedings, reports issued by sponsoring organizations, and materials such as announcements and programs of events. From these, I compiled an original data set that includes biographical data on over 2,000 individuals who participated in 150 conferences held between 1972 and 2002. My goal in compiling this data set was to include all terrorism conferences held in the United States or with significant US participation during this period. I cross-checked the completeness of this data set against journal articles and other contemporaneous materials for mentions of events that might not have resulted in published proceedings, and also against the recollections of interviewees.

To flesh out this history further, I consulted archival materials such as records from government committees and the personal papers of key experts, including documents from the Library of Congress, the Hoover Institution, the National Security Archive, and the archives of the RAND Corporation. I also examined secondary textual sources on the history of American terrorism expertise from the 1970s to the present day. These include review essays, evaluations of the field published in journals and collections of conference papers, and introductory essays in edited volumes. These documented the evolution of experts' assessments of the field over time.

There are three core journals in the area of terrorism research that can be used to document the changing nature of the substantive content of research, and as indicators of insiders' views of the development of the field over time (Gordon 2004a; Reid 1992): *Terrorism: An International Journal/Studies in Conflict and Terrorism*[13] (published 1978–present); *TVI (Terrorism, Violence, Insurgency) Journal* (published 1979–1999); and *Terrorism and Political Violence*

---

[13] *Terrorism* merged with the journal *Conflict* in 1992 and changed its name to *Studies in Conflict and Terrorism*.

(published 1989–present). My analysis focused especially on commentary pieces and review articles in which active researchers present their views of the current state of the field, editors' introductions, evaluations of the current state of research, and literature reviews. While some of the accounts found in such "first-order" histories of the field tend to assume that the rise of a specialty in terrorism expertise was a direct response to events (such as Laqueur 1999), and thus do not see the question of expertise itself as in need of explanation, some works of particular note include Alex Schmid's research, including his surveys of experts (Schmid 1993; Schmid and Jongman 1988).[14] I draw on these works as primary data, providing first-order accounts of the field.

In addition to these written sources, I conducted thirty-two semi-structured interviews with current and former researchers in the field, focusing on individual career histories and views of the field, including interviewees' judgments of what constitutes useful and legitimate knowledge. I recruited interviewees who were prominent in the development of the field, basing my judgments on conference presentations, journal articles and book publications, and the results of an earlier survey in which experts ranked others in their field (Schmid and Jongman 1988). I selected a mix of experts based at universities, think tanks, in government, and in the media, ensuring representation of both early and more recent entrants. At the conclusion of each interview, I also asked each respondent to recommend others whom I might talk to. Interviews generally lasted between forty-five minutes and one hour, and respondents were given the option of speaking anonymously or for attribution, with most choosing the latter. I also obtained transcripts from a series of eleven interviews conducted in the early 1980s by a student at the Claremont Graduate School (Hoffman 1984). Additionally, I attended several conferences on terrorism as an observer, and was a fellow in residence

[14] See also Ranstorp (2007), Silke (2004b), and Zulaika and Douglass (1996), along with Crelinsten (1989a, 1989b), Crelinsten and Schmid (1993), Gordon (1995, 1996, 1997, 1998, 2001, 2004a, 2004b, 2005), Reid (1983, 1992, 1993, 1997), Reid *et al.* (2004), and Sproat (1996).

at Stanford University's Center for International Security and Cooperation from 2006 to 2008, where I attended talks, meetings, and seminars with researchers on terrorism. At many of these events I was fortunate to have informal or off-the-record conversations with academics, think tank researchers, consultants, and current and former military personnel.

CHAPTER OUTLINE

Chapters 2 and 3 describe how the problem of terrorism first took shape, while Chapters 4, 5, and 6 focus on the shifting modes of governance through which the problem has been managed. Chapter 7 focuses on the emergence of a new pre-emptive logic in the post-9/11 war on terror, and analyzes how the historical analysis presented in the book helps us to understand these forms of discourse and governance that emerged in the wake of the attacks. Chapter 8 focuses on changes in the terrorism field of expertise after 9/11, and the conclusion highlights general implications for future research into knowledge and expertise.

Chapter 2, "The invention of terrorism and the rise of the terrorism expert," identifies how terrorism first came to be identified as a new and distinct sort of problem, and how there came to be an associated arena of terrorism expertise. I establish that it was only in the early 1970s that "terrorism" was diagnosed as a specific social problem associated with actors known as "terrorists." The chapter describes how events, actors, and projects formed new networks to create "terrorism" as a new object in the 1970s, illustrating that this was not just a discursive "construction" but the outcome of concrete events and relationships.

Chapter 3, "From insurgents to terrorists: experts, rational knowledge, and irrational subjects," analyzes how the concept of terrorism, and the role of the terrorism expert, were, from the beginning, intertwined with notions of morality, rationality, and politics, in ways that would deeply complicate ongoing relations between knowledge and policy. This chapter takes an in-depth look at how experts' very object of study took shape over the course of the 1970s. Expert discourses on bombings, kidnappings, and hijackings shifted from a framework organized around "insurgency" to one organized around the concept of "terrorism" – a shift that fundamentally transformed both understandings of political violence and the scope of possibilities for expert analysis of the phenomenon. Although the events they deal with may look similar, counterinsurgency and counterterrorism differ in their conceptualization of the problem, its causes, and the potential responses. While the discourse of counterinsurgency was based upon a mode of knowledge production in which moral, political, and rational evaluations of insurgents and insurgency were (at least in theory) separable from expert analyses, in the new discourse of "terrorism" the morality, politicality, and rationality of political violence were strongly intertwined with the production and evaluation of experts and expertise. Further, the nature of the relation between knowledge, experts, and the state shifted significantly with this reconceptualization, and this has led to persistent difficulties for the production of rational knowledge about political violence.

Chapter 4, "Disasters, diplomats, and databases: rationalization and its discontents," focuses on the concrete techniques of knowledge through which experts sought to make "terrorism" knowable and governable in the 1970s. I identify three key modes of analysis through which experts tried to enroll terrorism into knowledge projects and thus make it rationally understandable: legal rationality/ diplomacy, risk management/calculability, and crisis management/ routinization. Each sought to fit terrorism into an existing framework of managing social problems, and each not only implied a different understanding of terrorism as a problem, but also suggested a different set of strategies through which the problem might be managed. As the problem of terrorism took shape over the course of the 1970s, however, it resisted such rationalizing logics, and no single approach was able to "capture" successfully the management of the terrorism problem. Consequently, as I show in the next chapters, these logics were superseded by new modes of governance in the 1980s and 1990s.

Chapter 5, "'Terrorism fever': the first war on terror and the politicization of expertise," tells the story of how counterterrorism became a "war" in the 1980s. Claire Sterling, an American journalist based in Italy, argued that international terrorism was organized behind the scenes by the Soviet Union. Upon the inauguration of Ronald Reagan as president in 1981, his Secretary of State declared that "international terrorism will take the place of human rights" in the administration's foreign policy. This aligned terrorism as part of the Cold War, shifting its governance of terrorism from the focus on international law and crisis management in the 1970s to a more overt use of military force. This shift frustrated many experts within the nascent field of terrorism studies, who saw this theory as lacking in evidence and nakedly political. Conflicts over the proper role and form of terrorism expertise would subsequently be fought out on the terrain of claims to the politicization of knowledge.

Chapter 6, "Loose ca(n)nons: from 'small wars' to the 'new terrorism,'" traces how the "new terrorism" framework, which framed terrorism as something unfathomable, irrational, and capable of "mass destruction," crystallized as a new, powerful lens for making sense of terrorism in the 1990s. With the end of the Cold War and the occurrence of several new and spectacular terrorist events, along with fears of spreading "weapons of mass destruction," terrorism took on new salience as a preeminent threat. This chapter traces how new experts came together to produce this "new" discourse, and highlights some of the processes through which the central and ongoing role of rationality and irrationality in conceptualizations of terrorism has persisted.

Chapter 7, "The road to pre-emption," dissects the current state of terrorism expertise and governance, drawing on the previous six chapters to explain how the field has arrived at its contemporary condition. Specifically, I show how the three decades traced in this book can help us to understand the "war on terror" that emerged in response to 9/11. I argue that this war on terror, characterized by a Manichean world view of good versus evil, and a corresponding logic of pre-emption, was built on a pre-existing foundation of terrorism as a problem infused with morality, rationality, and politicization.

Chapter 8, "The politics of (anti-)knowledge: terrorism and expertise after 9/11," focuses on recent developments in the field of terrorism expertise. It argues that expert and popular discourse on terrorism after 9/11 were both characterized by a politics of "anti-knowledge" – the active rejection of explanation itself. It then asks whether terrorism expertise has moved towards institutionalization since 9/11, and how this might affect the politics of anti-knowledge. And in the conclusion, "The trouble with experts," I reflect on how this study speaks to the broader literature on the relation between expert knowledge and governance.

2 The invention of terrorism and the rise of the terrorism expert

Tell me what you think about terrorism, and I will tell you who you are.[1]

On September 5, 1972, eight members of the Palestinian nationalist Black September Organization stormed the dormitory of the Israeli athletes at the Munich Olympics site, killing two and taking nine others hostage. In exchange for the hostages, they demanded the release of 236 Palestinians imprisoned in Israel, as well as several members of the Red Army Faction imprisoned in West Germany, and a guarantee of safe passage out; they threatened to kill one hostage every two hours until their demands were met. All nine Israeli hostages, along with five of the Palestinians and a West German policeman, were killed in a gun battle following a failed rescue attempt by the West German police.

Although there had been a number of hijackings and other serious incidents of political violence from 1968 to 1972, it was the massacre at the 1972 Munich Olympics that took on central symbolic significance in the history of terrorism. The events at Munich have been inscribed in popular and expert histories of the problem alike as *the* spectacular event that inaugurated the era of modern terrorism. As one account reports, "Clive Aston, speaking for most experts, claimed that 'it was Munich which confirmed that terrorism as a political weapon had come of age'" (Naftali 2005: 52). Other experts, including J. Bowyer Bell (a terrorism researcher based at Columbia University), Robert Kupperman (who held appointments as an expert on terrorism at the US Arms Control and Disarmament Agency, at the Center for Strategic and International Studies, and at RAND), and

---

[1] Terrorism expert J. Bowyer Bell, quoted by Schmid (2011).

Brian Jenkins (who was for many years the head of RAND's research program on terrorism), also cited the impact of Munich when asked about the origins of terrorism expertise (Hoffman 1984).

The crisis reverberated around the world, broadcast live by the global media gathered for the Olympic Games to an estimated 900 million viewers worldwide.[2] But, even though Munich was a definite turning point, it was not yet clear what exactly "terrorism" entailed, or whether this was indeed the proper framework for making sense of such events. And, while "terrorism" was among the terms used to describe the events at Munich, the members of Black September were also denounced as criminals, madmen, and murderers. *The New York Times* wrote that "yesterday's murderous assault in Munich plumbed new depths of criminality" (*New York Times* 1972a), while a September 7 editorial described the events as "the depredations of such fanatical madmen" (*New York Times* 1972b). World leaders condemned the attacks as "insane terror" (Israeli premier Golda Meir), an "insane assault" (UK prime minister Ted Heath), "an abhorrent crime" and the work of "sick minds who do not belong to humanity" (King Hussein of Jordan) (*Los Angeles Times* 1972a). In the United States, President Richard Nixon condemned "[o]utlaws who will stop at nothing to accomplish goals" (*Los Angeles Times* 1972a), while Democratic presidential nominee George McGovern said that he was "horrified, as I think all Americans are, by this senseless act of terrorism" (Szulc 1972a). Both houses of Congress passed resolutions proposing that "the civilized world may cut off from contact with civilized mankind any peoples or any nation giving sanctuary, support, sympathy, aid or comfort to acts of murder and barbarism such as those just witnessed at Munich" (Szulc 1972b). The US stock exchange paused for a moment of silence in recognition of the events (*Los Angeles Times* 1972b).

---

[2] These events, in fact, would retain their position as key spectacle even up to the events of 9/11; as Peter Bergen noted in his book on the post-9/11 war on terror, "Not since television viewers had watched the abduction and murder of Israeli athletes during the Munich Olympics in 1972 had a massive global audience witnessed a terrorist attack unfold in real time" (Bergen 2011: 91).

Following the events at Munich, terrorism began to take shape as a problem in the public sphere and as an object of expert knowledge. It would take several years, however, before some of the most basic components of the problem as we now know it would coalesce. This is illustrated by some of the earliest official conceptualizations of "terrorism." An early list compiled by government counterterrorism officials included a wide-ranging plethora of troublesome incidents, generally linked to the international sphere in some way, but many seemed to lack any particular political message or intent, while others lacked any seeming connection to violence. The "incidents" included ranged from bomb threats to petty crime ("NYPD found hole in plate glass window of Aeroflot/Intourist office, presumed to be result of marble (found on the scene) propelled by slingshot") to peaceful demonstrations.[3]

While almost nothing had been written on terrorism at the start of the decade, by 1977 at least eleven bibliographic catalogues had been compiled to keep track of an ever-increasing number of publications.[4] And, although the term "terrorism" had previously been used infrequently, and in scattered fashion in the media, it came into much wider use during the 1970s. A survey of major newspaper and periodical indexes found that neither the *New York Times* index nor the London *Times* index included "terrorism" as a significant category before 1972.[5] Of the two major indexes of periodical literature, the British Humanities Index instituted the category in 1972, while the *Reader's Guide to Periodical Literature* had the category dating back continuously to 1959, but experienced a large jump in the number of

---

[3] NARA, Nixon papers.

[4] These were compiled by a variety of organizations, including the United Nations (UN), RAND, the US Army (1975), the US Air Force (Coxe 1977), the US Department of Justice (Boston 1977; Boston, Marcus, and Wheaton 1976; US Department of Justice 1975), the US Department of State (1976), the FBI, and the Central Intelligence Agency (CIA), as well as independent publications by academics and others (Mickolus 1976; Sabetta 1977).

[5] The *New York Times* index first included "terrorism" as a category in 1970, but listed no articles directly under that term until 1972, while the London *Times* index did not institute the category until 1972 (Crelinsten 1989a).

citations in the early 1970s (Crelinsten 1989a). A survey of two major bibliographies on terrorism found that over 99 percent of works on terrorism had been published in or after 1968 (Mickolus 1980; Norton and Greenberg 1980; Slann and Schechterman 1987: 3). By the end of the decade terrorism had become a hot topic of discourse within both political and academic realms, with one observer writing a few years later that "authors have spilled almost as much ink as the actors of terrorism have spilled blood" (Schmid and Jongman 1988: xiii). Why did terrorism take shape as a new and urgent problem in the 1970s? And how did a new literature on the problem so quickly emerge in such a brief period of time?

Two main explanations have been proposed for the rise of the terrorism discourse in the 1970s. The first suggests that the emergence of the terrorism discourse simply reflected events in the world: a new problem appeared, and the discourse followed. The second argues that the terrorism discourse is best understood as the creation of interested parties, generally identified as Western state elites and experts whose theories reflect the interests of these elites.[6] Yet, as I will argue, the emergence of the terrorism discourse cannot be explained as a simple reflection of concrete events, nor as a mere rhetorical creation. Instead, it is necessary to take account of changes in three dimensions of things, and the interactions among them: events, experts, and techniques of knowledge. The late 1960s and early 1970s witnessed dramatic shifts in the application of political violence by non-state actors. Whereas earlier airplane seizures had tended to play out in a relatively routinized way, with the hijackers demanding either money or transportation, the rise of hijacking as a *political/theatrical* tactic[7] in the late 1960s and early 1970s was indeed an innovation. In this reformulation, the spectacle of the incident became a crucial part of its intent and effectiveness, harnessing

---

[6] See Chapter 1 for a more detailed discussion of this literature.
[7] For a highly elaborated analysis of terrorism as "social drama," see the work of Robin Wagner-Pacifici (1986, 1995).

the global media to bring international attention to seemingly local social and political struggles.

But the events comprising this new category of terrorism were not purely novel. And, once the new coinage had solidified, experts began to apply the term retrospectively to past events, which were thus opened to the possibility of reconceptualization through the framework of "terrorism." As David Rapoport, a professor of political science at the University of California, Los Angeles (UCLA), and another prominent early academic terror expert, recalled: "In retrospect, people began to see the connection between this, not only in the earlier guerrilla movements or terror movements, but also in places like Cyprus and Palestine" (Rapoport, quoted by Hoffman 1984: 181). This is evident in many of the books on terrorism that began to appear during this decade (as in the preface to Richard Clutterbuck's (1977: 11) *Guerrillas and Terrorists*, wherein he declares: "The theme of this book is that terrorism...is as old as civilization itself." This is also evident in the construction of several of the large research projects that began to be developed after this time, such as the RAND database (founded in 1972) and the ITERATE database, which both began their chronologies at 1968, while another government-sponsored project traced the history of terrorism all the way back to 1870 (Mickolus, Heyman, and Schlotter 1980: 178–9).

Yet neither is it sufficient simply to conclude that the terrorism discourse was simply the rhetorical imposition of a powerful class. While the emergence of "terrorism" as a new problem was certainly a rhetorical achievement, this was not *only* a linguistic transformation. To account more fully for the emergence of the problem of "terrorism" as we now know it, we must focus on the trifecta of the emergence of new sorts of *events*, new sorts of *experts*, and the means by which these came together: the application of specific forms of expertise to the problem. This framework draws upon William Sewell's (1996: 844) characterization of "events" as not just happenings but processes through which incidents transform structures of meaning, and Foucault's (2003) similar notion of "eventalization," as well as the work of Latour, who argues that sociology of science must engage the role of "actor-networks" (Latour 1987, 1993 [1991]) in creating new objects of knowledge.[8]

The key factor drawing attention to the problem of terrorism at this time was the transnational character of the events. While the problem of terrorism would eventually come to encompass political violence against civilians in a very broad sense, the earliest concerns emanating from the US government were more focused. A 1972 White House memo specified that "practical objectives in the campaign against 'international terrorism'" did *not* include "traditional violence which is covered by established codes (e.g. common crimes), internal political disputes, civil strife, decolonization, bi-national or international armed conflict," but were targeted purely at "the prevention of the spread of violence to countries not directly concerned, the victimization of innocent persons, and the preservation of the vital machinery of international life."[9] Similarly, a 1976 speech given by the head of the Cabinet Committee to Combat Terrorism (CCCT) declared:

> With respect to the causes of terrorism, we have pointed out that none of the many states which have won their independence the hard way, including our own nation, engaged in the type of international violence which our draft convention seeks to control. Our proposal is carefully restricted to the problem of the spread of violence to persons and places far removed from the scene of struggles for self-determination.[10]

In other words, the US concern was less with insurgent violence, per se, than with the spread of such violence into the "international"

---

[8] See Chapter 1 for a more in-depth explication of these concepts.

[9] NARA, Nixon papers, Tufaro papers, box 1972–3, subject files, secret attachments no. 1, CCCT working group no. 2, memo headed "Wednesday December 13, 1972."

[10] "International terrorism: address by Robert A. Fearey" (reprint of speech given at World Affairs Council), article in *Department of State Bulletin*, March 29, 1976: 394–401, 401.

sphere. And as Jenkins has written recently, "The initial concern of Americans was not the conflicts themselves; rather we were concerned with preventing the conflicts from spilling over into the international domain" (Jenkins 2006: 8). The concern was with violence *out of place* – "spilling over" from local conflicts into the "international" sphere – and an attack at the Olympic Games, symbol of international cooperation, signified this perfectly.

THE RISE OF THE TERRORISM EXPERT

The Olympic attack spurred the US government to take action in ways that earlier hijackings and hostage-takings had not. The state played a key role in fostering the early growth of terrorism expertise: sponsoring and funding research, organizing conferences, and bringing experts and policymakers together. And a significant part of the early response to the problem took the form of recruiting experts who could make terrorism into something that could be known and subsequently (it was hoped) rationally acted upon.

Not long after the events at Munich, President Nixon established the first official US government body charged with focusing on the terrorism problem, the Cabinet Committee to Combat Terrorism.[11] The CCCT's first goals focused on improving security for specific populations for whom the US government felt a particular responsibility: US citizens at home and abroad, and official guests such as diplomats. Although its intended function was largely symbolic, signaling the administration's concern about the terrorism problem, the group was important in bringing together individuals interested in defining the terrorism problem and potential directions of response, and as one of the first institutional locations from which a

---

[11] My discussion of the CCCT is based on materials from the National Security Archive (a non-profit, non-government organization which collects documents related to US national security and foreign policy), which holds records from the CCCT and its working group, including reports and minutes of meetings. Many of these documents have been made available online, via the Digital National Security Archive (DNSA) project, at http://nsarchive.chadwyck.com. Citations to documents (e.g. TE 550) refer to the DNSA's document numbering system.

demand for terrorism expertise originated.[12] The CCCT and the Department of State (along with the Department of Defense, the CIA, and the FBI/Department of Justice) were major sponsors of terrorism expertise in the 1970s, and, as the problem of terrorism came to be addressed by more government agencies and organizations, the CCCT provided a location for coordinating these activities.

Although the committee proper met only a handful of times, it had an associated working group, chaired by Lewis Hoffacker (from 1972 to 1974, succeeded by Robert Fearey from 1974 to 1976, and then by Admiral Douglas Heck), that met on a regular (generally biweekly) basis from 1972 to 1977.[13] The working group sponsored several conferences on terrorism, and funded a number of research projects.[14] In late 1972 the RAND Corporation, soon to become one of the core locations for the development of terrorism expertise in the United States, was asked by the CCCT, the Department of State, and the Defense Advanced Research Projects Agency to do research on the

---

[12] A January 27, 1975, memo on whether the CCCT should continue to exist writes: "Although the CCCT has met only once since its formation, it continues to serve, in my view, two useful functions: it serves as a tangible expression of the President's concern with the still very acute problem of worldwide terrorism; and it serves as an umbrella for the extremely useful work which has been conducted by its Working Group in meeting the objectives set out in the President's memorandum to the Secretary of State of September 15, 1972, directing the formation of the CCCT" (DNSA document TE 371).

[13] The CCCT was disbanded in 1977, when President Jimmy Carter created a new working group on terrorism, which retained the same membership but was to "report to an executive committee of the NSC [National Security Council] – a new Executive Committee on Combating Terrorism – that would meet to determine counterterrorism policy" (Naftali 2005: 101). It was also at this time that a new terrorism intelligence subcommittee was formed in the CIA (Naftali 2005:102). Under Presidential Review Memorandum (PRM) 30, a new "special coordination committee" and a "policy review committee" was formed within the NSC to coordinate terrorism issues (Farrell 1982: 35). In 1978 the Department of State formed a new office for combating terrorism, to be headed by Anthony Quainton.

[14] The minutes of the meetings of the working group in the middle of the1970s regularly included reports on various research projects relating to terrorism, and fostering the production of such research appears to have been one of the primary activities of the group during this period. For example, in the fourth progress report (January 20, 1975) from the CCCT to the president, research was listed as one of the "priority areas of concentrated effort" (DNSA document TE 366, p. 11).

terrorism problem.[15] At first RAND was asked to focus on how to manage specific types of terrorist incidents – kidnapping and hostage incidents, including how to bargain in hostage situations (Jenkins and Johnson 1976). In 1976 the Department of State reported that the Office of External Research was managing a "quarter-million-dollar program of research and analysis on the subject," with funds coming from multiple federal agencies, including the Departments of State and Justice.[16]

At the start of the 1970s there were few, if any, terrorism experts. Recalling the state of affairs in terrorism studies at the beginning of the 1970s, one expert (Bell 1977: 481–2) wrote:

> There were really no general experts in the analysis of terror, only those with special academic skills (a knowledge of the Palestinian Fedayeen, or a career focused on deviant behavior) that could be related to the problem. Those threatened by the terrorists, however, needed advice, recommendations, aid, and comfort; if the recommendations worked, no matter how bizarre, so much the better.

Walter Laqueur, one of the first terrorism experts, and the author of many books on terrorism, including *The New Terrorism: Fanaticism and the Arms of Mass Destruction* (Laqueur 1999 – called "probably the best single volume...on terrorism and political violence" by a

---

[15] RAND, located in Santa Monica, California, was founded in 1948 as the "Research and Development" Corporation to provide consulting expertise to the air force, and subsequently became, among other things, the premier location of game theory simulations and debates over the possibility of rational nuclear war during the cold war (see Abella 2008).

[16] "Research has contributed significantly to the development of US policies to cope with international terrorism. The Office of External Research, Bureau of Intelligence and Research, for example, is currently managing a quarter-million-dollar program of research and analysis on the subject. Funds have come from the Department itself and half a dozen other agencies, notably the Law Enforcement Assistance Administration of the Department of Justice." Source: *Far Horizons* (Department of State newsletter), volume 9, issue 2 (spring 1976), article on "International terrorism" (report on the 1976 Department of State conference on international terrorism), p. 3.

former chief of counterterrorism operations at the CIA) recalled, similarly, that "[i]n the beginning, there were maybe half a dozen people... [T]his wasn't organized at all."[17] With these initiatives from the government, together with independent interest arising from academics and various others, however, the production of terrorism expertise expanded exponentially. Within the space of a few years terrorism was transformed from a problem with almost nothing written on it to a topic around which entire institutes, journals, and conferences were organized. One early bibliographic study of the field identifies 1973 as the year when the "systematic study of international terrorism began to develop," noting that virtually nothing was published on the subject prior to 1960, and only a handful of publications appeared before the middle of the 1970s, while 113 books appeared on the topic in 1976 and 161 in 1977 (Reid 1983: 104, 220).

The rapid growth of terrorism expertise is illustrated by the increase in conferences, a primary forum for communication among terrorism researchers at this time (see Figure 2.1). From 1972 to 1978 there was not only a significant growth in terrorism conferences but also growth in the interconnections between presenters and conferences. As H. H. A. Cooper, an early participant in the field, observed, "[F]rom about 1974 through 1978 was sort of the golden period, as it were; during this time, there were a tremendous number of conferences that brought together a lot of different viewpoints" (Hoffman 1984: 115). And, in the early 1980s, two experts recalled:

> One indicator of interest in antiterrorism is the proliferation of conferences concerning terrorism... Hardly a week goes by without witnessing some conference on terrorism. Security firms, entrepreneurs with few if any qualifications, college professors, non-profit institutions, universities and governments – they have all held their share of terrorism seminars.[18]

---

[17] Interview with Walter Laqueur, November 2006.

[18] Hoover Institution Archives, Claire Sterling papers: box 8, "A policy game about terrorism – draft," Hans Josef Horchem and Robert H. Kupperman (no date).

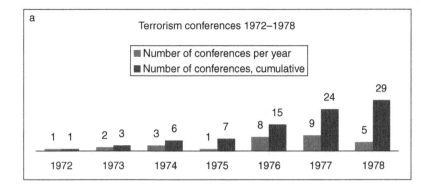

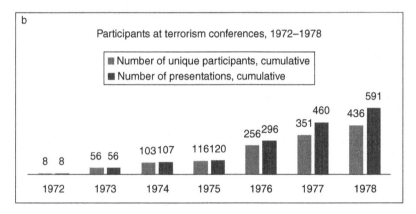

FIGURE 2.1 The growth of terrorism conferences, 1972–1978

The next section illustrates the increasing connections among terrorism experts via a network analysis of participants at conferences (comprising twenty-nine conferences and 436 individual presenters between 1972 and 1978). This shows not simply the quantitative increase in knowledge-producing activities, therefore, but also the growth of a set of relationships between those who were becoming "terrorism experts." In the diagrams that follow, conferences and individual presenters constitute the nodes (points), while each instance when an individual presented a paper at a given conference is marked as a tie (line), linking together individuals who presented at the same conferences, and conferences attended by the same individuals.[19] Each circle represents a conference, and each square represents an individual presenter at that conference. Tables 2.1 and 2.2 give further information on selected individuals and events portrayed in these figures.

In the first diagram (Figure 2.2), note that there are no ties (overlap) among the presenters at the first three conferences. In the second (Figure 2.3), representing conferences held from 1972 to 1975, it becomes apparent that there are now a handful of ties among the presenters. For example, J. Bowyer Bell of Columbia University (no. 56, in the lower right-hand corner of the diagram) attended both conferences 3 and 82, and thus constitutes a network tie between those events. Figure 2.4 illustrates the much more complex structure of ties among the conferences and presenters that has developed by 1976. Whereas in the period from 1972 to 1975 (Figure 2.3) there are only a handful of connections, by 1976 (Figure 2.4) multiple overlapping ties have emerged among conferences and presenters, and only a handful of conferences by this point have no overlap with over events. We can also see in this diagram that the majority of these ties are created through a small minority of the overall pool of presenters.[20]

---

[19] The figures were generated via the UCINET and Netdraw programs developed for social network analysis (Borgatti, Everett, and Freeman 2002). In the language of network analysis, the diagram here is represented as a two-mode network, in which it is not the case that the ties are direct links between people but, rather, that the ties between individuals are mediated by some second axis (in this case, conferences at which both individuals were present). Squares here represent individuals (presenters), while circles represent conferences (events). Individuals with only one tie (e.g. those who presented at only one conference during this time) have been excluded from the diagrams after 1975 for the sake of simplicity. These diagrams were constructed by modeling the network of ties among those who presented at the same conferences, which is taken as a proxy measure for the growth of social ties in the field. I take having presented at the same conference to be a valid proxy for actual connections, because of the relatively small size of most of these events.

[20] Figure 2.4 appears less visually dense because I have removed from it the relative isolates – that is, those presenters who appear at only one conference and do not form any further links. These relative isolates still compose the numerical majority of those presenting; I discuss this significance of this below.

Table 2.1 *Some prominent individuals in terrorism studies, 1972–1978*

ID number	Name	Background
1	Alexander, Yonah	Founding editor of *Terrorism: An International Journal*, professor of international studies and director of Institute for Studies in International Terrorism at the State University of New York (SUNY), Oneonta.
3	Hassell, Conrad V.	FBI, special operations and research unit.
4	Russell, Charles A.	Affiliated with Risks International, a consulting firm that quantified risks of terrorism (largely for corporate clients). Attorney, PhD in international relations from American University, formerly with US Air Force counterintelligence office.
6	Kupperman, Robert H.	PhD in applied mathematics from New York University (NYU). Chief scientist, Arms Control and Disarmament Agency. Member of CCCT working group, and chair of Interagency Committee on Mass Destruction and Terrorism.
9	Jenkins, Brian M.	Head of research on terrorism at RAND Corporation.
18	Mickolus, Edward F.	CIA analyst, PhD in political science. Constructed the ITERATE database of terrorist incidents; also compiled several bibliographies on terrorism.
52	Rapoport, David	Professor of political science, UCLA. Author of many books and articles on terrorism.
56	Bell, J. Bowyer	Senior research associate, Institute of War and Peace Studies, Columbia University. Published on terrorism, especially the Irish Republican Army (IRA); renowned as one of the few

Table 2.1 (*cont.*)

ID number	Name	Background
		early researchers to conduct first-hand research on terrorists.
120	Murphy, John F.	Professor of law, University of Kansas.
162	Crenshaw, Martha	PhD in political science, studied Algerian war. Later, professor of political science, Wesleyan University (Middletown, CT) and Stanford University.
407	Dror, Yehezkel	Professor of political science, Hebrew University, Jerusalem.
462	Horowitz, Irving L.	Professor of sociology and political science at Rutgers University (New Brunswick, NJ).

Note: ID numbers, which correlate to the labels in the network diagrams, are strictly arbitrary. The affiliations listed indicate individuals' affiliations during the period from 1972 to 1978.

Table 2.2 *Some important conferences on terrorism, 1972–1978*

ID number	Year	Conference name	Sponsors
2	1972	Department of State conference on terrorism	US Department of State
83	1973	"Conference on terrorism and political crimes"	International Institute for Advanced Criminal Sciences
3	1974	"International terrorism"	International Studies Association; Institute of World Affairs, University of Wisconsin, Milwaukee
9	1976	"Conference on terrorism in the contemporary world"	Glassboro State College, New Jersey Committee for the Humanities
6	1976	Department of State conference on international terrorism	US Department of State

Table 2.2 (*cont.*)

ID number	Year	Conference name	Sponsors
4	1976	"International terrorism, national and global ramifications"	Ralph Bunche Institute of the UN; City University of New York (CUNY); Institute for Studies in International Terrorism, SUNY
93	1977	"Research strategies for the study of international political terrorism"	Canadian government; US Department of Justice, Law Enforcement Assistance Administration (LEAA); International Centre for Comparative Criminology, University of Montreal; Institute of Criminal Justice and Criminology, University of Maryland
16	1977	"Terrorism and US business"	Georgetown University Center for Strategic and International Studies; Institute for Studies in International Terrorism, SUNY
11	1977	"Terrorism and the media"	Ralph Bunche Institute of the UN
15	1977	"Symposium on international terrorism"	John Bassett Moore Society of International Law
99	1978	International scientific conference on terrorism	Institute for International Scientific Exchange, Aspen Institute
202	1978	"Legal aspects of international terrorism"	US Department of State; LEAA; American Society of International Law

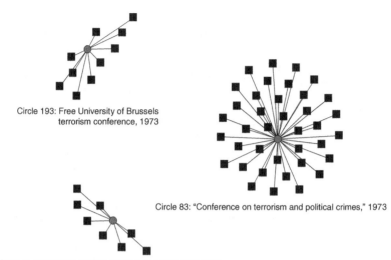

Circle 193: Free University of Brussels terrorism conference, 1973

Circle 83: "Conference on terrorism and political crimes," 1973

Circle 2: Department of State conference on terrorism, 1972

FIGURE 2.2 Presenters at terrorism conferences, 1972–1973

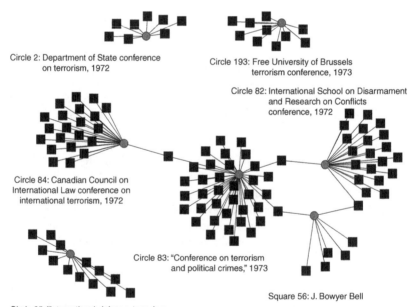

Circle 2: Department of State conference on terrorism, 1972

Circle 193: Free University of Brussels terrorism conference, 1973

Circle 82: International School on Disarmament and Research on Conflicts conference, 1972

Circle 84: Canadian Council on International Law conference on international terrorism, 1972

Circle 83: "Conference on terrorism and political crimes," 1973

Square 56: J. Bowyer Bell

Circle 85: "International violence: terrorism, surprise, and control," 1975

FIGURE 2.3 Presenters at terrorism conferences, 1972–1975

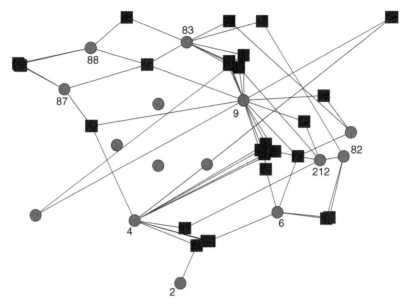

Circle 9: "Conference on terrorism in the contemporary world," 1976
Circle 88: "The impact of terrorism and skyjacking on the
             operations of the criminal justice system," 1976
Circle 87: "Hostage taking: problems of prevention and control," 1976
Circle 4: "International terrorism, national and global ramifications," 1976
Circle 2: Department of State conference on terrorism, 1972
Circle 83: "Conference on terrorism and political crimes," 1973
Circle 6: Department of State conference on international terrorism, 1976
Circle 212: "Terror: the man, the mind, the matter," 1976
Circle 82: International School on Disarmament and Research on Conflicts
             conference, 1974

FIGURE 2.4 Presenters at terrorism conferences, 1972–1976

Figure 2.5, representing conferences held through 1977, illustrates the further development of a 'web' structure, in which there are
multiple overlapping ties among the individuals and events. Conferences 5, 85, and 91 (in the upper left-hand corner) are the only
remaining events whose presenters fail to appear at any other events.
And, by 1978 (Figure 2.6), there is a highly complex pattern of overlapping connections among the conferences and presenters. Also of note
in these two figures is evidence that the 1972 Department of State

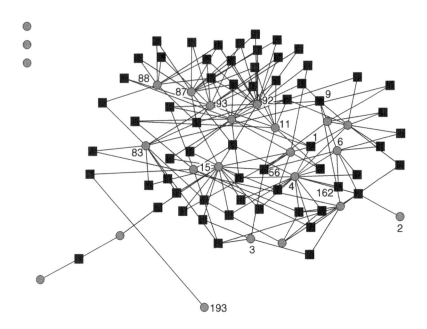

Circle 2: Department of State conference on terrorism, 1972
Circle 193: Free University of Brussels terrorism conference, 1973
Circle 83: "Conference on terrorism and political crimes," 1973
Circle 15: "Symposium on international terrorism," 1977
Circle 88: "The impact of terrorism and skyjacking on the
            operations of the criminal justice system," 1976
Circle 87: "Hostage taking: problems of prevention and control," 1976
Circle 93: "Research strategies for the study of international political terrorism," 1977
Circle 92: "Dimensions of victimization in the context of terroristic acts," 1977
Circle 11: "Terrorism and the media," 1977
Circle 4: "International terrorism, national and global ramifications," 1976
Circle 3: International Studies Association conference on international terrorism, 1974
Circle 6: Department of State conference on international terrorism, 1976

Square 162: Martha Crenshaw
Square 56: J. Bowyer Bell
Square 9: Brian Jenkins
Square 1: Yonah Alexander

FIGURE 2.5 Presenters at terrorism conferences, 1972–1977

conference on terrorism (no. 2) is a relative outlier, existing on the edge of the figure, illuminating the fact that most of the individuals presenting at this conference did not continue on in the field of terrorism studies.

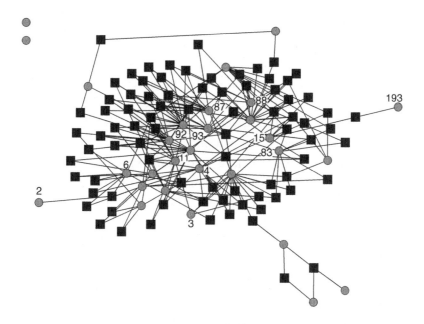

Circle 2: Department of State conference on terrorism, 1972
Circle 193: Free University of Brussels terrorism conference, 1973
Circle 83: "Conference on terrorism and political crimes," 1973
Circle 15: "Symposium on international terrorism," 1977
Circle 88: "The impact of terrorism and skyjacking on the
      operations of the criminal justice system," 1976
Circle 87: "Hostage taking: problems of prevention and control," 1976
Circle 93: "Research strategies for the study of international political terrorism," 1977
Circle 92: "Dimensions of victimization in the context of terroristic acts," 1977
Circle 11: "Terrorism and the media," 1977
Circle 4: "International terrorism, national and global ramifications," 1976
Circle 3: International Studies Association conference on international terrorism, 1974
Circle 6: Department of State conference on international terrorism, 1976

FIGURE 2.6 Presenters at terrorism conferences, 1972–1978

THE RISE OF THE "TERRORISM MAFIA"

As these diagrams illustrate, the growth of "terrorism studies" was not simply a quantitative increase in individual projects and experts. Rather, it took shape as a networked social arena. And this was not simply the emergence of a new arena in which pre-existing experts applied their skills to a new problem. Not only did the numbers of experts, conferences, and publications increase exponentially over the course of the 1970s, there was also a qualitative shift in the *types* of experts and expertise being applied to the problem, along with a shift in the very meaning of terrorism itself. The emergence of "terrorism" as a new problem occurred in concert with the creation of a new type of expert. Crucial to this development was the rise of "terrorism expertise" as a distinct position from which to speak.

The absence of specialized "terrorism experts" is apparent at the first US conference on terrorism, which was organized by the Department of State and the Cabinet Committee to Combat Terrorism on October 24, 1972. Most of those brought in as experts at this conference were called upon for their prominence in fields such as collective behavior, social movements, or social psychology, rather than for their expertise in the area of *terrorism*, per se. Nor did the presenters at this conference include any of those individuals who would come to constitute the core of the terrorism studies community in later years. Presentations were made by Thomas Thornton, of the Department of State, and author of the oft-cited (1964) essay "Terror as a weapon of political agitation"; sociologist Irving Louis Horowitz of Rutgers University; Karl Schmitt of the University of Texas; Carl Leiden of the University of Texas and the National War College; Edward Gude of the Adlai Stevenson Institute of International Affairs, who had written on counterinsurgency; and psychologist Sheldon Levy of Wayne State University, who had served as co-director of the Assassination and Political Violence task force of the Violence Commission under Presidents Johnson and Nixon.[21] The relative position of the earliest conferences as outliers in the later field of expertise is evident in the network diagrams: while most of the other conferences form a dense web of connections, this conference (labeled no. 2 in Figures 2.2 to 2.6) had very few ties to later events.

---

[21] *Far Horizons*, volume 6, issue 3 (September 1973), "External research at State: an overview of the FY 1973 program," page 11.

By contrast, presenters at a second conference on terrorism, organized by the Department of State in 1976, included a number of individuals who had done research specifically on terrorism, several of whom would go on to become prominent experts. Presenters at this conference included Brian Crozier, with a background in intelligence/counterinsurgency; Martha Crenshaw, an academic political scientist who had studied the Algerian resistance and would become one of the key figures in the terrorism studies field; Brian Jenkins, who would go on to head the terrorism research program at RAND; Paul Wilkinson, who would go on to head a terrorism research center at the University of St Andrews in Scotland; and J. Bowyer Bell, a researcher and adjunct instructor at Columbia University, and one of the few individuals to conduct fieldwork with terrorism organizations. The central role that the experts at the 1976 conference would go on to play in the emerging "terrorism studies" field is also illustrated in the network diagrams; see, for example, the relatively central positions of Crenshaw (no. 162), Bell (no. 56), and Jenkins (no. 9).

Jenkins, who would become one of the most prominent public faces of terrorism expertise, came to the study of terrorism with the sort of highly eclectic background that was more the rule than the exception for early terrorism experts. He began his career studying to be a painter, first at the Chicago Art Institute and Academy of Arts, and then receiving a BA in fine arts from UCLA in 1962. After graduation, Jenkins entered the Army Reserves, serving as a paratrooper, as a member of the Green Berets in the Dominican Republic, and with the Special Forces in Vietnam.[22] In 1968 he returned to Los Angeles, beginning work on a PhD in history at UCLA and coming to work at RAND as a consultant, and serving as a member of the Long Range Planning Task Group in Saigon, where he would spend time in 1968, 1969, and 1971.[23] Jenkins became an official

---

[22] RAND Corporation Archives (Los Angeles), Tanham files, folder "GKT Chiron January–June 1978," "Jenkins CV."

[23] RAND Corporation Archives, Tanham files, folder "GKT Chiron January–June 1978," "Jenkins CV."

RAND employee in April 1972, assigned to work on RAND projects relating to the war in Vietnam.[24] By 1976 he was associate head of the Social Sciences Department at RAND, and he also took on the role of the director of RAND's research into guerrilla warfare and international terrorism.[25]

By the middle of the 1970s we begin to see the appearance not just of individual actors who could claim to be terrorism experts but also the beginnings of networks, organizations, and social structures among these experts. By the late 1970s a core group of terrorism scholars, sometimes informally referring to themselves a "terrorism mafia," had emerged.[26] As Jenkins would write in 1979, "There is a kind of informal, international network of scholars and government officials with interests or responsibilities in the area of terrorism. A kind of 'college-without-campus' has emerged" (Jenkins 1983: 156).

The "mafia" consisted of a core group at the center of the emerging terrorism studies world, who took on the project of making the field a legitimate area of study. Institutional entrepreneurs organized projects, organizations, and activities that both facilitated the growth of experts' relations between themselves and communicated expert knowledge to other audiences. They organized events such as conferences and seminars, places to publish such as journals and edited books, and physical institutions such as research centers. These projects both provided methods of communication among experts and aimed to establish the importance of the terrorism research project itself. The projects of developing an expert identity, and of building the collective project of "terrorism studies," were thus intertwined with strategies to legitimate "terrorism" as an object of knowledge.

[24] RAND Corporation Archives, box "RAND items 1966–1974" (also marked "RAND items no. 40"), and "RAND items no. 425," "New employees,"April 11, 1972.

[25] RAND Corporation Archives, Tanham files, folder "GKT Chiron January–June 1978," "Jenkins CV."

[26] This phrase was introduced by some of these experts in interviews conducted by the author.

This strategy of network building and institutional entrepreneurship is perhaps best illustrated by the work of Yonah Alexander, a professor of international studies at SUNY Oneonta, and founder of the Institute for Studies in International Terrorism at that institution. Between 1976 and 1979 Alexander organized at least six conferences[27] and founded the first specialized journal on terrorism.[28] According to the "information for authors" included in the first issue, the journal aimed to "examine the types, causes, consequences, control, and meaning of all forms of terrorist action" and "present the results of original research without restrictions on the ideological or political approach of contributors."[29]

The first issues of *Terrorism* were largely populated by descriptive essays, typologies, and conceptualization work, as well as practical and policy-oriented pieces, but a relative lack of empirical research, consisting mostly of preliminary reports on work in progress. The authors came from a variety of backgrounds – academic, practical, and political. The next year, 1978, the journal *Conflict* (which did not focus solely on terrorism, although a number of articles in the first volume touched on terrorism), edited by George Tanham at RAND, was founded, and the following year, 1979, *TVI (Terrorism, Violence, Insurgency) Journal* made its first appearance.

A NEW DISCIPLINE?

This chapter has related what appears at first to be a tremendous success story. In 1979 Yonah Alexander wrote, "The study of terrorism has now 'arrived' internationally, as evidenced by the birth of a new

[27] These are "International terrorism, national and global ramifications," an interdisciplinary conference of the Ralph Bunche Institute of the UN (1976); "Terrorism and the media" (1977); two seminars sponsored by the Institute for Studies in International Terrorism (1977); "Terrorism and US business: (1977); and "The rationalization of terrorism" (1979).

[28] This journal, founded 1977, later merged (in 1992) with the journal *Conflict* to become *Studies in Conflict and Terrorism*, at which time George Tanham of RAND took over as editor.

[29] *Terrorism* volume 1, issue 1, inside the back cover.

international multidisciplinary journal, *Terrorism*; the proliferation of scientific conferences and papers; and the growth of university research and teaching on the subject" (Alexander, Carlton, and Wilkinson 1979: ix). This was not simply an assessment but, rather, a performative statement, meant to promote and consolidate terrorism studies as a field – a statement that seeks to enact the truth that it proclaims.

But had terrorism studies actually "arrived" at this time? Terrorism expertise was, at best, a semi-institutionalized field, with an overall lack of any significant structure or regulation among the pool of potential experts.[30] Although a nascent field of expertise was in evidence by the late 1970s, this "field" lacked many of the features that sociologists would generally expect to find in an established scientific field, including a formal structure, regulated boundaries, and highly defined criteria of certification and standards. Thus, even though the problem of "terrorism" was, by the end of the 1970s, circulating as an object of discourse and analysis, there was a marked lack of regulatory structure among the experts, making this "terrorism" problem open to (almost) all for speaking with but able to be (analytically) controlled by practically none.

The early development of terrorism studies did not result in the creation of a tightly organized field of cultural production, nor was the burgeoning area of investigation absorbed into or captured by any other pre-existing profession or discipline. Terrorism studies did not develop as an outgrowth of a pre-existing discipline or institutionalized field of knowledge but, instead, amalgamated individuals and knowledge from a variety of backgrounds. The new experts were drawn from a veritable hodgepodge of backgrounds, and the path to expertise was described as "accidental" by a number of early participants:

> The first time I discovered that I was a so-called expert is when
> I was at a major, highly selected conference of English and

---

[30] I revisit the question of whether the field has institutionalized since 9/11 in Chapter 8.

American scholars and government officials in England. I found
that I knew as much as anybody else did in that group, including the
government ministers (Robert Friedlander, quoted by Hoffman
1984: 97).

Brian Jenkins, a former art student who got into terrorism
accidentally, and myself, a respectable lawyer, as it were, got into it
equally accidentally, and would have been unlikely ever to have
met unless we had this common ground. You could say this in
regard to probably every person who's involved in it. They all came
into terrorism entirely accidentally (H. H. A. Cooper, quoted by
Hoffman 1984: 116–17).

My becoming a so-called expert on terrorism simply evolved
from the fact that I spent such a lot of time talking about it (Richard
Clutterbuck, quoted by Kahn 1978: 53).

Many of the most prominent experts were located in relatively
peripheral institutional locations. None were in tenured or tenure-
track positions at major research universities, and, even at think tanks
such as RAND, terrorism research was a relatively peripheral endeavor.
More concretely, we can also see that the backgrounds of many of these
new experts on terrorism were widely disparate, representing academic
disciplines ranging from psychology, political science, and sociology to
medicine, law, and criminology, along with individuals working in the
intelligence services, the police sector, and partisan and non-partisan
think tanks. When asked why there were so few academics in the early
years of terrorism studies, one expert suggested that – in addition to a
lack of data – it was considered too controversial, and too poorly
defined, to become the basis for a proper academic study, noting that
someone had once said that coming up with a proper definition of
terrorism was "like trying to nail a pudding to a wall."[31]

Furthermore, the self-identified "terrorism mafia" constituted
only a minor portion of those involved in some way in the production

[31] Interview with Martha Crenshaw, October 12, 2006.

of knowledge about terrorism at this point. There were a whole series of others, traversing this very porous boundary of the nascent world of "terrorism studies," coming in and making claims about terrorism and then disappearing. A large fraction of those publishing in journals or presenting at conferences had no particular background in the field, and often would not continue to do further work in the area.[32] Thus, although I emphasize in this chapter the emergence of a terrorism studies community and the "terrorism mafia," the larger arena of terrorism expertise continued to be dominated by people who were not (and perhaps did not want to be) terrorism experts in this specialized sense. Of 1,796 individuals presenting at conferences on terrorism between 1972 and 2001, 1,505 (84 percent) made only one appearance.[33] Similarly, a recent study of journal articles published on terrorism during the 1990s found more than 80 percent to be by one-time authors (Silke 2004b: 69), and another study found that core journals in terrorism studies had significantly higher rates of contributions from non-academic authors than journals in political science or communications studies (Gordon 2001).

These factors all contributed to the structuring of a relatively uninstitutionalized field of terrorism expertise with highly permeable boundaries. In contrast to theories of professions and scientific fields, which often tend to presume that the social structures of expertise will be composed of tightly bounded self-regulated units, the field of terrorism studies has been characterized by weak and permeable boundaries, a population of "experts" whose backgrounds and sources of legitimation are highly heterogeneous, and a lack of agreement not just over how expertise should be evaluated but even over how to define the central topic of their concern.

---

[32] This is evident in the relatively large proportion of participants in the conferences data set who make only one appearance (84 percent of those in my entire data set). This high degree of movement into and out of the research area continued to characterize the field as it developed; a recent study of journal articles on terrorism during the 1990s found that more than 80 percent were by one-time authors (Silke 2004b: 64).

[33] Source: author's data set on presenters at conferences on terrorism, 1972 to 2001.

While the sociological literature on cultural fields, disciplines, and professional projects tends to highlight the importance of institutionalization, terrorism experts have rarely succeeded in consolidating control over the production of terrorism discourse and terrorism expertise. Rather than looking like a discipline or a closed "cultural field," terrorism expertise is constructed and negotiated in an interstitial space between academia, the state, and the media. The boundaries of legitimate knowledge and expertise are particularly open to challenges from self-proclaimed experts from the media and political fields, and this has had significant consequences for the sorts of expert discourses that tend to be produced and disseminated. Experts, however defined, were not in control of the production of other experts, or the definition of their object of "terrorism," as illustrated in the continual tension over whether terrorism should be approached primarily as a moral problem or as a rational problem to be addressed through causal social-scientific analysis.

Further, it is important to note that terrorism studies and the "terrorism mafia" were, from the start, hybrid entities. Even though I use the "terrorism mafia" term here to refer to the core group of experts, and those who were most invested in maintaining a professional/academic direction to the field, this was not a homogeneous group. The members of the "terrorism mafia" were not all academics. And, in part because academic terror experts tended to occupy a relatively marginal place within academia, it was not necessarily the case that "academic" experts would be most oriented towards the reward system of the academic disciplines, as compared to those of the public or governmental arenas. Although, as the field of terrorism expertise went on to develop, this core group would most often come to represent the interest in making terrorism studies take on the characteristics of a scientific discipline, this was not a frictionless process, and several of the individuals who were central to building the field in this early period would later align with other approaches to the study of terrorism in the 1980s and 1990s.

In the next chapter I delve further into the question of how it was that "terrorism" took shape as a problem so imbued with tensions in meaning, creating great difficulties for the field of expertise. While the earliest discourse on terrorism took its cues from an earlier discourse on insurgency, over the course of the 1970s a new framework emerged in which "terrorism" was differentiated from previous understandings of political violence, and this shift would have significant effects on the production of experts and expertise.

3   From insurgents to terrorists: experts, rational knowledge, and irrational subjects

> The US Government recognizes the merit of elimination of causes of terrorism, including legitimate grievances which motivate potential terrorists.[1]

> Terrorism is "a new barbarism...fought primarily not to win territory or even to cause destruction, but to command attention, to instill fear, and to terrorize in the hope of forcing the world to listen and to right an alleged wrong."[2]

At the very first US conference on terrorism, held at the Department of State in 1972, there was a general consensus that "nearly every variety of political and ethnic group is likely under certain (generally desperate) circumstances to resort to terrorism," that terrorism "is a tool not confined to opposition forces" but could also be used by "established regimes," and that it "was the product of frustration induced by unresolved grievances" (Perenyi 1972: 4). But, just a few years later, most speakers at the 1976 Department of State conference on terrorism agreed that terrorism was the activity of sub-state actors, "doubted that the direct causes of terrorism could be discovered in political or socioeconomic conditions," and "were skeptical of the argument that the way to stop terrorism was to 'remove its causes'" (Johnson 1976: 17–18).

This chapter argues that, over the course of the 1970s, expertise on bombings, kidnappings, and hijackings shifted from a discourse organized around "insurgency" to one organized around the concept

---

[1] US government memo "Guidelines for dealing with terrorism with international ramifications," 1974.

[2] Preface to a collection of papers from a 1976 terrorism symposium, published by Marius Livingston, Lee Kress, and Marie Wanek (1978: 19).

of "terrorism." The discourse of counterinsurgency was based upon a mode of knowledge production in which moral, political, and rational evaluations of insurgents and insurgency were (at least in theory) separable from expert/scientific analyses. Within the new discourse of "terrorism," however, the morality, politicality, and rationality of political violence would come to be strongly intertwined with the production and evaluation of experts and expertise. This transform-ation would have significant consequences for the sorts of discourses and practices available to lay and expert commentators on political violence, affecting both the cultural frameworks applied to terrorism and the scope of possibilities for the production of terrorism expertise.

Although the actions and events they describe appear similar, the discourses of counterinsurgency and counterterrorism differed in their conceptualizations of the problem and its causes, and the poten-tial responses they suggest. Perhaps most significantly, the counter-insurgency discourse positioned insurgents and counterinsurgents as parallel roles, while the discourse on terrorism tended to characterize terrorists as evil, pathological, irrational actors, fundamentally differ-ent from "us." The discourse of counterinsurgency did not attach any *necessary* moral evaluation to the character of the insurgent, but the identity of the terrorist would become imbued with moral judgment (though some experts would then seek to divest the concept of terrorism of moral character).[3] Whereas insurgents were generally assumed to be rational actors, who could be countered with a similarly rational strategy of counterinsurgency, the rationality of terrorism, and thus the possibilities for a rational analysis and treat-ment of the problem, would be placed in perpetual doubt. And, while insurgency was generally considered to stem from political, even structural, motivations and goals, the question of whether terrorists even *have* political goals would come to be highly contested, with the nature of terrorists' goals a site of much contention. Consequently,

---

[3] For a sociological analysis of some of the conditions under which political violence can come to be seen as legitimate, see Fine (1999).

although the insurgency framework at least held out the possibility that political violence might be resolved by addressing grievances (even though, in practice, counterinsurgency has usually been characterized by violence, both symbolic and literal), the terrorism framework actively excluded such a possibility from consideration.

The new discourse of terrorism would come to be organized around three fundamental ambiguities – rationality, morality, and politics – each of which not only raised questions and created difficulties for knowledge about terrorism but also created difficulties for the *knowers* of terrorism. As a result of the formation of terrorism as a problem with a moral evaluation built into it, attempts to develop a morally neutral terrorism expertise, and sometimes even attempts to understand terrorism at all, became subject to discrediting attacks as – somewhat paradoxically – politicized knowledge, and this has led to persistent difficulties for those seeking to create rational knowledge about political violence. This chapter aims to clarify the relation between "counterinsurgency" and "counterterrorism," the distinctions between them, and the effects of the shift from one to the other upon experts and expertise.

TERRORISM VERSUS INSURGENCY

At a 1962 RAND symposium on counterinsurgency, "insurgent" and "counterinsurgent" were presented as parallel roles (Hosmer and Crane 2006 [1963]: 4). Similarly, Thomas Thornton's oft-cited 1964 essay "Terror as a weapon of political agitation" declared, "We are dealing, in a sense, with two continua of behavior – one of political agitation and the other of enforcement – which run parallel" (Thornton 1964: 74). Although there was an asymmetry between the positions within the counterinsurgency discourse, this was primarily conceived as a tactical and strategic opposition, and *not* generally a moral one. As French counterinsurgent David Galula (1964: 5) has written,

> [T]here is an asymmetry between the opposite camps of a
> revolutionary war. This phenomenon results from the very nature

of the war, from the disproportion of strength between the opponents at the outset, and from the difference in essence between their assets and their liabilities.

And Frank Kitson, who fought insurgents in Kenya, Malaya, Cyprus, and Northern Ireland as an officer in the British army, has written, "It is sometimes said that insurgents start with nothing but a cause and grow to strength, while the counter-insurgents start with everything but a cause and gradually decline in strength to the point of weakness" (Kitson 1974 [1971]: 29). Counterinsurgent writers and fighters frequently expressed a degree of respect for their opponents that would be quite unusual in the terrorism literature. As the preface to Roger Trinquier's *Modern Warfare* puts it, the author, who had served as an officer in the French armed forces, commanding counter-guerrilla units in Vietnam, approaches the insurgents with "the cold respect of a professional warrior. He describes an enemy who is deeply committed to his cause, and ingenious in its pursuit" (Trinquier 2006 [1961]: viii). But this equivalence would begin to slip away as the discourse of terrorism took hold. For, while insurgents were categorized first as enemies (a temporary, and potentially, honorable role), terrorists came to be considered essentially evil, and thus not eligible for the role of the honorable opponent.

Although the terms "terror" (and less often "terrorism") did sometimes appear within the counterinsurgency literature, these were generally treated as a tactic or tool, and not as the defining feature of individual or group identity. "Terror" was viewed as but one stage in a broader process of insurgency or revolution – a stage through which groups could pass without permanently tainting their reputations. In line with this view, counterinsurgency theorists wrote that insurgency "has usually included both guerrilla warfare and terrorism among its methods" (Paget 1967: 16), that terrorism is the first stage of resistance (Crozier 1959), that, "when the opportunity comes, the rebels will drop terrorism in favor of guerrilla activities" (Crozier 1960: 128), and that, "[i]f and when the guerrilla force grows in numbers and strength, terror assumes a less important role" (Thayer 1963: 124).

This view of "terror" as a tactic rather than an identifying feature of individuals or groups also meant that the counterinsurgency literature was more likely to approach terrorism as something that could be used by either insurgents or states. For example, Thornton suggested that "it is, however, by no means inevitable that the insurgents will initiate terrorism; in some instances, they may be 'counterterrorists' reacting to the terror of the incumbents" (Thornton 1964: 71–2). Participants at the 1962 RAND counterinsurgency symposium spoke of the possibility of "using terror wisely and selectively,"[4] while American guerrilla warfare manuals, during and after World War II, "made explicit reference to the utility – indeed, the necessity – of its use, from hostage-taking to selective assassination" (McClintock 1992: xvii).

Whereas counterinsurgency theory generally assumed (especially insofar as insurgents and counterinsurgents were imagined as *parallel* roles) that insurgents were rational actors, once the terrorism framework took hold the question of whether political violence could be rational was perennially up for debate. Counterinsurgency experts generally assumed that insurgents had rational, intelligible, political motives. As Thornton wrote in 1964, "We shall treat terror as a tool to be used rationally" (Thornton 1964: 71). The report from the 1962 Rand conference on counterinsurgency starts out by discussing structural problems that may lead to guerrilla movements in different parts of the world: problems such as unemployment, inequality, and colonialism (Hosmer and Crane 2006 [1963]: 1–2). An acknowledgment of the importance of a "cause" to insurgents and guerrillas was almost universal in the literature. As British soldier Julian Paget puts it, the first requirement of a successful insurgency is "a cause to fight

---

[4] "Terror" is not explicitly defined, but the meaning seems to be violence intended to impose fear upon the population (as opposed to the tactical use of violence) (Hosmer and Crane 2006 [1963]: 26).

for" (Paget 1967: 23). Similarly, Galula (1964: 18) emphasizes the importance of a cause in gaining the support of the population, Robert Thompson (1966: 21) writes that "[e]very insurgency, particularly a communist revolutionary one, requires a cause," John Pustay (1965: 16) cites problems of "cultural adjustment" and poverty, Brian Crozier (1960: 6) writes that "[f]rustration is the one element common to all rebels," and Charles Thayer (1963: 158) observes coolly that "the grievances that tear the country apart are those of other Latin American countries – mal-distribution of wealth and of land."

This emphasis on the role of motivations and grievances in the counterinsurgency literature imposed on counterinsurgency experts the importance of understanding insurgents' "minds, their mentality and their motives" (Paget 1967: 162). Yet, by the late 1970s, the role of concrete political grievances and motivations in understanding political violence had became highly contentious; so much so that a focus on "understanding" terrorism could expose experts to charges of "sympathy" with terrorists. As terrorism expert Brian Jenkins observed,

> When I was in the special forces, we read Mao, Guevara, etc. Not because we were ideologically enamored of Marxism, but this was the only way to understand the guerrilla warfare we confronted. But now, post-9/11, we consign terrorists simply to the realm of evil.[5]

The shift in the meaning of "terrorism" during the 1970s is clearly illustrated by a collection of over 250 definitions of the term collected recently (Easson and Schmid 2011). Practically every definition prior to 1972 refers primarily to state violence. But the definitions collected from 1972 and later either refer exclusively to insurgent violence or incorporate both insurgent and state violence within their purview, with very few referring primarily to state violence.

---

[5] Interview with Brian Jenkins, June 26, 2007.

The "counterinsurgency era"

The American "counterinsurgency era" of the 1960s brought together thinkers from academia, think tanks, and the military and civilian branches of the government. Although there had been a renewed interest in counterinsurgency since the end of World War II, President Kennedy was enamored of counterinsurgency theory, and encouraged its growth and institutionalization (McClintock 1992; Maechling 1988), with the result that the early 1960s marked a high point in elite interest, attention, and resources. Just before taking office, Kennedy set up the new Special Group on Counterinsurgency (Marlowe 2010), and four months later the army published the special report "Operations against irregular forces" (FM 31–15), which "opened with the premise that guerrilla warfare was merely the 'outward manifestation' of public disenchantment with certain political, social, and economic conditions," and emphasized that guerrilla movements relied on the support of the population and that insurgencies could be ended only by addressing their causes (Birtle 2006).

Over the next several years counterinsurgency would become institutionalized in field manuals and courses at the war colleges (Maechling 1988: 30). The US Department of Defense (DOD) provided contracts and grants for counterinsurgency research both to universities and to private federally funded research and development organizations such as RAND and the Institute for Defense Analyses (IDA). According to one source, the DOD's budget for research on counterinsurgency grew from $10 million to $160 million between 1960 and 1966, with $6 million of the latter figure devoted to social science research (Solovey 2001: 180), while another source estimates that overall DOD funding for social and behavioral sciences reached $27.3 million in 1965 (Gendzier 1998: 83), and a report commissioned by the US government found that "the amount spent for non-materiel research and development on counterinsurgency was $8 million in FY 64, and $10.8 million in FY 65, an increase of 35 percent" (Blumstein and Orlansky 1965: 11). Most of this work was performed at hybrid government/academic organizations such as the Special

Operations Research Office (SORO) at the American University and Project Agile of the Advanced Research Projects Agency (ARPA), though often by academic researchers at these locations.[6] And, while the percentage of university funding paled in relation to the overall DOD budget, it was not an insignificant amount for the universities. Nor was this work insignificant intellectually or policy-wise.

The counterinsurgency discourse of the 1960s merged ideas from American social scientists on international development with earlier schools of counterinsurgency thought from Europe, where (particularly British and French) colonial powers had elaborated theories of counterinsurgency to quell colonial rebellions. But, whereas the European counterinsurgency theorists tended to be soldiers, the US counterinsurgency theorists of the 1960s were largely academics and other civilian researchers. And, with development theorist Walt Rostow as Kennedy's deputy national security advisor, there was a convergence of thinking between ideas about insurgency and guerrilla warfare and development. A symposium on counterinsurgency, held at RAND's Washington, DC, office in 1962 in response to Kennedy's desire for information to aid in Vietnam, featured a number of military thinkers, including such luminaries of counterinsurgency theory as Charles T. R. Bohannan, Napolean Valeriano, David Galula, and Frank Kitson.[7] Counterinsurgency research funded by the Department of Defense in the 1960s included some of the most prestigious individuals and institutions in the academic world at the time, such as Seymour Martin Lipset at the University of California, Alex Inkeles at Harvard, S. N. Eisenstadt at the Hebrew University, Morris Janowitz at the University of Chicago, and researchers at the University of

---

[6] On this point, see Blumstein and Orlansky (1965: 16), who also write: "Universities are not being utilized to any significant extent in the research program on counterinsurgency. Twenty-six universities performed 32 studies and received about 14 percent of the total budget in FY65. The average size of these studies is small, i.e., $46,000 compared to an average of $96,000 for all studies" (Blumstein and Orlansky 1965: 31).

[7] This was a symposium held at the RAND office, sponsored by ARPA and organized and chaired by Stephen Hosmer (Hosmer and Crane 2006 [1963]).

Southern California, University of Pennsylvania, University of Florida, Indiana University, Stanford University, Princeton, the University of Illinois, and the Massachusetts Institute of Technology (MIT) (Blumstein and Orlansky 1965). Harry Eckstein's edited collection *Internal War* was produced at Princeton, and boasted contributions from many of the most prominent sociologists and political scientists of the time, including Talcott Parsons, William Kornhouser, Lucian Pye, Sidney Verba, Gabriel Almond, Seymour Martin, and Lipset (Eckstein 1964).[8] And a conference sponsored by SORO in March 1962, which had as a primary purpose to attract leading social scientists to counterinsurgency research, attracted representatives from leading schools and organizations such as the University of Wisconsin, the Russell Sage Foundation, the Brookings Institution, Yale, Princeton, the University of Chicago, the Social Science Research Council, the University of California at Berkeley, and MIT (Lybrand 1962).

The prominence of counterinsurgency theory, and the associated military–academic nexus, might well have persisted had it not been for two crucial breaking points: the controversy that erupted over Project Camelot in 1965, and the perceived failure of counterinsurgency in Vietnam. The primary role of academics in the development of counterinsurgency theory is visible in the roster of participants in Project Camelot, a research project conceived by SORO that was designed to seek the roots (and thus methods of prevention) of revolution and insurgency. Many of Project Camelot's consultants came from elite institutions, and were of high status in their respective disciplines: its consultants included some of the most eminent names in the social sciences, such as Jessie Bernard, Lewis Coser, Neil Smelser, S. N. Eisenstadt, James Coleman, and William Gamson (Solovey 2001: 181). And with a projected budget of $4 to 6 million, it was to have been "the largest single grant ever provided for a social

---

[8] See www.rand.org/pubs/reports/R412–1. Note, however, that most of those who did – successfully – make the transition in the United States from counterinsurgency to terrorism were from the military/government/think tank side, not the academic side.

science project" (Horowitz 1967: 4), a "veritable Manhattan Project for the behavioral sciences" (Herman 1998: 103).[9]

But the project was cancelled on July 8, 1965, before it had even got off the ground, disrupting the prior seemingly stable relations between government and the social sciences in the United States (Gendzier 1998; Herman 1998; Lyons 1969; Solovey 2001). Just two years later a volume on the affair declared that the Camelot controversy "is now recognized as a fundamental watershed in the relations between social science and practical politics," and that "[t]his project has had perhaps the worst public relations record of any agency or subagency of the US government" (Horowitz 1967: v–vi). The official goal of the study, according to a description in a document mailed to scholars about the work in December 1964, was "to determine the feasibility of developing a general social systems model which would make it possible to predict and influence politically significant aspects of social change in the developing nations of the world" and to identify "actions which a government might take leading to potential internal war" (Horowitz 1967: 4–5). But after word of the study had leaked to the public, and a letter sent out by Johan Galtung of the International Peace Research Institute in Oslo accused the project of using social scientists for spying to further the interests of US imperialism in Latin America, the subsequent outcry spread from social scientists to Congress and the mass media, leading to its cancellation (Horowitz 1967).

The outcry was so great that hearings were called in the Subcommittee on International Organizations and Movements of the House Committee on Foreign Affairs on the same day the project

[9] Note, however, that the relative impact of such funding was highly inflected by local circumstance. Whereas the Camelot budget seemed like a "virtual Manhattan project" to many social scientists, it was more of a proverbial drop in the bucket to the overall Department of Defense budget. As Horowitz has suggested, "A set of different perceptions arose as to the importance of Camelot: an Army view that considers a four-to-seven million dollar grant as one of many forms of 'software' investment and, in contrast, a social science perception of Project Camelot as the equivalent of the Manhattan Project" (Horowitz 1967: 27).

was cancelled (Herman 1998: 104). The solution settled upon was to impose greater oversight, with all "foreign area research" in the future to be cleared through a new agency located within the Department of State (Herman 1998: 104). One significant outcome of the Camelot controversy was a shift from the use of university-/disciplinary-based intellectuals, to primarily nonacademic researchers for military and foreign affairs research in the social sciences,[10] signaling a break in the location of counterinsurgency research. Government sponsorship of social science research significantly increased during the late twentieth century, but underwent a shift in location from the university to the private sector, particularly in relation to foreign policy and national defense.[11]

It was not until the end of the Vietnam War, however, that counterinsurgency begin to be thought of as an irredeemable failure (McClintock 1992; Spjut 1978) – so much so that the author of an intellectual history of counterinsurgency wrote, "When I started this project in late 1980, many people told me that counterinsurgency was passé...a rapidly fading and best forgotten moment in American foreign policy" (Shafer 1988: ix). And, even more strikingly, an instructor at one of the military colleges was reportedly told, on seeking books on counterinsurgency at the JFL Special Warfare Center and School at Fort Bragg, North Carolina, that "all material on counterinsurgency and Vietnam had been discarded in 1975 on direct order from the senior Army command" (Hoffman 1991: 2). As I show in the next section, although the counterinsurgency discourse was already on a steep decline when the problem of "terrorism" first began to emerge, it

---

[10] This break was most vehement in the discipline of anthropology, and has continued to guide the central norms of the field to this day (see, for example, the hostility that anthropologists have evinced towards the attempts of the military to enlist them into the current "war on terror" as "human terrain specialists" (Gonzales 2009; Kelly *et al.* 2010; Network of Concerned Anthropologists 2009).

[11] The rise of "think tanks" as new sites for the production of knowledge and policy-related expertise more generally has been documented elsewhere, but more attention has been paid to the arena of domestic affairs in this regard (Medvetz 2012; Smith 1991; Weaver 1989).

was still coherent enough to be the first framework applied to the nascent terrorism problem as it took shape in the 1970s.

BREAKS, CONTINUITIES, AND AMBIGUITIES ON THE ROAD FROM COUNTERINSURGENCY TO COUNTERTERRORISM

I have, up until this point, painted the shift from "counterinsurgency" to "counterterrorism" as a fairly clean break, highlighting the contrasts between the two approaches.[12] But, stark as the contrasts appear, some of the individuals and organizations who would become central to the production of terrorism expertise had roots in the study of insurgency. Brian Jenkins, who would go on to become the head of terrorism research at RAND, had earlier worked on the study of guerrillas and insurgency (Jenkins 1971, 1972),[13] and others who made the transition include Brian Crozier, Robert Moss, and Walter Laqueur.

The earliest expert commentaries on "terrorism" drew heavily upon the counterinsurgency literature (together with studies of social movements, and violence more generally). A bibliographic study of the early terrorism literature (Reid 1983: 224) found frequent references to figures best known for their work on counterinsurgency such as Feliks Gross, Joseph Roucek and Eugene Walter, and Brian Crozier, Robert Moss, and Richard Clutterbuck. And among the speakers at

---

[12] I do not mean here to deny that there were significant differences and disagreements *within* the counterinsurgency framework, as documented by researchers such as Teresa Rangil (2010) and Ron Robin (2001), who frame this difference in terms of a struggle between "demand-siders" and "supply-siders," or the "hearts and minds" versus a "cost-push" economics approach to counterinsurgency. Both these approaches treat rebellion and insurgency as a problem to be approached rationally through traditional social science methods, however, and this is a key difference that frames the distinction between both counterinsurgency schools and the new discourse on terrorism.

[13] In the latter of these works on guerrillas, it is apparent that concerns about what would soon be called "international terrorism" were already rearing their head: "Perhaps in response to the difficulties in sustaining an urban guerrilla movement in the politically more advanced nations, a new type of international terrorist may be appearing. Guerrillas have discovered mobility. Almost every major city in the world is linked by jet with twenty or thirty cities in other countries. Why storm embassies and corporate offices at home when you can deliver your destruction to your enemy's capital city?"(Jenkins 1972: 3).

the 1972 Department of State conference was Edward Gude, who had authored a number of projects for the army at SORO, including "Internal (revolutionary) wars as instruments and processes of socio-political change (REVOLT)," and "Country operations information requirements (REQUIRE)," which aimed to "improve the Army's capability to assess relevant strategic, tactical, and operational options vis-à-vis a given country under selected facts or assumptions of the international situation, and to improve the efficiency of research for country-oriented operations by considering the target country from all aspects of potential Army interest" (Blumstein and Orlansky 1965: D-13). A number of experts at RAND, such as Jenkins and Nathan Leites, who had earlier worked on counterinsurgency, headed up the emerging research program on terrorism there. And a short memo on the "History of terrorism research at RAND" made this connection explicitly, noting:

> Even prior to launching a research effort to study terrorism in 1972, RAND had been very involved in studying the threats, causes and methods of dealing with low-level conflict and insurgencies... By the time RAND's research evolved to include terrorism, studies had already been conducted on insurgencies in Manchuria, South Vietnam, Guatemala, Colombia, Thailand, the Philippines and Iraq... In 1971, Brian Jenkins wrote "The five stages of urban guerrilla warfare: challenge of the 1970s," which began setting the stage for RAND's work on terrorism.[14]

There were significant continuities that carried over from one discourse to the next, with some of the themes that would become most central to the terrorism discourse already present within the literature on counterinsurgency. Although I have emphasized the extent to which the counterinsurgency literature tended to affirm the importance of grievances, disavowals of insurgents' motives were also

---

[14] Karen Treverton, "History of terrorism research at RAND," unpublished report, RAND Corporation, Santa Monica, CA.

sometimes present. For example, Paget (1967: 85–6) argued that insurgents' claimed grievances were unfounded, and that they were driven by envy, resentment, and emotion instead. And, although the counterinsurgency literature most often treated "terror" as just another tactic, some authors did single it out for moral opprobrium: Crozier (1960: 127) declared that "rebellion may or may not be 'good,' but terrorism cannot be anything but 'bad,'" while Trinquier (2006 [1961]: 16, 18) wrote:

> What characterizes modern terrorism, and makes for its basic strength, is the slaughter of generally defenseless persons. The terrorist operates within a familiar legal framework, while avoiding the ordinary risks taken by the common criminal, let alone by soldiers on the field of battle or even by partisans facing regular troops... The terrorist claims the same honors while rejecting the same obligations. His kind of organization permits him to escape from the police, his victims cannot defend themselves, and the army cannot use the power of its weapons against him because he hides himself permanently within the midst of a population going about its peaceful pursuits.

Some of these themes were picked up on by critical contemporaries, such as Eqbal Ahmad, who wrote in an essay on counterinsurgency, "The reduction of a revolution to mere insurgency also constitutes an a priori denial of its legitimacy" (Ahmad 2006 [1971]: 27), "Counterinsurgents share a conspiratorial theory which views revolutionary warfare as being primarily a technical problem, i.e., a problem of plotting and subversion, on the one hand, and of intelligence and suppression, on the other" (Ahmad 2006 [1971]: 46), and, foreshadowing a theory of terrorism that would become especially influential in the 1980s, "A logical extension of the conspiratorial theory is the belief, held with particular tenacity by counterrevolutionary army officers, that any revolutionary movement is inspired, directed, and controlled from abroad" (Ahmad 2006 [1971]: 50).

A number of aspects of the insurgency framework, in which "terror" was seen as more a tactic than a morally defining act, carried over into the earliest expert analyses of terrorism. For example, presenters at the 1972 Department of State conference on terrorism suggested that states and insurgents/opponent groups might both be terrorists; and that almost any group might take up terrorism (Perenyi 1972: 1). Terrorism was still treated, at this early stage, as a tactic, not an identity linked to a particular (morally or politically identified) type of actor. Further, the link of terrorism to specific grievances and motivations was emphasized, thus framing terrorist actions as both rational and understandable. At the 1972 Department of State conference, "[t]he participants agreed generally that terrorism was the product of frustration induced by unresolved grievances or, in Professor Levy's terms, 'punishing circumstances.'"[15] Similarly, the report from a 1973 conference on terrorism (Bassiouni 1975: 5) reports on a 1972 UN study on

> measures to prevent international terrorism which endangers or takes innocent human lives or jeopardizes fundamental freedoms, and study of the underlying causes of these forms of terrorism and acts of violence which lie in misery, frustration, grievance and despair and which cause some people to sacrifice human lives, including their own, in attempt to effect radical changes.

This emphasis on the role of grievances remained central to the earliest expert analyses of terrorism, as the excerpts from the 1972 Department of State conference at the opening of this chapter illustrate. And the tenor of the debate within the Department of State and its associated Cabinet Committee to Combat Terrorism retained this interest in concrete motivations for terrorism through the middle of the decade. A 1973 report noted that "the unresolved Middle East question still spawns sufficient Arab frustration to produce a steady flow of the type of the type of terrorist who perpetrated dastardly crimes such as the murder of Belgian and American diplomats in

---

[15] Copy of summary of report from 1972 Department of State terrorism conference, NARA, Nixon papers.

Khartoum," declaring: "We are not unmindful of the motivations inspiring frustrated political terrorists, but they must be dissuaded, by reason or by preventive measures, from striking at innocent bystanders."[16] A 1974 memo on "Guidelines for dealing with terrorism with international ramifications" took a focus on grievances as the root cause of terrorism, condemning the use of violence, while acknowledging that underlying motivations might be legitimate:

> The US Government recognizes the merit of elimination of causes of terrorism, including legitimate grievances which motivate potential terrorists... While political motivations such as the achievement of self-determination or independence are cited by some individuals or groups to justify terrorism, such issues should be addressed in appropriate fora rather than by resort to violence against innocent bystanders.[17]

And a 1975 progress report from the CCCT to the president concluded, "Last but not least, there seems to be no shortage of political, economic, and social frustrations to spawn terrorists on all continents."[18] In sum, there was a serious recognition of the fact that terrorism could stem from specific grievances, and that the proper response on the part of the government to terrorism was to investigate and possibly act upon these grievances.

Even as the decade wore on, counterinsurgency experts were among those considered as potential terrorism experts, and some aspects of the counterinsurgency discourse persisted in the new terrorism framework. Brian Crozier, Robert Moss, and Ted Gurr were among those considered as speakers for a 1976 Department of State conference on international terrorism,[19] a 1976 conference on "Terror: the man, the mind, the matter" included presentations from

---

[16] CCCT, DNSA document TE 285.
[17] DNSA document TE 340, memo to CCCT on "Guidelines for dealing with terrorism with international ramifications" (1974).
[18] CCCT, DNSA document TE 366.
[19] DNSA document TE 441, "Agenda for meeting 92 WG/CCCT" (1975).

Felicks Gross and Nicholas Kittrie, while RAND counterinsurgency expert Nathan Leites was one of the speakers at a 1978 international scientific conference on terrorism (Rapoport and Alexander 1982).

Yet, by the late 1970s, the question of attributing rationality to terrorists would become quite contentious, and as the terrorism discourse developed the very question of whether terrorists had rational, objective motives would become highly politically charged. As the editor to an edited volume composed of papers from a 1976 terrorism conference saw it (and as quoted at the start of the chapter), terrorism in this day was "a new barbarism...fought primarily not to win territory or even to cause destruction, but to command attention, to instill fear, and to terrorize in the hope of forcing the world to listen and to right an alleged wrong" (Livingston, Kress, and Wanek 1978: 19). We must, he emphasized, "never forget for a moment that terrorists can never be depended upon to act rationally," and that there is a "fanatical and truly irrational element among terrorists"(Livingston, Kress, and Wanek 1978: 20), who are "fanatics incapable of accommodation," best characterized as "naive, emotional, impulsive, often irrational, and fundamentally uninformed" (Livingston, Kress, and Wanek 1978: 20–2). Similarly, an article on "out-inventing the terrorist," published in 1979, reported that "we see the likelihood of terrorism increasingly becoming an end in itself. This would result from a nihilist attitude that already appears to be quite prevalent over other actually ideological motivations" (Russell, Banker, and Miller 1979: 35–6).

As the decade progressed it became more common for analysts to claim that terrorists' goals were not rational, and perhaps not even recognizably political at all. If terrorists were conceded to be political, their goals were often categorized as not normally political but, rather, pathological. By the middle of the 1970s the discourse had begun to move towards a reconceptualization of terrorism as a practice that defined a certain type of actor. At the 1976 Department of State conference on international terrorism, the question of whether terrorists could ever be "freedom fighters" was hotly debated, with (according to the official report), the majority of presenters arguing that the categories were mutually exclusive. In other words, "terrorism" was in the process of being redefined as a category with *a moral evaluation intrinsically built into it*. The question of whether "terrorists" could be "freedom fighters," though seemingly a matter of arcane semantics, is actually indicative of a crucial turning point in the history of conceptualizations of political violence. This very opposition, between "terrorists" and "freedom fighters," which would become a statement of cliché just a few years later, would have been relatively nonsensical within the earlier counterinsurgency discourse, which did not pose these as mutually exclusive categories. By the late 1970s the moral evaluation of terrorists, and rejection of attention to grievances, had become firmly entrenched within the terrorism discourse. In 1979 an entire conference was devoted to the notion of terrorism as psychopathology (Mickolus 1980), and to the question of how terrorists could justify their horrific acts, while another took as its guiding question how (immoral) terrorists justified their unthinkable acts, suggesting that "it is precisely because terrorists always violate accepted norms, and their actions are unprecedented sometimes by the practices of the terrorist group itself, that justifications can never cease" (Rapoport and Alexander 1982: 3).

EXPLAINING THE SHIFT

I have argued that, although the earliest terrorism expertise drew upon a previous discourse on political violence, that of insurgency, by the late 1970s the counterinsurgency framework had been supplanted by a new approach, which conceptualized terrorism as an entirely new sort of problem: irrational, fundamentally immoral, and with a complicated relationship to the political realm. How can we explain this transformation? A partial answer can be derived from the observation that there was a shift in the key governmental site of terrorism discourse during this time, to a more public realm. The state was the key instigator of terrorism expertise in the early 1970s. The development of terrorism discourse and expertise was at first located primarily within the relatively quiet executive branch

Cabinet Committee to Combat Terrorism. In 1974, however, there were eight congressional hearings on terrorism held in the House of Representatives and the Senate.[20] This moved the debate on terrorism into a more public venue, and a site in which discussions were likely to take a more contentious tone as senators and representatives aimed – through the witnesses they called, the questions they asked, and the very topics put forth as subjects of hearings – to advance their political agendas. Thus, one reason for this shift can be attributed to the growth of "terrorism" as a problem in the public eye.

Another contributing factor is that "terrorism," as opposed to earlier forms of political violence that were labeled "insurgency," seemed to be more of an imminent threat to the domestic US population. This was both because it targeted Americans and, especially, because it targeted sites of international connection identified with a peaceful civilian realm, such as airline travel, diplomacy, and the Olympic Games. And, while this shift to a more publicly oriented debate does not, in and of itself, explain the emergence of the particular characteristics that I have attributed to the new discourse, framing terrorism as evil, irrational, and inexplicable, it is noteworthy that a parallel landmark shift occurred in the realm of criminological policy. As David Garland (2001) convincingly argues, over the course of the 1970s criminological policy in the United States shifted from a rehabilitation orientation, heavily informed by social-scientific research emerging from sociology and criminology, to a punitive framework, oriented towards public sentiment against criminals and a fear of crime. Furthermore, the earlier criminological rehabilitative framework and the counterinsurgency framework can both be situated within a broadly progressive and modernist view of the world, which linked state policy and social science research in ambitious projects that aimed to remake

---

[20] There was one Congressional hearing related to terrorism in 1973, but this hearing, on the Anti-Hijacking Act of 1973, was characterized by a focus on particular tactics, such as hijacking and kidnapping as criminal acts, rather than as part of a larger problem of "terrorism." There were no hearings on terrorism in 1972.

individuals and society (as discussed by James Scott 1998), while the punitive criminological framework and the new "terrorism" discourse are both grounded in a rejection of that project (as Jal Mehta argues in a forthcoming book: Mehta forthcoming).

In transcripts from the 1974 congressional hearings on terrorism, the contrasts and interactions between members of Congress and expert witnesses are telling. Members of Congress were likely to assert that terrorism was evil, irrational, and meaningless while expert witnesses varied in their approach, from analysts who stressed the role of political grievances to those who viewed terrorists as mentally disturbed. For example, at the opening of the first part of the 1974 hearings on terrorism before the Committee on Internal Security in the House of Representatives, Representative Richard Ichord commented:

> I wish we could find some other more suitable expression than "political kidnappings" or "political terrorism" particularly as the subject is used by the news media which seem to suggest somehow that what are purely and simply criminal acts can be justified because they are perpetrated in the name of politics or social reform.[21]

In line with this anti-political sentiment, the witnesses for this portion of the hearings were three psychiatrists, who testified as to how they saw hijackers as mentally abnormal or as having a "terrorist personality," and a representative of the International Association of Chiefs of Police. And, later that year, in a hearing on "International terrorism before the House Subcommittee on the Near East and South Asia," witness Eugene Methvin (editor at *Reader's Digest*)[22] declared

---

[21] "Terrorism, part 1" hearings before the Committee on Internal Security, House of Representatives, February 27–28, March 21, 22, 26, 1974, p. 2952.

[22] Methvin also suggested in this same testimony that the KGB played a role in international terrorism – a view that would (as I discuss in Chapter 5) take on great significance during the 1980s, and that the *Reader's Digest* (among other publications) would help to promulgate.

that analyses of terrorism that linked it to social grievances were not just untrue but politicized opinions rather than factual analyses:

> The liberal view that they are a response to justifiable social grievances is a deceptive part-truth. They are also a regular response of human nature to myriad and random circumstances. They are a result of the individual human penchant for hate, and of the tendency of haters to communicate, to congregate, and via a process of mutual reinforcement to concentrate, magnify, and focus their hate energies. You will find terrorism occurring with a frequency as usual and normal in human societies as such other normal human pathologies as alcoholism or suicide.[23]

Some of the hearings later that year did bring witnesses who contextualized terrorism within a context of political motivations and grievances, but these witnesses were often subject to objections from the members of Congress to whom they were speaking. Some of the most interesting moments in the transcripts occur in these contentious interactions between representatives and witnesses. Members of Congress were most likely to take issue with approaches that contextualized terrorism in relation to political grievances, that appeared to justify terrorism, or that questioned the utility of a "hard-line" policy response. During the hearings, witness Dr. Frederick Hacker, a psychiatrist, kept trying to contextualize violence and terrorism, in response to which the congressmen would persist in returning to the question of whether terrorists were mentally ill. In one telling instance, Hacker specified:

> I disagree with the former Vice President of the United States who made the distinction between fighting criminality by supporting the police no matter what, on the spot, and investigating to get to the root causes of it. As you know, he

---

[23] Testimony of Eugene Methvin, "International terrorism" hearings before the Subcommittee on the Near East and South Asia of the Committee on Foreign Affairs, House of Representatives, June 11–24, 1974, p. 32.

expressed himself by stating he would be in favor of fighting it rather than investigating. But the two have to go together.[24]

In the hearings on "International terrorism," held in June 1974,[25] the exchanges between those witnesses who attempted to contextualize terrorism and the members of Congress are quite interesting, and follow a similar pattern. Lewis Hoffacker, of the Cabinet Committee to Combat Terrorism, in his testimony cited the "frustrations that feed terrorism," and argued:

> We as a government must maintain a position of firmness – and I might add, sensitivity – in responding to these vicious attacks against our citizens and other interests. As we seek to defend ourselves against this viciousness, we are not unmindful of the various motivations, both real and conjured of individuals and organized terrorist groups who have chosen terrorism as the way to attain their objectives.[26]

In response, Representative John Buchanan emphasized the importance of establishing terrorism as "barbaric" and "unspeakable," declaring:

> Mr. Ambassador, I think that there must be a way that we can establish an international climate in which barbaric acts of terrorism against innocent people will be treated by the world community as barbaric and as something that is simply an unspeakable policy in a civilized setting,[27]

and continued:

> It is a matter of great concern to me that it has become respectable in some Arab circles to boast of the murder of innocent children, and I think only an unbalanced mind could conceive of acts of terrorism as an acceptable element of any kind of struggle.[28]

---

[24] "Terrorism, part 1" hearings, February–March 1974.
[25] "International terrorism" hearings, June 1974.
[26] Hoffacker, "International terrorism" hearings, June 1974, p. 5.
[27] Buchanan, "International terrorism" hearings, June 1974, p. 11.
[28] Buchanan, "International terrorism" hearings, June 1974, p. 11.

These same hearings on "International terrorism" brought as witnesses Bert Lockwood, of the NYU Center for International Studies, and Richard Falk, of the Center for International Studies at Princeton, on June 19. Both Lockwood and Falk emphasized the importance of international law, human rights, and justice in fighting terrorism – an approach that drew strong responses from those present. Lockwood testified:

> If the United States is truly concerned about combating international terrorism then I recommend – if I may borrow the jargon in vogue in this administration – that in addition to its developing a defensive strategy replete with security measures, that it take the offense, meaning that it should press for laws and international agreements on both terrorism and "state terrorism."[29]

Falk took a similar approach, arguing for a new emphasis on human rights, and stating that

> I think the fundamental issue here is that one can't have a stable international environment merely by facilitating order in the world. A serious – and not merely rhetorical – concern for justice is integral to achieving any kind of meaningful stability.[30]

He continued:

> I think it is often true that the perpetrators of terror are fanatical individuals, perhaps psychologically unstable, but I think it is more to the point to acknowledge that their recourse to desperate politics arises from objective grievances that are widely endorsed by the international community.[31]

In response, Representative Benjamin Gilman objected, stating:

> Gentlemen, the main thrust of your joint statement seems to be that we should examine more closely the reasons for terrorism and

---

[29] By this he means human rights violations, primarily; Lockwood, "International terrorism" hearings, June 1974, p. 84.

[30] Falk, "International terrorism" hearings, June 1974, p. 111.

[31] Falk, "International terrorism" hearings, June 1974, p. 113.

to try to satisfy some of these grievances, perhaps change our foreign policy in some instances. Is my understanding of the statements correct? [...] We are studying criminal acts against society, against individuals. In studying claims and in dealing with crimes and persons dealing in acts against society, shouldn't our first objective be to find the crime and mete out the punishment in order to deter further crimes?[32]

Representative Jonathan Bingham raised similar objections:

I am troubled to some extent by both of these papers. I think one thing that I find missing in your presentation, Dr. Falk, is the kind of indignation against the killing of innocent people that I recall you expressing very vividly in connection with Vietnam. I don't find a distinction between violence on the one hand directed at the opposition, and terrorism which I would define as trying to use innocent people in a way to influence the political situation. I don't find the kinds of distinction between types of terrorism that it would seem to me scholarly analysis ought to provide.[33]

A similar pattern of contention occurred during the testimony of Brian Jenkins of RAND, who was called as a witness on June 24, and who began by describing terrorism as a new form of warfare, stating that "[t]errorism is often described as mindless violence, senseless violence, or irrational violence. None of these adjectives is correct." He asserted, instead, that "terrorism is a means to an end, not an end in itself; in other words, terrorism has objectives." This seemingly moderate approach drew questioning, however; Representative Lee Hamilton questioned Jenkins as follows:

It seems that there may be two broad approaches by our various witnesses to the question of how to deal with the terrorists. One emphasizes the criminal nature of the terrorist and suggests very

---

[32] Gilman, "International terrorism" hearings, June 1974, p. 123.
[33] Bingham, "International terrorism" hearings, June 1974, p. 132.

strong counterforce measures. The other school of thought emphasizes the legitimate concerns of many terrorist groups and says that the way to deal with them really is to deal with these underlying political, social, and economic injustices. Which school of thought would you put yourself in here as between the two?

To this Jenkins responded:

> I would fall somewhere between the two. I don't think it will be possible to outlaw terrorism... Insofar as solving all injustices in the world as a means of eliminating terrorism, I doubt that can be done.

Jenkins went on to disavow both the idea that "terrorist" was a fixed identity and the idea that terrorism could be understood without a larger social or political context:

> I don't believe terrorists belong to a separate country of the world called "terrorism," and therefore we can deal with them apart from various local struggles. Their actions take place within a political context. In some cases their actions result from injustices that are understandable. In some cases not.

He continued by distancing himself from the claims that terrorists were irrational and lacked political motives, advising that US policy towards terrorists should not

> take the position that they are international thugs who exist in the world only to create pain for us or that they are lunatics. They are seldom lunatics.

Representative Bingham questioned Jenkins as to whether governments can commit terror. Jenkins answered in the affirmative, declaring:

> Within any dispassionate definition of terrorism – that is, if one does not deliberately attempt to use the word in a pejorative sense – we would have to recognize a state or official terrorism which would fall within the purview of our discussion. I don't think terrorism is limited to nongovernment groups. Indeed, if one had

some means of counting all of the victims of totalitarian regimes in recent years, I am sure that state terror would be far ahead of revolutionary or nongovernmental terror.

Clearly displeased with this response, Bingham replied, "Don't we perhaps need a different word for that?"

One of Jenkins' most contentious statements at this hearing was his classification of terrorism as a form of warfare. Representative Gilman objected to calling terrorism a form of warfare, saying: "I think that when we characterize these as acts of warfare we are giving them a cloak of legality that really does not belong to the terrorists and to their acts of terrorism." In response, Jenkins asserted that, while he did consider terrorism a form of warfare, "[c]alling terrorism a form of warfare does not legitimize it," and that, further, the question of terrorism's legitimacy should be seen as entirely separate: "By calling terrorism a kind of warfare I have neither accorded it a legitimate status nor have I branded it to be totally illegitimate."[34]

This chapter has now identified some of the more macro causes of the shift from insurgency to terrorism, including the shift to a more public realm of debate. But there were also changes at the level of expert action that contributed to the transformation. First, there was a growing move on the part of experts to distinguish "terrorism" from insurgency and guerrilla warfare – a problem that seems particularly keen to an era of transition. In 1973 Irving Horowitz stated that, as soon as one "attempts to profile the terrorist, enormous problems of definition arise that inhibit possible remedial action" (Horowitz 1973: 147), but that it was of particular importance to distinguish between terrorist and guerrilla actions. Others tried to specify what these differences were. According to Walter Laqueur (1974: 48),

Seen in historical perspective, guerrilla warfare, per se, is neither good nor bad, certainly not more reprehensible morally than war

---

[34] All the above quotations come from the "International terrorism" hearings, June 1974, pp. 137, 144, 144–5, 145, 148, 150, 151, 154, 155, respectively.

itself. On many occasions it has been a perfectly legitimate, sometimes the only possible, method of resisting national or social oppression... But at the same time it has become more and more obvious that what was once known as guerrilla warfare is gradually giving way in many countries to terrorist tactics, pure and simple, on the part of small groups...trying to impose their will on the majority in the struggle for power.

The next year Paul Wilkinson (1974: 16–17) wrote:

What fundamentally distinguishes terrorism from other forms of organized violence is not simply its severity but its features of amorality and antinomianism. Terrorists either profess indifference to existing moral codes or else claim exemption from all such obligations. Political terror, if it is waged consciously and deliberately, is implicitly prepared to sacrifice all moral and humanitarian considerations for the sake of some political end.

In addition, there was, as I have detailed in Chapter 2, a significant entry of new experts into the field. And the somewhat smaller number of experts who made the transition from counterinsurgency to counterterrorism scholarship, such as Laqueur, quoted above, were often some of the most insistent upon the need to draw distinctions between the two forms of violence.

Effects upon expertise

As "terrorism" solidified as an object of expert knowledge, it did not, as studies of scientific knowledge often find, become "purified" of its political or moral character. Rather, the expert discourse became *more* characterized by an interweaving of moral, political, and scientific/ analytical concerns and approaches at this time. This led to persistent difficulties for those seeking to create rational knowledge about political violence, and the nature of the relation between knowledge, experts, and the state shifted significantly with this reconceptualization.

As "terrorism" developed throughout the 1970s, ideas about morality became intertwined with definitions and explanations of terrorism. At the same time, however, morality also became intertwined with the production and evaluation of terrorism experts and expertise. Experts faced increasing difficulty presenting themselves and their work as legitimate, yet morally detached and separable from their object of "terrorism." For example, Bernard Avishai, in a 1979 essay in *The New York Review of Books*, criticized terrorism experts for not being sufficiently critical of terrorists. Avishai writes that two of the authors under review "are social scientists who claim to be experts on terror and give advice on how to deal with it," yet critiques them for having "little patience" for moral argument and for writing in a style such that their "tone is casual and clear of indignation," evincing a "stoic attitude toward the suffering of others" (Avishai 1979: 41).[35] In a similar fashion, Conor Cruise O'Brien, in a 1976 review of two books by J. Bowyer Bell in *The New York Review of Books*, writes (O'Brien 1976):

> Mr. Bowyer Bell writes about terrorists with a degree of sympathy
> which the present reviewer, being perhaps oversensitive on the
> subject, finds moderately repugnant. He sometimes, though not
> consistently, adopts the language of the terrorists themselves,
> terming their killings "executions" or, even worse, using coy
> euphemisms like "elimination," and he is impressed by the "logic"
> or "elegance" of various bloody deeds. He thinks that "the

---

[35] Avishai even goes so far as to suggest that some authors' work may not just encourage terrorists but even provide scientific rationales for their behavior: "It is of particular interest that behavioral scientists concerned with terrorism should share so many methodological assumptions with the revolutionaries they study. That [J. Bowyer] Bell [1978] and [Jan] Schreiber [1978] describe terrorists in much the same language as the latter describe themselves is evident in the recent interview with German terrorist Michael "Bommi" Baumann, in *Encounter*, September 1978... Moreover, behind terrorists' (and, I dare say, Bell's and Schreiber's) apparent indifference to argued analyses of right and wrong – and necessary to that indifference – is in fact an argument about right and wrong, namely, that what has come to seem necessary, in view of the frequency or intensity of its occurrence, action, etc., also has claims to be right. Whatever their pretensions to acting merely by response to history's stimulus, terrorists could not have begun to speak their 'scientific' language without having absorbed moral and epistemological views that have a long history" (Avishai 1979: 44).

practitioners of terror can largely be categorized on the basis of their aspirations" and resists other methods of categorizing them, such as those which would include among others the categories of lunatics and gangsters.

A second set of dilemmas arose around the question of whether terrorism was susceptible to rational analysis. If terrorism, and terrorists, are irrational, how could it be possible to understand them through scientific analysis? The contested nature of terrorists' rationality thus impacted not only understandings of terrorism but the very form and possibility of terrorism expertise itself. In a 1977 review, Anthony Arblaster writes: "A second popular myth about terrorists figures rather more prominently in these books. This is the belief that the terrorist is – must be – psychologically warped, if not actually mentally deranged" (Arblaster 1977: 421–2). As Arblaster points out, one common strategy adopted by experts in response to such difficulties was to take an ambiguous, or even contradictory, stance: straddling the line, as it were. A final set of difficulties emerges from the question of whether expertise can be separable from politics. Is terrorism experts' work necessarily political? Ought it to be? Or can terrorism expertise be separated from political inflections and goals? While experts have attempted to "strip the term of its abusive connotations, and thus make it 'objective' or 'scientific'" (Rapoport and Alexander 1982: 3), such strategies achieved limited success.[36]

The discourses of "insurgency" and of "terrorism" not only presumed a different understanding of the problem of political violence, they also each set up a different relation through which the expert speakers of these discourses relate to their objects of study. "Terrorism" became newly problematic as an object of expert knowledge along three key axes in the new discourse of terrorism expertise, both in terms of the possibilities for the creation of expert knowledge and in terms of conceptualizations of terrorism and terrorists

---

[36] I take up this issue of the attempts at subjecting "terrorism" to rational analysis, and the difficulties this project faced, in greater detail in the next chapter.

Table 3.1 *Three newly problematic dimensions of "terrorism" discourse*

	Morality	Rationality	Politicization
As pertaining to *terrorism/ terrorists*	Necessarily immoral (slightly contested)	Rationality of motives and tactics always in question	Whether terrorists have political motives/ goals is contested
As pertaining to *terrorism experts (*and their relation to the problem/ data)	Requirement to condemn; possibility of moral detachment; value-neutral research is questioned	Possibility of rational analysis in question	Possibility of apolitical expertise continually in question

themselves. These were: morality, rationality, and politicization. Tables 3.1 and 3.2 illustrate this shift.

The 1960s discourse of counterinsurgency was (perhaps surprisingly, from the contemporary point of view) formally morally neutral: neither the moral character of either insurgents or counterinsurgents, nor a moral evaluation of the practices and outcomes of insurgency or counterinsurgency, was integral to the discourse, and within the counterinsurgency discourse even "terrorism" was a concept that could be set apart from morality. A studied neutrality towards insurgent and guerrilla violence was common throughout the counterinsurgency writings of the 1960s and early 1970s. As Crozier wrote in 1960 (Crozier 1960: 159),

> Terrorism is a weapon of the weak. This is a factual observation: it does not exonerate those who use terrorism as a weapon from any moral blame that may be put on them by their victims or by outsiders. Nor, on the other hand, does it imply that the weak are morally inferior to the strong. All acts of violence are open to criticism on moral grounds.

Table 3.2 *"Insurgency" versus "terrorism"*

	Insurgency/ counterinsurgency	Terrorism/ counterterrorism
Morality of *actors* part of definition?	No	Yes (contested)
Rationality of actors in question?	No	Yes (contested)
Political motives of actors in question?	No	Yes (contested)
Morality of *experts* in question?	Yes[a]	Yes
Possibility of rational analysis in question?	No	Yes
Possibility of apolitical analysis in question?	Yes[b]	Yes
Insurgents/terrorists considered parallel to their opponents?	Yes	No
Insurgents/terrorists resist application of the label?	No	Yes
Expertise defined by a "problem of definition"?	No	Yes

Notes:
[a] The moral relation between experts and their object of study undergoes a fundamental shift between counterinsurgency and counterterrorism, however.
[b] Although the relation between politics and knowledge was highly contested under both counterinsurgency and counterterrorism, the form of this contestation would shift significantly.

Frank Kitson, in the introduction to his 1971 classic *Low Intensity Operations* (Kitson 1974 [1971]: 8), felt the need to clarify that "there is some right and some wrong on both sides," and to make the case that *counter*-subversion could be morally defensible:

> One final matter which requires mentioning in this introduction, concerns the moral issues involved in preparing to suppress subversion. Many regard subversion as being principally a form of

redress used by the down-trodden peoples of the world against their oppressors, and feel, therefore, that there is something immoral about preparing to suppress it. Undoubtedly subversion is sometimes used in this way, and on these occasions those supporting the government find themselves fighting for a bad cause. On the other hand subversion can also be used by evil men to advance their own interests in which case those fighting it have right on their side.[37]

Similarly, Robert Moss opened his 1972 book (Moss 1972: 16) by stating:

> This is neither a "how to do it" nor a "how to bash them" book. Its aim is analytical rather than polemical... But it would be tendentious to talk about the guerrilla movement in Guatemala (for example) without mentioning the glaring social injustices and the short-sighted and self-seeking economic practices of foreign corporations like the United Fruit Company that explain its popular following... [A]rmed rebellion is usually the symptom of a deep-seated social malaise. No one would quarrel with the idea that some governments are so corrupt or repressive that they deserve to be overthrown, or that violence is sometimes justified as a last resort for men who have no other avenue for protest.

And this carried over into the role of the experts themselves, and their relation to their topic of study. As Crozier (1960: 159) writes,

> I shall try, therefore, to avoid passing moral judgments. My purpose is to examine the weapon of terrorism, to find out whether it brings results, and to guess whether similar results could have been achieved by other means, either at all or within the same time. If I mention moral reactions, such as popular or official indignation, it

---

[37] This concern, and Kitson's response to it, apparently persisted, as several years later another writer also opened his book on guerrilla warfare with that same quote (Fairbairn 1974: 8).

will be because such reactions have bearing on the efficacy of the
terrorist weapon; not because I agree or disagree with them.
Emotion is a foe of impartiality.

Likewise, Geoffrey Fairbairn emphasizes his neutrality, but also
takes pains to make it clear that this *does not* imply a lack of sympathy for those he discusses (Fairbairn 1974: 358; emphasis in original):

> In retrospect, the author has misgivings about an implication that
> might be drawn from his mode of treating the subject. Treating
> revolutionary guerrilla warfare primarily *as warfare* might seem to
> have implied a lack of sympathy for poor men in the Third World
> who have every reason to seek all available means of liberation
> from often appallingly wretched conditions. This is certainly not
> the attitude of the author. As the descendant of a Scottish farmer of
> poor circumstances who "made good" in Australia, he is
> temperamentally disinclined to discount, let alone to denigrate, the
> motives that might well move poor farmers of the Third World to
> join guerrilla units.

Note that this is precisely the opposite maneuver that would later be
required of terrorism experts – of whom the display of sympathy could
be utterly discrediting, and neutrality possible only on a finely bal-
anced sword. Wilkinson (1974: 21) sums up these tensions, writing:
"As we shall have cause to note frequently in our analysis there is a
constant tension apparent in the literature on terrorism between
judgment and prescription and the presumed demands of scientific
impartiality or historical objectivity."

Terrorism experts have been subject to delegitimating claims of
politicization from both the left and the right, and, although some
experts have devoted significant time and resources in attempts to
purify and reform terrorism studies into an apolitical knowledge field,
their work has been continually open to challenge. Recent analyses of
terrorism expertise have suggested that the research area has suffered
from prolonged difficulties in attaining the status of an accepted

scientific field (Jackson 2005; Ranstorp 2007; Silke 2004b; Stampnitzky 2011). This chapter has suggested that the roots of these difficulties may be traceable to the origins of the discourse on "terrorism," and its differentiation from the discourse of "insurgency," in the 1970s, when the concept of "terrorism," and the expected relations between experts and political violence as an object of study, were both transformed. I return to this question of "politicization" and its effect upon expertise in Chapter 5, and again in Chapter 8. In the next chapter I take on the question of rationality, and the various rationalizing practices through which experts and policymakers attempted to deal with the seemingly irrational problem of terrorism.

4 Disasters, diplomats, and databases: rationalization and its discontents

> *The primary target was...Ruritania, a small but economically strong European nation....beset by its own terrorists, terrorist groups espousing a nihilist philosophy... The terrorists, who call themselves HATAF, threaten the Ruritanian government with a technologically sophisticated but not excessively lethal weapon... HATAF had threatened the Ruritanian government with more killings if the Ruritanian government did not comply with its demands.[1]*

The above does not describe an actual event but was the fictionalized background distributed to experts and policymakers who were going to role-play the parts of the terrorists and the government in an exercise. Such games were not intended to predict the future, or as a straightforward test of current response capabilities. They were framed as a way to spur participants to think about potential situations that might be faced, and the need for advanced planning. As the authors of this scenario put it, "Gaming hypothetical incidents, i.e., simulating possible futures, is a technique that can reduce the risk of making rash decisions."[2]

The previous chapters have shown how the meaning of terrorism first took shape. But, once "terrorism" had emerged as a problem, its meaning was not settled. Rather, it was subject to a variety of logics of governance through which it was understood and managed. These logics corresponded to practices by which experts sought to rationalize it: to make it easier to manage by subjecting it to routines

---

[1] Hoover Institution Archives, Claire Sterling papers, box 8, "A policy game about terrorism – draft," Hans Josef Horchem and Robert H. Kupperman, no date, p. 11.

[2] Hoover Institution Archives, Sterling papers, "A policy game about terrorism – draft," Horchem and Kupperman, p. 6.

of action that increase predictability. In order to understand how the problem of terrorism took shape, we must analyze not just the events that comprised – and the people who compiled – the category but also the practices through which it was made knowable. This chapter analyzes the techniques of knowledge through which the problem of terrorism was made subject to expertise and governance in the 1970s: legal analysis, scenarios and simulations, and terrorism databases. Each of these methods not only implied a different understanding of terrorism as a problem but also enabled a different mode of governance, or set of practices by which the problem might be managed. Table 4.1 outlines this alignment between experts, their ways of knowing, and their tools for governing the problem of terrorism in the 1970s.

The earliest US responses to terrorism envisioned international law as a key method for its governance. This reflected the primary role of the Department of State, which saw this as an issue to be handled through diplomatic channels. A second approach that emerged in the 1970s focused on developing practical strategies for managing and responding to terrorist events. By developing planned, routine, responses for various potentialities, experts and policymakers sought to tame the frightening and seemingly unpredictable terrorist event. While the legal approach sought to manage terrorism at the level of the world system through treaties, the operational approach focused on managing terrorism at the level of the *incident*. A third approach sought to rationalize terrorism by quantifying it. The production of chronologies, in which counts of terrorist events and deaths/casualties are plotted over time, and databases, in which events are correlated with the characteristics of perpetrators, victims, and methods of attack, aimed to make terrorism subject to calculable technologies of risk management such as insurance. Further, databases were also used to inform the governance of terrorism through logics of crime and punishment, and of crisis management.

Each of these modes of knowledge sought to fit terrorism into an existing logic, and each also enabled a different mode of governance, or set of practices through which the problem might be managed. As

Table 4.1 Logics of governance applied to terrorism in the 1970s

Logic of governance	Key time period	Archetypal knowledge technique	Corresponding techniques of management	Associated experts	Key actors	Object of governance
Legal; crime and punishment	Early/mid-1970s	Legal analysis	International law/diplomacy; extradition; use of national and international courts	Lawyers; diplomats; criminologists; law enforcement	States and the international system	Terrorist actors and organizations; the international system
Crisis management	1970s	Simulation	Routine procedures for managing (crisis) events	Emergency responders; terrorism experts; police	Emergency responders: police, doctors, etc.	Events/incidents
Risk management	1970s	Databases	Forecasting; insurance; precautionary behaviors	RAND; statisticians; CIA/intelligence agencies; analysts	Insurance/security organizations (public or private)	Risk (possible events)

the problem of "terrorism" took shape over the course of the 1970s, however, it resisted such rationalizing logics, and no one of these approaches was able to "capture" successfully the management of the terrorism problem. None of these techniques of analysis was able to make terrorism understood in an unproblematic way, and terrorism proved incapable of being fully subsumed within prevailing logics of risk management.

TERRORISM AS A LEGAL/DIPLOMATIC PROBLEM

The Department of State and the Cabinet Committee to Combat Terrorism envisioned terrorism as an issue to be handled through diplomatic channels. Indeed, this had a certain logic, since it was, at this time, a problem largely aimed at diplomats and other prominent international actors (who were some of the most common targets at the time). The impetus for the legal/diplomatic approach originated with states and international organizations such as the UN as well as with lawyers and legal organizations, who themselves began to concentrate on terrorism as a problem to be governed through law.[3] Within this framework, terrorism was largely to be governed by regulating *terrorists*, understood as lawless individuals, or lawbreaking groups, who could nonetheless be corralled and controlled within an existing framework of international laws and treaty agreements. Practices aligned with this approach included determining what "terrorism" is, and how it should be defined; determining how terrorism could be made to fit into existing laws and treaties; and producing international agreements, such as extradition policies, agreements about procedures for hijackings, and laws against harboring terrorists.

---

[3] In 1973, for example, the American Bar Association sponsored a student essay contest on "Possible legal solutions to international terrorism." NARA, Nixon papers, WHSF, Tufaro papers, box 1972–3, subject files, box 1, press release, American Bar Association Law Student Division, ABA-LSD 1973 "Henry C. Morris International Law Essay contest."

Records from this time underscore the central role that law played in the American state's early approach to the governance of terrorism. For example, a September 18, 1972, memorandum from Secretary of State William P. Rogers to President Nixon on "measures to combat terrorism" noted:

> The Legal Adviser has contacted several nongovernmental organizations in the field of international law and protection of human rights to enlist their assistance in contributing ideas and in possibly adopting statements or resolutions deploring the spread of terrorism and calling on governments to fulfill their international obligations to prevent terrorism and to punish terrorists.[4]

Similarly, a 1972 memo from Henry Kissinger, the US national security advisor, to President Nixon on "actions to combat international terrorism" noted that "Secretary Rogers and Ambassador [George H. W.] Bush have been very active in pressing for international conventions to control terrorism, particularly as it concerns civil aviation."[5] The minutes of the November 9, 1972, meeting of the working group of the CCCT reported: "The Chairman reviewed recent US actions in various international fora to establish a stronger legal foundation for combating international terrorism."[6] And a 1973 report of the president's Science Advisory Committee's subpanel on hijacking, while focusing on concrete security measures, began by noting that "the panel wants to emphasize that the elimination of

---

[4] NARA, Nixon papers, NPMP, WHSF, Tufaro papers, box 1972–3, box NSC files, subject files, CCCT, box 310.

[5] He continued, "In my opinion, we are making progress but still face formidable problems, particularly in trying to persuade other states to stand firm in the face of terrorist blackmail. We also face a major task in finding workable sanctions against nations that abet terrorism," foreshadowing the ultimate abandonment of the legal approach by the United States as the primary approach to governing terrorism, when it would come to be seen as too difficult. NARA, Nixon papers, NPMP, WHSF, staff member and office files, Tufaro papers, box 1972–3, subject files, secret attachments no. 1, CCCT working group no. 2, box 1.

[6] NARA, Tufaro papers, box 1972–3, subject files, secret attachments no. 1, CCCT working group no. 2, box 1.

safe-haven countries through international agreement would have a major impact on the problem and such agreements should continue to be pursued energetically."[7]

The US government began to sponsor a number of research projects looking into how terrorism might be governed through international law. In 1974 the CCCT sponsored research on "laws relating to terrorist acts,"[8] and the following year it solicited bids for a legal research project (with cost estimated at $50,000) to develop "an international compendium of laws and practices for combating terrorism." From this research, the CCCT hoped to gain insight into "strategies for getting quicker signatures and ratifications or international agreements."[9]

One of the largest of these projects was a study sponsored by the US Department of State and the LEAA, and carried out by the American Society of International Law (ASIL) (Evans and Murphy 1978; Murphy 1980). The aim of the study was to develop a plan to use international law to prevent terrorism, and the report was followed by a conference, held in late 1978, that aimed at evaluating its recommendations and developing a future agenda for experts and governments to use to combat terrorism (Murphy 1980: vii). Discussions at the conference focused on the following six priorities: "(1) apprehension and prosecution of international terrorists; (2) practical problems of law enforcement; (3) state responsibility, state self-help and problems of public international law; (4) technological vulnerabilities; (5) personnel and property of transnational business operations; (6) international initiatives" (Murphy 1980: vi).

This emphasis on legal and diplomatic remedies is also reflected in the records of conferences on terrorism held in the 1970s. Quite a few of the earliest conferences focused specifically on the role of law

---

[7] NARA, Tufaro papers, box 2, folder "Terrorism 3," "Report of the PSAC's subpanel on hijacking," March 1973, p. 5.

[8] DNSA document TE 335 (October 1974).

[9] DNSA document TE 369, p. 3 (notes from the seventy-fifth meeting of the CCCT working group, January 22, 1975).

in combating terrorism, including the one mentioned above, and lawyers were a significant component of those presenting at conferences in the first decade of terrorism expertise. One of the earliest terrorism conferences focused on the role of international law in fighting terrorism, organized by law professor M. Cherif Bassiouni, gathered together lawyers specializing in criminal and international law, who framed terrorism explicitly as a "crime," to be dealt with through the force of law. Themes covered at the conference included "perspectives on the origins and causes of terrorism," "wars of national liberation," "hijacking," "kidnapping," "jurisdiction and extradition," and the "international control of terrorism" (Bassiouni 1975).

Lawyers and legal experts were among the first to take on the problem of terrorism. Robert Friedlander (then professor of law at Ohio Northern University, and author of a number of articles on terrorism) suggested in a 1984 interview that it was lawyers who were actually the first organized entrants into the field of production of expertise about terrorism, putting forward the view that work on terrorism was considered more legitimate in law than in other disciplines (Hoffman 1984: 95):

> I think the lawyers grabbed hold of it first and, in addition, only in law is it considered to be a thoroughly legitimate academic field. If you are a historian and you work on that, you are suspect...but, in law, it is an absolutely substantive, legitimate field, and we get full credit for everything we do in the field of terrorism.

In fact, the application of legal knowledge to the component problems that would come to comprise the new problem of terrorism actually *pre-dated* the concrete formulation of terrorism as a problem itself, which may aid in explaining both the early role of the legal approach and its relatively early demise (or at least decline). H. H. A. Cooper, whose qualifications included, at various times, head of a security consulting firm, consultant on terrorism to the International Association of Chiefs of Police, professor of law at New York University, and staff director of the National Advisory Committee Task

Force on Disorders and Terrorism, stated in an interview (Hoffman 1984: 115):

> Most of the early studies...were done principally by lawyers, and there was little concern by people from other disciplines... [T]he first terrorist topic that generated a great deal of literature was skyjacking. You'll find that skyjacking articles generally go back to about 1966 in law journals, a little bit before that in popular sources; they proliferate through about 1972, and then interest starts to wane. After 1972, after Munich, hostage taking starts to make its debut, but terrorism as a general subject doesn't really "hit the stands," as they would say, until about 1974.

Despite the prevalence of the legal framework in the early years, the attempt to treat terrorism as a primarily legal/diplomatic problem would encounter a number of roadblocks, and ultimately founder, as illustrated by figures 4.1 and 4.2. Legal experts took on the problems,

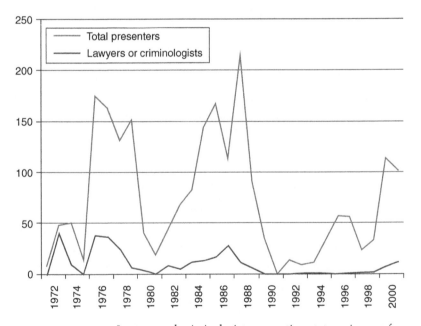

FIGURE 4.1 Lawyers and criminologists presenting at terrorism conferences, 1972–2001

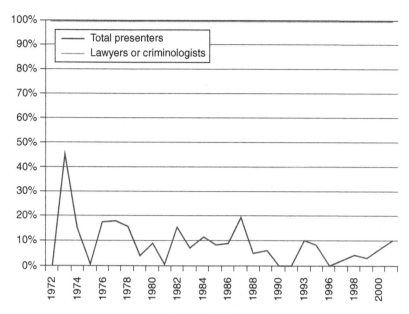

FIGURE 4.2 Lawyers and criminologists as a percentage of conference presenters, 1972–2001

such as "skyjacking,"[10] even before the problem of "terrorism" had taken shape. Yet, once terrorism had taken shape as a composite problem, the legal approach began to have less traction. In contrast to many of the later analysts who would take on the problem, lawyers did not necessarily style themselves as terrorism experts. Rather than developing grand theories of terrorism, legal experts tended to focus on how international law might apply to a particular situation. And, as we will see, once the nature of the problem to be governed evolved away from relatively concrete problem formation such as "skyjacking" and into the more complex, politically inflected, and difficult-to-define "terrorism," the legal/diplomatic approach to the governance of terrorism would become increasingly difficult to apply in an effective manner. By the middle of the 1980s very few terrorism conferences were legally oriented, lawyers constituted a declining

---

[10] This is an early synonym for airliner hijacking.

percentage of those acting as experts, and the United States had largely given up on international law as a means of fighting terrorism.

In a 1975 speech before the Federal Bar Association, Robert A. Fearey (chair of the working group of the CCCT, and special assistant to the Secretary of State, coordinator for combating terrorism at the Department of State) noted that the "the basic dilemma" for dealing with terrorism internationally was that

> [m]any third world countries, particularly newly independent
> countries which used terrorism to help achieve their freedom, view
> terrorists as patriots, believing their causes justify their terroristic
> acts... And for different reasons many advanced countries are also
> disinclined to be tough on terrorists... Because of these attitudes, a
> US-proposed convention to prevent the export of terrorism from
> one country to another failed of adoption by the 1972 UN general
> assembly... The prospects for effective international measures for
> the apprehension and punishment of terrorists are not good.[11]

In a speech the following year before the Los Angeles and Orange County World Affairs Councils, Fearey explained that there were three primary ways to combat terrorism: "intelligence," "physical security," and "apprehension and punishment of terrorists" (he then noted a fourth: addressing grievances). He noted that the third (apprehension and punishment) had been of only limited success, however, as it required international cooperation, and

> [t]oo few countries are willing to arrest, try, and severely punish
> international hijackers and saboteurs, or indeed international
> terrorists of any kind... How are we to achieve more effective
> international cooperation for the apprehension, trial, and
> punishment of international terrorists? This objective is as
> intractable as it is central.[12]

---

[11] Hoover Institution Archives, Robert A. Fearey papers, notes, box 5, folder "Writings and speeches: terrorism: before the federal bar association July 1, 1975."

[12] Hoover Institution Archives, Fearey papers, notes, box 3, folder 1, "Excerpt from Department of State Bulletin March 29, 1976" ("International terrorism," address by Robert A. Fearey, pp. 396–8).

Similarly, a 1976 CIA report (Milbank 1976: 27–8; emphasis in original) declares that international conventions on terrorism

> presently [sic] do not, singly or in combination, constitute much of an effective constraint on terrorist activity...the conventions lack teeth... The obstacles which have blocked more effective international action are formidable. They have, as previously indicated, included the controversy over *justifiable* versus *illegal* political violence and broad resistance to such further infringements of national sovereignty as would be implied in any inflexible curtailment of the right to grant political asylum.

Although legal scholars aimed to fit terrorism into legal paradigms, it proved to be a continually shifting subject. Obtaining international agreement for counterterrorism conventions proved difficult, as states were unable to agree upon a definition of "terrorism." Within the legal/diplomatic perspective, there was a need for precision of definitions in order to pursue remedies effectively. Furthermore, as time went on, even individual states often did not want to be bound permanently to a singular definition. Audiences at a 1977 event on the "Control of terrorism in international life" were told that the primary obstacle to the control of international terrorism was the

> inability of the world community to agree on a definition of that term... It has proven difficult, particularly at the global level, to distinguish between terrorism – international, transnational, or domestic – and such common crimes as murder, assault, kidnapping, or hijacking.[13]

In the legal approach, the need to resolve the definitional problem applied equally to the academic theoreticians/analysts and the practical practitioners. In a non- or extra-legal approach to counterterrorism, however, the lack of a stable definition may actually be

---

[13] DNSA document TE 578, April 21, 1977, "Control of terrorism in international life: cooperation and self-help," co-sponsored by the World Affairs Council of Northern California, moderator John F. Murphy, University of Kansas Law School, p. 18.

beneficial for practitioners, while remaining a problem for academics and analysts.

Simulating disaster, routinizing unpredictability

A second key technique for making terrorism knowable during the 1970s was the use of simulations and scenarios: fictionalized events through which terrorism experts, first responders, and policymakers could develop routines for responding to terrorist attacks. By developing planned responses for various potentialities, experts and policymakers sought to tame the frightening and seemingly unpredictable, unknowable terrorist event, to build up bureaucratic knowledge and routines, and to practice skills of improvisation for dealing with the unpredictable. As with the legal/rational approach, the impetus for routinization came both from the government and from experts themselves. Whereas the legal approach sought to manage terrorism at the level of the international world system through international legal regulations and treaties, however, the operational approach focused on managing terrorism at the level of the *incident*, through the development of routine procedures for responding to terrorist events.

A key technique for the development of this form of knowledge was the *simulation*: games in which experts, policymakers, and first responders took the parts of various actors in a terrorist drama, with the aim of testing potential sets of responses, and then establishing and practicing routines for dealing with such events. Scenarios, fictionalized situations that could be enacted with decision-makers taking different roles, including those of terrorists, counterterrorists, and first responders, were used for developing practical strategies for managing and responding to terrorist events such as hijackings, kidnappings, and hostage situations. The simulations and scenarios that became popular in the study of terrorism were a subset of the more general practice of gaming, a significant technique for US military planning in the middle of the twentieth century. The use of scenarios and political gaming took broad hold in the American defense and foreign policy arena in the late 1950s, with RAND, MIT, the

Pentagon, and the CIA as key sites (Bloomfield and Gearin 1973; DeLeon 1973; Mandel 1977).[14]

A 1973 RAND report emphasized that scenarios should be "used to focus research efforts, encourage interdisciplinary perspectives on crisis situations, and provide an education in crisis management for potential decisionmakers" (DeLeon 1973: v). Gaming was intended to "sensitize" policymakers to the potential results of their actions, to "focus research actions" and to identify possible weak spots in planning (DeLeon 1973: 5). They were not, it was repeatedly emphasized, to be seen as a "predictive or operational tool" (DeLeon 1973: 5). A 1974 RAND report defined gaming, as often used in international relations and strategy, as "human beings acting as themselves or playing simulated roles in an environment which is either actual or simulated," while "simulation" was described as "the representation of a system or organism by another system or model, which is designed to have a relevant behavioral similarity with the original system,"[15] continuing: "A common feature of nearly all gaming activities is the scenario. Scenarios range in style and complexity from the elaborate, fully articulated version often used in free-form games to implicit scenarios embedded deeply within hard, all-machine models" (Brewer 1974: 28).

One of the key proponents of the use of simulations and "games" in counterterrorism planning was Robert Kupperman of the Cabinet Committee to Combat Terrorism. Having earned a PhD in math, Kupperman had worked since 1973 for the US Arms Control and Disarmament Agency, conducting studies of terrorism and other security problems. He had previously worked for the government Office of Emergency Preparedness and the military think tank the

---

[14] Scenarios as a tool for strategic planning were first developed by American nuclear strategist Herman Kahn in the middle of the twentieth century, and then adopted by the petroleum companies Shell and ELF during the first oil crisis (Cooper 2010: 5). For a key early statement on scenarios from RAND, see Goldhamer and Speier (1959).

[15] In other words, all games are simulations, but not all simulations are games, as simulations can be performed by computers (Brewer 1974: 3).

Institute for Defense Analyses.[16] Kupperman was active in organizing a number of conferences, and international networks, including the Evian seminar of 1977 and the Berlin conference of 1978, and was one of the key drivers behind efforts to make use of simulations and "games" for crisis preparation and training. In planning for the Berlin terrorism conference of 1978, Kupperman wrote to conference organizer Jacov Katwan that "your conference is becoming a mecca," and that public officials were interested in attending.[17] Kupperman designed a simulation to be played at this conference, writing to Katwan that he hoped this would move the conference in a new direction:

> Thus far, I have given some 50 speeches and have attended 20 or 30 conferences on the subject of terrorism... The sad fact is that very little new is being said. The material I read, the conferences I attend, and the legislative hearings with which I am involved, regurgitate the same issues with no resolution in sight... I hope for a novel, interesting, and constructive conference... I doubt the causes of antiterrorism and human welfare would be served in the slightest by having another vague, discursive conference.[18]

A second center of innovation for the use of scenarios and simulations for developing crisis response plans was the Study Group on International Terrorism at the University of Oklahoma, led by Professor of Political Science Stephen Sloan (Sloan, Kearney, and Wise 1978). This group led simulations for groups including the security department of the University of Oklahoma, the Norman, Oklahoma, police department, a US Army special forces unit, and airline flight attendants (Sloan, Kearney, and Wise 1978: 323). According to Sloan, "Each of the scenarios was based on a composite of actual incidents of political

---

[16] Hoover Institution Archives, Robert H. Kupperman papers, box 6, folder "European trip May 1976," "Curriculum vitae."

[17] Hoover Institution Archives, Kupperman papers (accession no. 95022–101.05/06), box 5, letter to Jakov Katwan (Berlin), October 24, 1978.

[18] Hoover Institution Archives, Kupperman papers (accession no. 95022–101.05/06), box 5, letter to Jakov Katwan, June 22, 1978.

terrorism related to hostage-taking incidents" (Sloan, Kearney, and Wise 1978: 323). Similarly, "Each simulation was subjected to a detailed post-operation evaluation in order to provide the Study Group with the opportunity to refine its simulation techniques and to help the participant agency strengthen its procedures" (Sloan, Kearney, and Wise 1978: 323–4).

A number of such conferences brought together police and other emergency responders and government officials along with researchers. The focus here was often on the question of dealing with terrorist events as crisis situations, taking into account both the immediate motive of resolving the crisis and the questions of whether certain modes of response might have a deterrent effect upon future terrorism and terrorists. A conference on "Research strategies for the study of international political terrorism" was held in 1977 (Crelinsten 1977), which had three main sessions: crisis management, emergency preparedness and technological issues, and international cooperation, with participants from the "terrorism mafia," including Jenkins, Yehezkel Dror, and Kupperman. Another conference focusing on the question of developing routines for crisis management was "Hostage taking: problems of prevention and control," sponsored by the University of Maryland's Institute of Criminal Justice and Criminology and the University of Montreal's International Centre for Comparative Criminology, and funded by the Canadian government and the US LEAA (Crelinsten, Laberge-Altmejd, and Szabo 1976). Government interest in the use of scenarios and the development of routines for the management of terrorism events is evident in a variety of additional sources. President Nixon's staff in 1972 compiled a memo entitled "Contingency plans concerning terrorist attacks" suggesting plans of action to be taken in case of four categories of hypothetical terrorist attacks.[19] Another document laid out in detail

---

[19] NARA, Nixon papers, NPMP, WHSF, staff member and office files, Tufaro papers, box 1972–3, subject files, "Scenarios," "Terrorism no. 4"; box 2, "Scenarios," memo: Thomas J. Kelley to Martin R. Pollner, subject: "Contingency plans concerning terrorist attacks," October 6, 1972.

plans for action to be taken in the case of four potential scenarios: the kidnapping and taking hostage of a foreign official in Washington, DC; terrorists taking over a foreign embassy in Washington, DC; the kidnapping and taking hostage of a US official in a foreign country; and the seizure of a US embassy overseas.[20]

Simulations were seen as particularly valuable for preparing for potential "extreme" events. Kupperman, in particular, used his position within the government to call attention to the potential consequences of terrorism,[21] and was especially concerned about the need to prepare for future possibilities of catastrophic events, warning (Kupperman 1977: 2):

> Western nations, even the United States, are ill prepared to cope with any form of warfare other than conventional military response. A clever terrorist who understands the potential failure modes of government can inflict grievous harm, possibly more harm than war. Unless governments take basic precautions, we will continue to stand at the edge of an awful abyss.

Crisis management and the specific techniques of simulations and routinization persist to this day. Scenarios once again became a key technique in the 1990s, when fears of "weapons of mass destruction" took center stage in the terrorism debate, and they were among the techniques used by the Department of Homeland Security after 9/11. Although the scenarios of the 1970s were based chiefly upon actual events (although composited/fictionalized), and were aimed largely at planning for future events of a similar type, the sorts of scenarios that would gain attention later on would move beyond modeling the sorts of unpredictable, yet knowable events that were the focus of terrorism gaming in the 1970s. Instead, with scenarios

---

[20] NARA, Nixon papers, NPMP, WHSF, staff member and office files, Tufaro papers, box 1972–3, subject files, "Scenarios," "Terrorism no. 4," document "Draft: contingency plan," "Four core scenarios," 1972.

[21] See, for example, Kupperman's (classified) 1975 "Mass destruction terrorism" study, cited by Kupperman (1977).

such as Project Megiddo, gaming in the 1990s would take on an increasingly speculative cast, aiming to truly "outthink" the terrorist not just in terms of moves in the game but in terms of the very structure and logic of the game itself. As the prospect of ever more destructive and "irrational" terrorism took hold of the national imagination, there grew demands for reactive and preventive approaches. While simulations and routinization proved to be useful techniques for *responding* to terrorist events, and routinization could aid first responders in doing their jobs better, it could not fill the larger discourse about what terrorism was or what we ought to do about it.

Making terrorism count(able): quantification and risk management

The third primary technique for making terrorism knowable in the 1970s was quantification.[22] As historians and sociologists of science have argued, quantification – making things subject to counting and numerical analysis – can be seen as a means of standardizing entities that may have an unruly presence in the world, and of making them subject not just to science but also to governance (see, for example, Bowker and Star 1999; Espeland and Stevens 2008; Lampland and Star 2009; Porter 1995). A major theme in the sociological literature on quantification has been that counting and commensuration are social processes, and, as such, require work to make them happen (Martin and Lynch 2009; Timmermans and Epstein 2010; Espeland and Stevens 1998). Quantification is a process of classification; it entails

---

[22] This method of "counting" was not always seen positively by researchers who advocated a more holistic approach. In a 1981 review, Augustus Norton (1981: 607) lamented the prevalence of the practice of "counting of cases or victims" as a mainstay of terrorism research, and, in an article from four years earlier, J. Bowyer Bell (1977: 479) wrote, "One of the first responses to the advent of the new terrorists on the part of the concerned – other than speculation, and there was plenty of that – was to count. The result is that, although no one is any closer to understanding the phenomenon, still the course of events can be followed in the detailed chronologies of violence provided by RAND or HERO [Historical Evaluation Research Organization], or in the appendices to various studies or Congressional committee reports."

determining which things are alike and not alike, and may include both the construction of new categories and the determination of which sorts of things do and do not fit into a particular category (Martin and Lynch 2009).

Some of the largest projects in the early years of terrorism expertise were efforts to quantify terrorism. These consisted largely of efforts to construct chronologies of terrorist events, and then event databases that could be used to run statistical regressions (Jenkins and Johnson 1975, 1976). Chronologies, in which counts of terrorist events and deaths/casualties are plotted over time, and databases, in which events are correlated with characteristics of perpetrators, victims, and methods of attack, instantiate "terrorism" as a particular sort of problem (by virtue of the particular events included and not included in the chronologies) and certify some types of information (such as the countries of origin of the perpetrators) as significant, and others (such as terrorists' motives) as less so. Databases were developed at RAND, the Historical Evaluation and Research Organization, and the CIA (Mickolus, Heyman, and Schlotter 1980), as well as by private companies engaged in security and risk consulting, and at the US Department of State, the Defense Intelligence Agency (DIA), and by individuals at the University of Southern California and the American University (Fowler 1981: 2–3). Terrorism databases were used not only by the state but also by private companies engaged in security and risk consulting, to advise clients (governments and businesses) as to the risk of terrorism in different areas of the world. For example, Pinkerton Government Services and a company called Risks International used such databases to calculate the potential risk of terrorism in various parts of the world for their clients, usually multinational corporations.

Researchers at RAND constructed the first database of terrorist incidents, and conducted a number of studies of hostage incidents, aimed at providing direct assistance for the management of such events. One of RAND's first projects on terrorism was to develop a chronology of events comprising the category "international terrorism." The first version covered the period from 1968 to 1974, and later editions incorporated additional years. The project of constructing the RAND database was headed up by Brian Jenkins, with the assistance of Janera Johnson and Geraldine Petty.[23]

A key problem faced in any knowledge project on terrorism is the problem of how to define "terrorism" itself. As a RAND report on terrorism databases notes (Fowler 1981: v, 9):

> The major problems in the collection of terrorism data are the definition of terrorism itself and the determination of the scope and content of the data. Most of the data bases discussed here have implicit conceptual definitions of terrorism which were developed to meet the needs of particular missions or application domains...
> There is no universally accepted definition of terrorism. The word is used to describe a number of mostly illegal activities committed by a variety of political, criminal, and even psychopathic groups and individuals... The definitional problem has two aspects: developing conceptual definitions that delineate the interests of the researcher and the general needs of the application, and translating the conceptual notions into operational definitions with which information can be selected and formed into a coherent data base.

Thus, in deciding whether to include an incident in the database, the RAND researchers were also determining what events counted as "terrorism," and which deaths counted as terrorist-related.

The RAND database began with a series of chronologies: lists of terrorist events by year. These were originally compiled on index cards, and then later entered into a computer program. The aim was to establish a more empirical and authoritative source of data, to advance upon the use of relatively anecdotal sources.[24] This focus

---

[23] Later contributors to the database included Bonnie Codes and Karen Gardela Treverton, who assumed management of the database from 1988 to 1994. In 1994 the database moved to the terrorism research center at St Andrews University in Scotland, to return to RAND in 1998, and eventually to be transferred to the University of Maryland after 2001.

[24] Interview with Karen Treverton, June 12, 2007.

on events provided a means of beginning to collect empirical information on terrorism, while partially sidestepping the thorny question of how exactly terrorism ought to be defined, although this very "problem of definition" was one that the RAND experts necessarily struggled with in the very constitution of the database itself. As an early version of the chronology (Jenkins and Johnson 1975: 2) notes:

> The problem of defining *international* terrorism is complicated by international politics. Apart from a few categories of incidents that most nations would define as international terrorism – airliner hijacking or the kidnapping of diplomats, for example – few nations agree on what international terrorism is. Definitions strongly reflect political points of view.

Further, the authors note:

> Some governments apply the word terrorism to all violent acts committed by their political opponents, and, by the same token, antigovernment extremists frequently claim to be victims of terror committed by government security agencies.

Moreover, in theory the RAND database tracked incidents rather than perpetrators, but the practice was rather different (Jenkins and Johnson 1975:2):

> Incidents of state terror are not included in the chronology, primarily because such terrorism tends to be internal rather than international, but it should be recognized that governments may also employ terror at home and abroad.

Consequently, while RAND analysts acknowledged in principle that states could also commit terrorism, in practice the deaths resulting from political violence by states were not included in their calculations.

This process of determining what ought to be included in the database can be seen as a debate over the construction of the category of "international terrorism" itself – and the determination of what counted as "international" was a matter of deciding where national and international boundaries lay. The boundaries were not always as clear as one might imagine, and say something about the construction of these borders. So, for example, a decision was made that attacks by Irish terrorists in Northern Ireland against British targets were not included in the international chronology, but incidents perpetrated by Irish terrorists in the United Kingdom were. Attacks by Puerto Rican terrorists on the US mainland were included. Attacks by Corsican separatists against French targets in Corsica were excluded, but attacks by Corsicans in France were included. Terrorist attacks in the West Bank, the Gaza Strip, and the Golan Heights were not included, yet terrorist attacks in Jerusalem and the rest of Israel were.

The chronologies consisted of lists of terrorist events, ordered by year. Databases took this information, and put it into a computerized format, which could be used to perform statistical analyses. These were *event* databases; the unit of analysis was the terrorist event. And several important distinctions were made during this process: the decision to track events, as opposed to some other category of things, the category level decision being made for each case, which determined what events "counted" and did not count as members of the category of terrorism; and the decision as to which factors were more or less relevant (at least in this instance) to an understanding of terrorism (such as the nationality of the victims, the nationality of the perpetrators, and the mode of weaponry used), and which factors (often including the broader political context) were deemed excludable, at least in this case.

According to RAND, a focus on events rather than perpetrators allowed for more objectivity.[25] As a 1980 RAND report (Fowler 1980: 3) noted,

---

[25] "Of course, the concept of 'terrorism' is subject to differences of interpretation and perspective: nations, government agencies, and individuals often have quite different definitions of the term. For the RDWTI, RAND has defined terrorism by the nature of the act, not by the identity of the perpetrators" (RAND website, accessed 2011).

Each entity in the data base seeks to answer the question "who did what to whom and when?" The information represented by the incident is the most disaggregated act that can reasonably be called "international terrorism." The approach is designed to reduce, as much as possible, potential research problems caused by the inherent complexity and ideological sensitivity of political terrorism.

And, at least in these early years, this presented a possible inductive approach towards the definition of the problem, as noted by Jenkins and Johnson (1975): 3):

Common characteristics do emerge from the list of incidents included in the chronology: The violence is often directed against civilian targets; the attacks are often carried out in a way that will achieve maximum publicity; the use or the threat of violence is often coupled with specific demands; the lives of hostages are often at stake.

The overt purpose of these databases was to guide policymakers and practitioners in decision-making. Databases were used to track potential responses to terrorist incidents and suggest what techniques might be more fruitful. A primary goal was to make the problem of terrorism somewhat more predictable, not in the sense of predicting what would happen in the future but in the sense of being able to rationalize responses to particular types of events, and guide these responses by police, emergency responders, and negotiators. It was also hoped that databases might be used to solve cases of terrorism when the perpetrators were unknown.

Funding for the RAND database and similar projects came largely from the government, including the US Defense Nuclear Agency, the US Department of Energy, and Sandia Laboratories (Fowler 1981: iii). William Fowler at RAND (Fowler 1980: 11) suggests:

The goal of the program is to understand terrorism in terms of actual terrorist behavior... The research design could culminate in a comprehensive system for monitoring and forecasting changes in the volume, dispersion, and nature of international terrorism.

But the construction of event databases did not just serve practical aims in the governance of terrorism; the databases aided in the very construction of the field of terrorism studies itself. Terrorism event databases served to illustrate the extent of the terrorism problem, and the possibility of subjecting terrorism to rational analysis. Because terrorism was seen often as inherently irrational, the very question of whether terrorism could be studied according to rational methods would become an ongoing axis of contention in the field. Bruce Hoffman (author of *Inside Terrorism*, formerly a terrorism expert at RAND, and now at Georgetown University) makes this point explicitly, telling me that "the idea of databases was to put some academic rigor... [I]t was to give [the field] the rigor and an empirical foundation that it lacked, move it away from the anecdotal."[26] Similarly, Edward Mickolus, the author of the ITERATE database, one of the first (and still in use) terrorism databases, has written (Mickolus 1981: 1–3):

> This study's central thesis is that international terrorist behavior
> forms discernible patterns. Discovery of these patterns through
> even the simplest of statistical procedures can be helpful in
> combating terrorism. The popular myth of terrorist randomness
> and irrationality confuses terrorist tactics to influence public
> perception with their predictability... Unfortunately, while
> this menace has generated a cottage industry of writers,
> self-appointed security experts, apologists, symposium organizers,
> and novelists, the literature in the field has been unsystematic,
> noncumulative, and distressingly unhelpful to the policy-maker,
> as well as the general public. The study of terrorism has been
> marked by unsupported generalizations based upon lack of
> hard data.

[26] Interview with Bruce Hoffman, November 7, 2006.

The enthusiasm for database construction in the early years of terrorism expertise can thus be understood as an attempt not simply to make sense of terrorism but to communicate the importance (and the plausibility) of terrorism as an object of knowledge. Techniques of quantification served to communicate the magnitude of the problem and also to establish the scientific legitimacy of its analysis.

The application of databases and quantification to the terrorism problem has persisted, but has also been subject to perennial difficulties. Quantification sought to rationalize terrorism and make it subject to techniques of risk management, largely through the creation of terrorism event databases. Nevertheless, although a number of such databases have been constructed, at great time and expense, they have also been subject to continual critique. Each of the databases has defined the scope of what "terrorism" is in a different way, making comparison and communication difficult tasks. And, as each database is constructed, the authors must decide case by case whether any individual incident should be included, often leading to ambiguities or inconsistencies within each data set as well. In fact, even today, as acres of data are compiled, the question of what this data means, or how it might be applied to solving the problem, remains highly contested.

Rationalization and its discontents

This chapter has discussed three modes of knowledge creation through which early terrorism experts attempted to constitute terrorism as a governable problem. The earliest US response to terrorism envisioned international law as one of the primary methods for governing terrorism, reflecting the Department of State's primary role, as it saw this as an issue to be handled through diplomatic channels, and indeed, to a certain extent, a problem aimed primarily at diplomats. The second approach focused on developing practical strategies for managing and responding to terrorist events (particularly hijackings, kidnappings, and hostage situations) through routinized event management responses developed via fantasy scenarios. And the third approach sought to rationalize terrorism and make it subject to techniques of risk management, largely through the creation of terrorism event databases, which aimed to make terrorism subject to calculable technologies of risk management such as insurance. Each logic not only implied a different understanding of terrorism as a problem but also enabled a different set of practices through which the problem might be managed.

As the problem of terrorism took shape over the course of the 1970s, however, it resisted such rationalizing logics. Not one of these approaches was able to capture successfully the management of the terrorism problem. Rationalization is not a given; as with terrorism itself, problems, people, and events can and do act back upon the attempts of experts and others to impose reason upon them, and this shapes and constrains the analytical, political, and governmental actions we can enact in response.

But, even though these practices were unable to capture the problem fully, they would not disappear, but would persist alongside other approaches. And practices of knowledge, even relatively marginalized ones, have effects upon what we can, and what we seek to, know. While the shift from "insurgency" to "terrorism" (which I traced in Chapter 3) marginalized attempts to understand the meanings and motivations of terrorists at the discursive level, the practices associated with the logics of law, routinization, and quantification accomplished the same at a technical level. Turning terrorist events into points in a database, reducing attacks to situations to be managed, and dealing with terrorists as international criminals all presented practical modes of managing terrorism that made the consideration of terrorists' motivations unnecessary, even irrelevant.

As I have shown in this chapter, the first decade of terrorism expertise focused on trying to govern terrorism through three core modes of rationalization, yet none of these was able to capture the problem. Experts and rational techniques of governance were not able to capture either how we know terrorism as a problem or how we govern it. This opened the door to other interpretations of the problem and how it ought to be managed. Instead of highly rationalized, bureaucratized responses and techniques of regulation, we see a problem that seems to spiral out of control, both in terms of what it encompasses and the techniques used to combat it. The more dangerous and uncertain terrorism becomes, the more extreme the modes of governance that arise in response. In the next chapter I explain how terrorism came to be understood in the 1980s as an attack upon civilization, which had to be governed through war.

5 "Terrorism fever": the first war on terror and the politicization of expertise

Terrorism fever became epidemic in Washington and on Capitol Hill with the inauguration of the Reagan administration.[1]

Terrorism is a revolting phenomenon undertaken by those who by choice stand outside the pale of civilized people.[2]

The word "terrorist" is not – like "communist" and "fascist" – being abused; it is itself an abuse.[3]

I used to think terrorism was a pretty non-partisan subject.[4]

On January 28, 1981, one week after the inauguration of President Ronald Reagan, the new Secretary of State, Alexander Haig, in his first official press conference, accused the Soviet Union of "training, funding and equipping" international terrorists (Woodward 1987: 93). With the Iran hostage crisis dominating the nightly news, terrorism had taken on a central role in the 1980 presidential election, and it would come to play an unprecedented role in the Reagan administration. This chapter analyzes how terrorism came to be governed through a logic of "war" in the 1980s.

Counterterrorism policy under Reagan shifted away from the focus of the 1970s on diplomacy and crisis management, and towards military retaliation, accompanied by a new narrative that reframed terrorism as a civilizational struggle, between "the democracies" or

---

[1] Richard Braungart and Margaret Braungart (1981: 264).

[2] Robert C. McFarlane, assistant to the president for national security affairs, speaking at the "Defense strategy forum," National Strategy Information Center, International Club, Washington, DC, March 25, 1985, quoted by Cline and Alexander (1986: 47).

[3] Christopher Hitchens (1986: 68).

[4] Former senior advisor in the US Department of State, Office of the Coordinator for Counterterrorism, interview, March 18, 2007.

"the West" against a network of terrorists backed by the Soviet Union. The adoption and dissemination of the new framework intro-duced shock waves into the nascent expert community – some of whom adopted this new framework, while others remained wary. And the conspiratorial tenor of the new narratives opened up a space for the rise of a counter-discourse from critics who dismissed "terrorism" as a biased concept, critiqued terrorism experts as propagandists, and dismissed any possibility of real expertise on terrorism. These conflicts took the form of a series of claims and counterclaims over the "politicization" of expertise, with each group trying to seize the high ground of neutral, apolitical knowledge.

The reframing of terrorism as a war was not just a discursive shift; it also shaped how the Reagan administration (and the subsequent administrations of George H. W. Bush and Bill Clinton) concretely responded to the problem. While the governance of terrorism in the 1970s was dominated by the logics of law, risk, and crisis management, in the 1980s a military logic came to the fore. But, in contrast to the pre-emptive "war on terror" that would arise after 9/11, this first war on terror was driven by a logic of retaliation, in which military counterterrorism strikes were akin to punishment for a crime. This reframing of terrorism as war was an explicit technique of delegiti-mization: terrorism was redefined as *outside* the laws of war and crime, and thus illegitimate in both means and ends (Vitas and Williams 1996: 25).

The event that perhaps best exemplifies this retaliatory logic took place in April 1986, when the United States bombed Libyan cities in response to a bombing at a disco in Berlin that had killed an American soldier. L. Paul Bremer, the ambassador-at-large for counterterrorism, defended the attack with reference to law and the failure of legal tactics: "Ultimately, after years of economic and political sanctions and in the face of clear evidence of Libyan involvement in terrorist acts, we had to resort to military action... [T]he law amply justified our action" (Vitas and Williams 1996: 26). The *9/11 Commission Report* cites both this attack and the 1991 US-led attack on Iraq as key incidents that "symbolized for the military establishment effective use of military power for counterterrorism – limited retaliation with air power, aimed at deterrence" (National Commission on Terrorist Attacks 2004: 98). This shift towards an explicitly retaliatory policy was formalized in Reagan's National Security Directive 138, which called for "a shift...from passive to active defense measures" (National Commission on Terrorist Attacks 2004: 98). Shortly thereafter Reagan called terrorism "an act of war" in a July 1985 speech before the American Bar Association (National Commission on Terrorist Attacks 2004: 99).

This chapter analyzes three episodes that were key to the shift to viewing terrorism as a war: the 1979 Jerusalem conference on international terrorism, the controversy surrounding the publication of Claire Sterling's 1981 book *The Terror Network*, and the 1981–1986 Senate Subcommittee on Security and Terrorism (SST) hearings. In each of these episodes, experts and politicians argued that international terrorism was orchestrated by the Soviet Union, and, as they proceeded, the possibility of neutral, unbiased expertise about terrorism was increasingly called into question. These events interacted to produce an unprecedented level of conflict in the field, redefining both "terrorism" and when, how, and by whom credible knowledge about it might be produced.

THE 1979 JERUSALEM CONFERENCE

It was at the July 1979 Jerusalem conference on international terrorism that the new narratives of Soviet terrorism sponsorship and of terrorism as an attack on civilization were first introduced to a number of the individuals who would go on to be crucial to their dissemination. The conference was sponsored by the Jonathan Institute, an Israeli think tank founded by future prime minister Benjamin Netanyahu, and named for his brother, who had been killed in the operation at Entebbe.[5] While formally a non-governmental organization, the

---

[5] Operation Thunderbolt (July 4, 1976) was an Israeli rescue of hostages from Popular Front for the Liberation of Palestine hijackers at Entebbe Airport in Uganda.

Jonathan Institute had close ties to the Israel state, as illustrated by an administrative committee dominated by current and former members of the government. Its honorary president was Israeli president Ephraim Katzir, former prime minister Golda Meir served as chairman, and other members of the "public committee" included the prime minister, Menachem Begin, the foreign minister, Moshe Dayan, the minister of defense, Ezer Weizman, the minister of agriculture, Ariel Sharon, a former prime minister, Yitzhak Rabin, and a former minister of defense, Shimon Peres. The event received significant media coverage, and was attended by prominent American experts and political figures, including several US senators and representatives, future vice president (and president) George H. W. Bush, writer George Will, Richard Pipes of Harvard University's Russian Research Center, and representatives of the American Enterprise Institute (AEI), the Center for Strategic and International Studies (CSIS), and *Commentary* magazine, all of whom helped to carry these narratives back to the United States.

Although this conference was framed as an apolitical truth project exposing the "politicized" knowledge of others, its stated goals were explicitly to awaken the Western world to the problem of terrorism as defined by the conference organizers. Thus this "apolitical" project was directly about the politics of knowledge. As Netanyahu wrote in the widely distributed book that came out of the conference, "[T]he major contribution" of the conference was to counter "a curious reticence about the massive evidence of Soviet involvement with terror movements" and to "reveal the nature and full extent of this involvement" (Netanyahu 1980: 7). Judging the conference a success, he reported, "Whatever else was achieved, international terrorism can no longer be examined without considering the pivotal role played by the Soviet Union" (Netanyahu 1980: 9). This goal of sharing the truth, and exposing the "politicized" knowledge of others, was echoed in the talks of many of the presenters.

Most terrorism conferences until this point had been conceived either as exercises in academic knowledge production or as events at which policymakers could consult with researchers who might provide technical advice about the problem. In contrast, the Jerusalem conference was explicitly framed as an intervention to change the international discourse on terrorism. The conference was organized with the goal of bringing together experts who shared this view and political leaders who might be persuaded to adopt and disseminate a new framework of understanding, comprising several interrelated narratives about terrorism: that terrorism was a movement as well as a tactic, that terrorism was a threat directed specifically at "civilization," "democracies" and "the West," and that terrorism was a (more or less directed) product of the Soviet Union in its struggle against the West. The first of these is clearly articulated in Netanyahu's introduction to the conference report: "The means and ends of terror groups, it was suggested, are indissolubly linked, and both point to a single direction: An abhorrence of freedom and a determination to destroy the democratic way of life" (Netanyahu 1980: 2).

The second set of claims at the conference asserted that terrorism was directed specifically against "democracies," "civilization," and "the West," which were thus amalgamated into a contiguous group with a common enemy. Senator John Danforth's talk articulated this framing most clearly in its title: "Terrorism versus democracy" (Netanyahu 1980: 120). Senator Henry M. Jackson's talk, "Terrorism as a weapon in international politics," asserted (Netanyahu 1980: 33) that

> international terrorism is a modern form of warfare against liberal democracies. I believe that the ultimate but seldom stated goal of these terrorists is to destroy the very fabric of democracy.

Similarly, Ray Cline of the Washington-based think tank CSIS[6] (Netanyahu 1980: 90–1) stated,

---

[6] Cline, who had a PhD from Harvard, had arrived at CSIS in 1976. He had previously worked in intelligence for the government, serving as deputy director of intelligence at the CIA from 1962 to 1966 and director of the Bureau of Intelligence and Research at the Department of State from 1969 to 1973.

> Terrorism is part of a war! We, the open societies are the target! [...]
> Terrorism is intended by those who finance it, arm it and
> ideologically inspire it, to weaken and ultimately dissolve the fabric
> of civilized behavior in open, pluralistic societies.

Israeli diplomat Gideon Rafael declared terrorism the "antithesis of
democracy," asserting (Netanyahu 1980: 111–12) that terrorists

> are part of an international demolition squad disguised as freedom
> fighters, presented by perverted publicity as glamorous guerrillas,
> idolized by a disoriented community of alienated adolescents.

And Netanyahu, in his 1984 book *Terrorism: How the West Can Win*
(Netanyahu 1984: ix), which draws upon this conference as well as
a subsequent event in 1984, takes the sweeping view

> that the battle against terrorism was part of much larger struggle,
> one between the forces of civilization and the forces of barbarism,
> and that, if left unchallenged, terrorism would continue to spread
> with disastrous consequences.

The third, and most controversial, aspect of the new war narrative was the claim that international terrorism was sponsored by the
Soviet Union. The majority of speakers at the Jerusalem conference
not only affirmed the Soviet sponsorship of terrorism but paired this
with an assertion that this truth had been suppressed, due to the
naivety, mendacity, or willful ignorance of Western politicians, journalists, and academics. Thus, US Senator Jackson argued that Western
governments were involved in a "coverup...to muffle the facts about
Soviet-bloc support for international terrorism" (Netanyahu 1980: 34).
Cline asserted that "[t]he Soviet Union has provided the logistic
support and political rationale that ties the terrorists together stra-
tegically in ways they themselves may not fully realize and which
American scholars, journalists, and political leaders have failed to
focus on" (Netanyahu 1980: 91–2). Robert Moss's talk, "The terrorist
state," accused those who hoped to achieve détente with the Soviet
Union of perpetuating "a conspiracy of silence" (Netanyahu 1980:

128), proclaiming: "International terrorism [is] exploited by the Soviet Union and other interests in the effort to undermine Western societies" (Netanyahu 1980: 133). And Representative Jack Kemp, stating that international terrorism was "a transnational weapon," declared: "I am pleased to see an emerging consensus as to the ultimate source of international terrorist support in an overwhelming number of cases – the Soviet Union" (Netanyahu 1980: 189, 195). Only a few presenters took a more skeptical view of these claims, dissenting from the otherwise unified vision.[7]

From this point onward, accusations about the "politicization" of knowledge and expertise would become a key mode of contention. Although many subsequent critics would view this conference as an attempt to politicize the field, the organizers worked to establish their position as the baseline of neutrality, while attempting to stigmatize dissent with the tag of politicized knowledge. This involved a balancing act, between asserting a new political framework, while claiming to be apolitical, and dismissing opponents as biased. As Netanyahu writes in the conference report (Netanyahu 1980: 1–2),

> As some nowadays satisfy themselves with the easy moral relativism of "One man's terrorist is another man's freedom fighter," it was important to establish at the outset the fact that a clear definitional framework exists, regardless of political view.

Similarly, George Keegan Jr., former chief of intelligence for the US Air Force, declared that the conference had "rendered a great service by piercing through the fog of causation and making clear, possibly for the first time in an open forum, the true nature of the Soviet Union's perfidious role in the direction and support of global terror as an instrument of strategic warfare" (Netanyahu 1980: 35).

[7] David Barrett, from the Canadian New Democratic Party, and Joop den Uyl, from the Dutch Labour Party, questioned the narratives of terrorism as a threat to civilization and of the Soviet sponsorship of terrorism. And nuclear experts Edward Teller (who did not attend but sent a talk to be read out) and Thomas Schelling both attempted to reframe the primary problem as the possibility of nuclear terrorism and nuclear proliferation.

The conference received extensive media coverage. Articles about the conference appeared in publications around the world, including *The Daily Telegraph* (London), *Deutschland Magazine, National Review,* and the *International Herald Tribune.*[8] Conference organizers reported that "the major themes of the Conference were echoed in newspapers, magazine, radio and television in many parts of the world... [T]he Conference's message penetrated into many of the leading newspapers and journals in the United States, Western Europe, South America, and elsewhere" (the Jerusalem conference publication *World Press Coverage,* quoted by Paull 1982: 19–20). A documentary entitled *The Russian Connection* aired across the United States on the Public Broadcasting Service (PBS) on September 25, 1979, including interviews with Brian Crozier, Ray Cline, and Shlomo Gazit.[9] Congressman Jack Kemp and Senator Robert Packwood inserted materials from the conference into the *Congressional Record* (Paull 1982: 20). *The Wall Street Journal* reported: "Terrorism, the institute people think, is one of those issues dramatizing the fact that the forces threatening Israel are the same as those threatening the West in general... Many speakers during the conference echoed this theme: A necessary step in fighting terrorism is to educate democratic nations about how massive a moral and practical threat it is to their beliefs."[10] The Jonathan Institute was pleased with the media coverage, writing in its October 1979 *Bulletin* that the conference had "had a decisive impact on the Western perception of international terrorism and the central role of the PLO [Palestine Liberation Organization] in it."[11]

[8] Library of Congress, Ray S. Cline papers, box 53, folder 1, "Conferences and meetings," Jonathan Institute *Bulletin,* October 1979.
[9] The Jonathan Institute *Bulletin* also went so far as to compare, side by side, claims made at the conference and statements made in the PBS television show as proof of their influence. Library of Congress, Cline papers, box 53, folder 1, "Conferences and meetings," Jonathan Institute *Bulletin,* November 1979, "TV documentary confirms Jerusalem conference revelations."
[10] Library of Congress, Cline papers, box 53, folder 1, "Conferences and meetings," *Wall Street Journal,* Suzanne Weaver, "The political uses of terror," July 26, 1979.
[11] Library of Congress, Cline papers, box 53, folder 1, "Conferences and meetings," Jonathan Institute *Bulletin,* October 1979.

THE STERLING AFFAIR: "IN '81, ANOTHER EXPERT
APPEARS, LIKE A SUPER NOVA"[12]

The second episode that publicized the "terrorism as war" frame
was the emergence of Claire Sterling as a new expert. Sterling was
an American journalist living in Italy, whose 1981 book *The Terror
Network* became a best-seller in multiple countries, including the
United States, turning into the most formally influential book on
terrorism to date (Sterling 1981b). It was promoted by the Reagan
administration: Secretary of State Haig distributed excerpts from
the book to members of Congress, and the US International Communications Agency promoted it overseas through its cultural centers
(Schlesinger, Murdock, and Elliot 1983: 7).

Some of the most contentious public debates over the politicization of terrorism were spurred by the Reagan administration's
adoption of the Soviet "terror network" theory, first popularized in
the United States by two articles in *The New York Times Magazine*;
Robert Moss's November 1980 article "Terror: a Soviet export"
(Moss 1980) drew directly on the 1979 Jerusalem conference, while
Claire Sterling's March 1981 cover story "Terrorism: tracing the
international network" (Sterling 1981a) drew on her forthcoming
book, asserting that "for the last decade the Soviet Union and its
surrogates have provided support for terrorists around the world."
Sterling (1981a) summarizes:

> Such connections within the terrorist network have long been
> evident. What is now beginning to emerge is the degree to which
> the links in this network have been purposefully forged – and
> continue to be maintained – by the Soviet Union and its two chief
> proxies in this regard – Cuba and the Palestinians.

Daniel Schorr wrote in *The New York Times* that *The Terror
Network* "bursts upon the scene like an answer to a Reagan prayer,"
noting: "The publisher's ads proudly claim that the book 'proves'

---

[12] Interview with Timothy Naftali, June 2006.

what Secretary of State Alexander Haig proclaims – that Moscow consciously fosters international terrorism" (Schorr 1981). He called the book "important" and "a considerable feat of research, organization, and literary craftsmanship," yet found the argument somewhat "conspiratorial" (Schorr 1981). Others were more critical. Alexander Cockburn and James Ridgeway, in the *Village Voice*, wrote of "calculated misrepresentations of reality," while Aryeh Neier in *The Nation* wrote that the book "shows nothing" in support of its claims (both quoted by Wilson 1981: 34–5).

James Q. Wilson's *Commentary* piece is itself an exercise in rhetorical positioning with regard to the question of "politicization." Wilson calls the *Village Voice* piece a "serious assault," and the *Nation* review "a piece of systematic misrepresentation." Wilson also asserts that Sterling's critics themselves refuse to commit to a definition of terrorism: "Instead of proposing a definition of terrorism and then attempting to deal with it in all its ugly manifestations, we seem locked into the familiar rhetorical tactic of answering a charge by leveling a charge." Wilson proposes adopting the definition put forth at the 1979 Jerusalem conference, namely "deliberate, systematic murder, maiming, and menacing of the innocent to inspire fear in order to gain political end." A second interesting aspect of Wilson's piece is the way in which it highlights the importance of ambiguity in the production and reception of Sterling's book, and the "terror network" theory more generally. Is Sterling claiming that the Soviets orchestrate international terrorism, or merely that they enable it? Her texts appear purposefully ambiguous, while other supporters of the terror network theory range from more or less strong versions of these claims in their public statements. Wilson claims that Sterling is merely claiming Soviet "complicity," and thus that critics charging her with promulgating an unsupported conspiracy theory are guilty of misreading her (Wilson 1981). Sterling herself makes similar claims in her defense: a *Chicago Tribune* article reports her unhappiness with Haig's use of her book to support his accusations that the Soviets are responsible for international terrorism, and that her work has been misinterpreted (Worthington 1981).

> For the first time in my 30-year career as a reporter," Sterling said, "I have suddenly become an extreme right-wing hawk! [...] First, they (the liberal left) tried to discredit the book, saying it was just propaganda; a knee-jerk, undocumented, no-credibility, anti-Soviet book. And *then* they (both liberals and conservatives) said that *I* said the Russians *masterminded* the terrorists."

In contrast to its enthusiastic reception at the White House, *The Terror Network* received a more skeptical reception from established experts and the broader media. While some accepted the terror network theory, Sterling's work was dismissed by other researchers as a conspiracy theory unsupported by serious evidence. Brian Jenkins of RAND observed archly (Jenkins, quoted by Schmid and Jongman 1988: 105):

> A friend of mine recently observed that at the moment there are three kinds of people in Washington: those who have always believed the Soviet Union is responsible for terrorism; those who want to believe that it is; and those who, in order to maintain their influence in government, must pretend to believe.

Elsewhere, Jenkins suggested that the Soviet theory was actually impeding practical counterterrorism efforts (Kempe 1983: 22). According to Schmid (1988)'s overview of the field, most credible individuals were skeptical, and he quotes "Another insider, who works for the CIA, found the book 'poorly researched' and called the 'use of evidence flawed,' with 'quotations taken out of context,' 'biases creeping in on every page,' and 'data impossible to reproduce'" (Schmid and Jongman 1988: 105).

Official promotion of Sterling's thesis encountered perhaps the strongest resistance when it ran up against the professional autonomy of the CIA intelligence analysis corps.[13] Timothy Naftali, author of

---

[13] My account of the conflict between the CIA and the Reagan administration is based primarily on Woodward (1987) and Persico (1990).

Blind Spot: The Secret History of American Counterterrorism, identified this as a crucial turning point in the history of US counterterrorism, noting that "the terrorism elite within the US Government balks and says this is just not right."[14] William Casey, who had directed Reagan's 1980 presidential election campaign, was sworn in as director of Central Intelligence one week after the presidential inauguration (and would serve until 1987). Casey was also becoming convinced by the Soviet network theory. After reading Claire Sterling's *New York Times Magazine* story,[15] he encouraged the CIA intelligence corps to follow up. Tasked with verifying Sterling's claims, however, the analysts found her method and findings flawed. "Our analysis showed that what she claimed often didn't stand up," John McMahon, CIA deputy director of operations, said. "It just was not true" (McMahon quoted by Persico 1990: 287–8). The senior national intelligence officer responsible for looking at the Soviet Union wrote a report that "took a strong anti-Sterling line" and "pretty much cleared the Soviets of involvement in terrorism" (Woodward 1987: 125). Casey, in response, reportedly advised his analysts: "Read Claire Sterling's book, and forget this mush" (Woodward 1987: 125), adding, "I paid $13.95 for this and it told me more than you bastards whom I pay $50,000 a year" (Woodward 1987: 126). Casey and Sterling had a meeting. When the skeptical conclusions of the CIA analysts were broached, according to McMahon, who was present at the meeting, "Claire Sterling...jumped all over Bill. She said, 'Your people aren't pursuing this thing because half of them are leftist sympathizers'" (Persico 1990: 286–7).

Definitional problems plagued attempts to bridge the gaps between Soviet theory fans and skeptics. While the CIA analysts resisted Sterling's framework, Bobby Ray Inman, deputy director of the CIA, and Eugene Tighe, director of the Defense Intelligence

[14] Interview with Timothy Naftali, June 2006.
[15] It was reportedly Richard Nixon who originally alerted Casey to this story, sending Casey a letter in March 1981 telling him to read the article (Persico 1990: 286).

Agency, were both sympathetic to the theory. Casey asked Tighe to have the DIA analysts prepare a report on the topic, and the DIA draft that emerged supported Sterling's hypothesis. A few weeks later, Woodward says, Casey received a memo from Lincoln Gordon, former president of Johns Hopkins University and "one of three members of a senior review panel at the CIA charted with bringing non-intelligence professional and academic review to the formal estimates" (Woodward 1987: 126). Gordon wrote that the CIA report used too narrow a definition of terrorism, while the DIA's was perhaps too broad, and Casey asked Gordon to write his own report on the matter. Gordon's report, presented at a meeting on May 14, 1981,[16] was said (Woodward 1987: 127–8) to have

> arrived at something between the CIA and DIA extremes. Part of the problem was the confusion over what constituted terrorism. Clearly, the Soviets supported Third World wars of liberation... But, he said, the intelligence provided no evidence that the Soviets were playing a mighty Wurlitzer of terrorism.

These findings were released to the White House in a report stating that there was "insufficient evidence" to support claims that the Soviet Union was orchestrating international terrorism,[17] alongside which Casey reportedly commented, "Of course, Mr. President, you and I know better" (Persico 1990: 288).

A final irony in this affair comes from accusations that Sterling's book was based on "blowback." The concrete accusations she makes, and several of her sources, had their origins in CIA disinformation campaigns linking the Italian Red Brigade to the Soviet Union (Woodward 1987: 129), with another writer finding that Sterling's

---

[16] On May 13 there had been an attempt to assassinate Pope John Paul II, which Sterling and others, including Casey, attributed to Soviet-sponsored terrorists. Casey pushed his analysts to investigate this connection, but they reported that they saw no evidence to support it.

[17] Gordon's report was classified and the findings were not released to the public.

CIA quotations were "exact replicas of the misquotes published by the Jonathan Institute" (Paull 1982: 4–5).[18]

THE SENATE SUBCOMMITTEE ON SECURITY
AND TERRORISM

The Terror Network would have perhaps its most lasting effect in the form of a series of congressional hearings that sought to substantiate the claims made at the Jerusalem conference and in Sterling's book. The hearings began on April 24, 1981, chaired by Senator Jeremiah Denton and initiated by the new Senate Subcommittee on Security and Terrorism created by Senator Strom Thurmond, chair of the Senate Judiciary Committee following the Republicans' victory in the 1980 congressional elections. The purpose of the hearings was to establish the veracity of the claims of a Soviet connection to international terrorism in a public forum. As *The New York Times* claimed several weeks into the hearings, they were "without any real legislative purpose," and Senator Denton, chair of the hearings, acknowledged that their main purpose was "to raise public consciousness" (Wicker 1981).

Almost all the experts called as witnesses at the hearings affirmed the Soviet theory. Of the total of sixty-five witnesses testifying before the hearings of the Senate Subcommittee on Security and Terrorism between 1981 and 1986, thirty-two were US government employees or elected officials, and eighteen testified as former members of terrorist organizations or as victims of terrorism. Of the remaining twenty-five, seven were prominent advocates of the Soviet theory of international terrorism, including two (Cline and Moss) who had also presented at the 1979 Jerusalem conference.[19]

[18] For more on the "terror network" theory as blowback, see Persico (1990: 288) and Herman and O'Sullivan (1989: 63).
[19] The remaining eighteen witnesses included two representatives of the airline industry, three members of local law enforcement, four attorneys, two representatives of the energy industry, the director of the Woodrow Wilson International Center for Scholars, a former coordinator of the Ministry of Popular Culture in Nicaragua, the deputy general counsel of the US Nuclear Regulatory

But the hearings did not invite any of the previous experts involved in organizing the new would-be discipline of terrorism studies in the 1970s. And this is true despite the fact that members of this so-called "terrorism mafia," such as Brian Jenkins, Paul Wilkinson, Martha Crenshaw, and Ronald Crelinsten, were frequently called to testify in other congressional hearings during this same period.[20] The expert witnesses at the Senate hearings were not, for the most part, the academics seeking to develop "terrorism studies" as a new field of research. Nor were they the technical and quantitative analysts who had been developing databases and statistical analyses at RAND, an organization whose claims to authority rested upon its strictly disinterested, non-partisan approach to analysis. Instead, a new group of individuals, tightly networked and affiliated with a small number of more politically oriented think tanks and organizations such as the Center for Strategic and International Studies, were invited.

Think tanks, key among them CSIS, were an important development in the spread of the Soviet terror narrative, providing an institutional platform to promote and coordinate its dissemination. CSIS was founded in 1962, "at the height of the Cold War, dedicated to the simple but urgent goal of finding ways for America to survive as a nation and prosper as a people."[21] It was affiliated with Georgetown University until 1987, when the two split following an investigation prompted by allegations that CSIS was "promoting a conservative agenda and catering to the news media, rather than on pursuing scholarly research" (New York Times 1987). CSIS became the hub

Commision, the president of the Association of Former Intelligence Officers, a political scientist from the University of Arizona, a journalist of Latin American affairs, and a law professor at the University of Virginia.

[20] Brian Jenkins of RAND testified at congressional hearings in 1983, 1984, 1985, and 1989. Robert Kupperman (former advisor to the CCCT) testified in 1983, 1988, and 1989. J. Bowyer Bell testified in 1985 and 1986. Political scientist Martha Crenshaw testified in 1985 and 1986, and Bruce Hoffman of RAND testified in 1988. Source: Lexis-Nexis, "Congressional hearings" file.

[21] See CSIS, "A brief history", available at www.csis.org/about/history/#1960 (last accessed July 11, 2008).

of a new type of terrorism expertise – one that was explicit in its advocacy. CSIS-affiliated experts' advocacy of the Soviet conspiracy theory of international terrorism made it a crucial link between the Jerusalem conference, the Claire Sterling book, and the Senate hearings. CSIS affiliates were key witnesses at the Senate hearings on terrorism, attended the Jonathan Institute conference and disseminated its findings, and promoted Sterling's book and her ideas in the United States.

CSIS was home to a number of terrorism experts during the 1980s who were sympathetic to the Soviet theory, including Ray Cline, Yonah Alexander, and Walter Laqueur. Cline, a senior associate at CSIS since 1974, had previously worked in the US government for over thirty years, including as deputy director of intelligence for the CIA from 1962 to 1966, and director of the Bureau of Intelligence and Research at the Department of State from 1969 to 1973.[22] Alexander was professor of international studies and director of his own center, the Institute for Studies in International Terrorism, at SUNY Oneonta, as well as a research associate at CSIS. Exceedingly well networked, Alexander also held various affiliations with the University of Chicago Institute for Social and Behavioral Pathology, the Tel Aviv University Center for Strategic Studies, and the International Institute for Strategic Studies in London, and was the founder and editor in chief of the journal *Terrorism*, as well as author or editor of fifteen books on the subject.[23] And, although Alexander had been a part of the early "terrorism mafia" of the 1970s, he had split from most of that group in becoming an advocate of the terror network theory.

Cline and Alexander's book *Terrorism: The Soviet Connection* (1984) argued, as the title suggests, for the Soviet theory. Senator Jeremiah Denton hosted a news conference announcing the publication, and a reception was held at CSIS to celebrate the publication, with guests including William Casey, Jim Woolsey, Neil Livingstone, and representatives of the American Jewish Committee, the Heritage

---

[22] Library of Congress, Cline papers, box 28, folder 7.
[23] Library of Congress, Cline papers, box 28, folder 7.

Foundation, the Department of State, the FAA, and the Federal Emergency Management Agency.[24] Arnaud de Borchgrave (an editor at the conservative *Washington Times*, and co-author, with Robert Moss, of *The Spike*, a best-selling novel about terrorism) blurbed the book, saying that it was essential "reading for thousands of professors and journalists who still refuse to believe the steadily-growing evidence of links between the Soviet KGB and its proxy services on the one hand and international terrorist groups on the other."[25] Copies of the book were sent to members of Congress, and the book was distributed by the Department of State in response to public requests for information about terrorism (Herman and O'Sullivan 1989: 147).

The first hearing, on "Terrorism: origins, direction and support," investigated Soviet support for international terrorism. Expert witnesses at this hearing included former CIA director William Colby, Claire Sterling, Michael Ledeen,[26] and Arnaud de Borchgrave. Shortly before the hearings began *The New York Times* reported: "De Borchgrave's novel is about a Kremlin 'blueprint' for taking over the West, with the help of KGB dupes and agents of influence in academia, the press, and even the White House" (Lardner 1981: A11), while the book review section had earlier reported: "The authors acknowledge that the controversial plot, about a Russian plan to manipulate the Western press in order to blunt public awareness of Soviet intentions, is not intended solely as escapist fare" (McDowell 1980). These first four witnesses all affirmed the Soviet theory. Sterling testified on the "role of Soviet Union in supporting terrorist activities in democratic societies; questioned candor of Western governments regarding Soviet involvement in terrorism; explanation of supranational common bonds among terrorist groups."[27]

---

[24] Library of Congress, Cline papers, part I, container 9, folder 15.

[25] Library of Congress, Cline papers, part I, container 9, folder 15.

[26] Ledeen was, more recently, an advisor to the George W. Bush administration and a proponent of links between Saddam Hussein and "weapons of mass destruction."

[27] All the quotes in this section come from Lexis-Nexis "Congressional hearings" summaries.

The second hearing, on "Historical antecedents of Soviet terrorism," followed up on these claims, bringing James Billington (of the Woodrow Wilson International Center for Scholars) and Stefan Possony (of the Hoover Institution, who discussed "current Communist terrorist group activities worldwide" and the "likelihood of Soviet-directed international terrorist networks," along with "related Soviet intelligence service activities") as witnesses. A hearing later that year on "Terrorism: the role of Moscow and its subcontractors" called Robert Moss, a London-based journalist alleged to have CIA affiliations, who had been one of the presenters at the 1979 Jonathan Institute conference, and one of the first to introduce the Soviet thesis to the United States, through his 1980 article "Terror: a Soviet export" (Moss 1980), which discussed "Soviet involvement in international terrorism," "US vulnerability to Communist terrorist groups," and the "extent of Soviet intelligence service activities in Latin America and Europe."

The hearings would continue for five years, and, although they would face charges as biased, partisan, and detached from reality, their organizers sought to reclaim for themselves the ground of neutrality, detachment, and seriousness. In an interview with *The Washington Post*, Joel Lisker, the chief counsel for the Senate Subcommittee on Security and Terrorism (and formerly of the FBI), is quoted as saying: "If we used the classic witnesses, from the intelligence agencies, I think they'd be looked on as representing vested interests, not as objective as they should be," whereas the witnesses they have called "will be taken more seriously" and "bring a fresh perspective to the problem" (Lardner 1981: A11).

According to scholar Michael Gold-Biss, these hearings, and the sort of witnesses called to them, indicate that during the 1980s "the discursive space on political violence...was taken over by a small but vociferous community of interpretation" (Gold-Biss 1994: 2), whom he labels the "terror cabalists" (Gold-Biss 1994: 3). Gold-Biss charged that "[t]he themes and subjects the SST explored were open to the charge of being *prima facie* preposterous, in view of their lack of scholarly underpinnings or practical merit," and the purpose of the hearings was to construct such a threat where none existed (Gold-Biss 1994: 113, emphasis in original). Gold-Biss's book is not only a useful overview of these hearings but is also representative of a new trend that took shape in the middle of the 1980s: the rise of a critical "counter-discourse" in response to the perceived bias of the mainstream terrorism discourse.

POLITICIZATION: CLAIMS AND COUNTERCLAIMS

As terrorism came to take on a more prominent role in American political discourse, and the narratives spun around the terrorism problem began to take on an ever more elaborated character, a counter-discourse arose, with two main sets of claims. The first, which some labeled a reverse conspiracy theory (Schmid and Jongman 1988: 106), turns the narrative of Soviet sponsorship of terrorism on its head, highlighting the role of the United States in sponsoring sub-state violence abroad.[28] A quintessential text in this vein is Edward Herman's *The Real Terror Network: Terrorism in Fact and Propaganda*, published in 1982, which argues that the United States was a perpetrator of terrorism, and that the concept of terrorism is commonly understood in a biased way, given that most of what has been labeled "terrorism" in the West pales next to the sub rosa violence sponsored by the United States (Herman 1982).[29] Herman's subsequent book (co-authored with Gerry O'Sullivan), *The "Terrorism" Industry*, argues not only that "terrorism" is an essentially politicized concept put forth by Western powers to "obscure and justify further

[28] Interestingly, while Schmid and Jongman assess both these as "conspiracy theories of terrorism," they evaluate the counter-discourse as more credible: "Which of the two conspiracy theories of terrorism one wishes to believe is a question of political choice. It is safe to assume that both theories contain elements of truth. From the point of view of documented hard evidence, the Chomsky/Herman book [Chomsky and Herman 1979] is, however, qualitatively different and superior to Sterling's work" (Schmid and Jongman 1988: 107).

[29] For additional examples of the growth of such a counter-discourse, see also Douglass and Zulaika (1990); Gold-Biss (1994); Hocking (1984); Paull (1982); Said (2001 [1988]).

Western-based primary violence" (Herman and O'Sullivan 1989: 56) but also that terrorism experts "meet a 'demand' for intellectual-ideological service by states and other powerful interests, analogous to the demand for tanks by the army or advertising copy by the producers of soap" (Herman and O'Sullivan 1989: 7). "Terrorism" could potentially be an unbiased concept, these authors hold, if state violence were to be included within its parameters, and it was only the overarching ideological power of the state that kept the concept in this biased state. Other works taking similar approaches released at this time included Noam Chomsky's *Pirates and Emperors: International Terrorism in the Real World* (1986) and Edward Said and Christopher Hitchens' (2001) edited volume *Blaming the Victims: Spurious Scholarship and the Palestinian Question.*

An alternative version of the counter-discourse held that "terrorism" did not hold any potential for analytic neutrality, and therefore was an essentially politicized concept that ought to be scrapped altogether. For example, Christopher Hitchens' 1986 article "Wanton acts of usage: terrorism: a cliché in search of a meaning"[30] opens with the problem of definition, asking, "How can a word with no meaning and no definition...have become the political and media buzzword of the eighties?" (Hitchens 1986: 67–8). Unlike those who would reclaim the term, however, Hitchens (1986: 68) rejects the notion of "terrorism" altogether:

> In a defensive reaction to this hypocritical and ideological
> emphasis, many liberals have taken simply to inverting the word,
> or to changing the subject... This is all right as far as it goes, which
> is not very far. You don't draw the sting from a brainless propaganda
> word merely by turning it around. The word "terrorist" is not – like
> "communist" and "fascist" – being abused; it is itself an abuse.

[30] This essay was a review of several books on terrorism, including *Terrorism: How the West Can Win* (Netanyahu 1984) and *Terrorism as State-Sponsored Covert Warfare: What the Free World Must Do to Protect Itself* (Cline and Alexander 1986).

Despite widespread criticism of Sterling's book, and of the Soviet theory more generally, *The Terror Network* continued to exert a strong influence upon popular and political discourse on terrorism throughout the 1980s. The terror network thesis was promulgated at a number of conferences, and in a series of publications by an increasingly intertwined set of authors. In 1985 Jillian Becker published *The Soviet Connection: State Sponsorship of Terrorism*, referencing works by Roberta Goren (whose 1984 book *The Soviet Union and Terrorism* she had edited), John Barron's book *KGB Today: The Hidden Hand*, Claire Sterling's *The Terror Network*, and Raphael Israeli's work on similar themes, sending a copy to Sterling with her "warmest best wishes."[31] The book's preface, written by Gerald Frost, the head of the Institute for European Defence and Strategic Studies, derides "the reluctance of Western politicians and opinion-forming elites to recognize unpalatable truths... [W]hat researchers such as John Barron, Claire Sterling, and Mrs Becker have shown about the extent of Soviet support for terrorism is either ignored or derided; whatever hard evidence of Soviet involvement has been produced publicly is soon forgotten" (Frost 1985: 6).

A number of other conferences on terrorism, following the Jerusalem conference and the publication of *The Terror Network*, also picked up these themes. A 1985 conference at the Fletcher School of Law and Diplomacy at Tufts University on "Terrorism and other 'low-intensity' operations: international linkages" attempted to "assess phenomena that have not received adequate attention, namely, the utilization of terrorism by states, including the Soviet Union," and argued: "Despite impressive evidence of Soviet complicity, there remains a pervasive incapacity or unwillingness in both Western Europe and the United Sates to face the reality of what is known" (Institute for Foreign Policy Analysis [IFPA] 1985).[32] The

---

[31] Hoover Institution Archives, Sterling papers, box 69.

[32] This conference was sponsored by the "International security studies program" of the Fletcher School of Law and Diplomacy, Tufts University; the report, copyright

conference program included talks by Claire Sterling, along with other advocates of the Soviet network theory such as Neil Livingstone, Michael Ledeen, and Douglas Feith, but none by the members of the "terrorism studies mafia" that had taken shape in the 1970s. And a 1986 conference sponsored by the Department of Defense incorporated discussion of terrorism within a broader framework of "low-intensity warfare," and incorporated the Soviet framework into this conceptualization. This conference report opened with a paper from Caspar Weinberger, the secretary of defense, in which he declares: "Tonight, one out of every four countries around the globe is at war. In virtually every case, there is a mask on the face of war. In virtually every case, behind the mask is the Soviet Union and those who do its bidding" (Weinberger and US Department of Defense 1986: 3).

Although the proponents of the "terror network" theory were remarkably successful in propagating their expertise in the public sphere throughout the 1980s, this approach was treated with skepticism by analysts at the CIA, the military, RAND, and most of the scholarly terrorism experts, who viewed terrorism as a problem to be managed and understood. One instance of such conflict can be seen in the internal struggle at the CIA over the Sterling thesis, as detailed above. A similar but somewhat less public clash can be read in the evaluation of a report prepared by experts at the Center for Strategic and International Studies. In 1984 CSIS received a contract to produce a report on state-sponsored terrorism for the US Army, to be prepared by Ray Cline and Yonah Alexander, and submitted the following year. The report was lauded by Senator Denton, who distributed it to members of Congress, and a book based on the study, titled *Terrorism as State-Sponsored Covert Warfare*, was published the following year (Cline and Alexander 1986). The book, which was promoted with blurbs from Arnaud de Borchgrave of *The Washington*

IFPA, was later published as *The Hydra of Carnage*. Hoover Institution Archives, Sterling papers, box 69, pp. v, 3.

Times and Senator Richard Lugar, declared that international terrorism had become "an indispensable tactical and strategic tool of totalitarian dictatorships" and that terrorism was now "one of the gravest threats to the strategic interests of the West" (Cline and Alexander 1986: 1, 12).

But the US Army's evaluation of the report was not nearly as positive. Responses to the initial draft, submitted in December 1984, were quite harsh, with critiques focusing on problems of definition, the distinction between facts and opinion, skepticism towards the Soviet theory of terrorism espoused in the report, and issues of measurement. One evaluation complained that the report contained "dogmatic statements that have not yet been proven," and relied on "journalistic accounts" and statistics that were "highly suspect."[33] Other army readers emphasized that the report "lacked balance," failed to address right-wing terrorism, and contradicted the US Army's definition of terrorism;[34] that "the authors' political preferences, prejudices, and emotionalism should be eliminated from the text so that the 'facts' can speak for themselves";[35] and that the concept of state-sponsored terrorism "is not sufficiently defined to be useful in the development of Army doctrine."[36] An evaluation of a later version of the report expressed concern that the study had a "strong political bias," and that the report did not make a clear distinction between "documented fact" and "opinion."[37]

---

[33] Memo from Lieutenant Colonel Preston L. Funkhouser, DAMI CIC [Department of the Army Military Intelligence, Combat Information Center], to chairman of Study Advisory Group [SAG] re CSIS study on state-sponsored terrorism, December 18, 1984. Library of Congress, Cline papers, box 33, folder 17.

[34] Library of Congress, Cline papers, box 33, folder 17, "Document: state-sponsored terrorism."

[35] Library of Congress, Cline papers, box 33, folder 17, "Comments on state-sponsored terrorism study – draft," December 5, 1984.

[36] Memo from Lieutenant Colonel Richard M. Swier to SAG re CSIS study on state-sponsored terrorism, December 19 1984. Library of Congress, Cline papers, box 33, folder 17.

[37] Memo from LTC Funkhouser to chairman SAG, attn. DAMO-SSP [Department of the Army Management Office – Strategic Systems Programs], re CSIS study on state-sponsored terrorism, April 4 1985. Library of Congress, Cline papers, box 33, folder 17.

DEPOLITICIZING TERRORISM STUDIES?

What became of the rest of the "terrorism mafia," those who had first begun to develop the field of terrorism studies in the 1970s? Worry at the increasing charges of politicization leveled against terrorism studies would spur a number of these experts – composed largely of those centered at RAND and at academic institutions – to attempt to depoliticize the field. The reaction of most of the members of the "terrorism mafia" to the Soviet theory was one of skepticism. In June 1984 Brian Jenkins wrote to Senator Denton on terrorism legislation that "I think it will be extremely difficult to create a list of countries sponsoring terrorism that will not fall victim to partisan wrangling and pressures from numerous interest groups lobbying for the inclusion of this country or the exclusion of that country."[38] Martha Crenshaw, in a review of a later book by Netanyahu, would write: "This book is not a product of academic research or scholarship but of what Avishai Margalit, in his review..., defines as Hashara,[39] a Hebrew term meaning literally 'explanation' but implying a mixture of propaganda, preaching, indoctrination, apology, rhetoric, and even self-righteousness" (Crenshaw 1996: 177). The Soviet network theory of terrorism was seen to undermine this project of trying to develop a legitimate field of terrorism studies; as Martha Crenshaw has reflected more recently, "[U]nder the Reagan administration, the attempt to blame terrorism on the Soviet Union in many ways discredited the study of terrorism."[40] Academically inclined terrorism studies researchers were stung by the charges of politicization that were leveled at their field, even when they themselves partially agreed with the critiques.[41] Crenshaw told an interviewer in the early 1980s (Hoffman 1984: 132–3):

---

[38] RAND Corporation Archives, George K. Tanham files, folder "G. K. Tanham chronological file, January–July 1984," letter from Brian Jenkins (program director, security and subnational conflict) to Senator Jeremiah Denton, June 20, 1984.

[39] The word appears thus; it was probably intended to read "hasbara."

[40] Interview with Martha Crenshaw, June 28, 2006.

[41] In interviews conducted in 2006 and 2007, several individuals spontaneously brought up the book The "Terrorism" Industry (Herman and O'Sullivan 1989).

It also creates political problems, both for governments and for researchers because of the polemical nature of the term. This is not really a definitional problem; it's a problem of political discourse or political terminology in that the minute you use the term "terrorism," you get everybody's back up.

A subset of terrorism researchers reacted to these events by attempting to reclaim a space insulated from the logic of the political sphere, in which, they hoped, neutral, scientific, apolitical expertise could be produced. Terrorism studies, in the view of these actors, needed to be defended on two fronts – both against those, particularly from the universities, who saw terrorism analysis as an essentially political (and thus illegitimate) project, and against those who would so mold the concept into their particular political framework as to make it difficult for there to be a rational/scientific study of the topic.

This was an unusual form of boundary maintenance (Gieryn 1983), however, for terrorism studies researchers needed to maintain boundaries around their field sufficient to maintain the appearance of autonomy and yet simultaneously keep these boundaries flexible enough to maintain engagement with both academia and the state. The primary reaction of the "terrorism mafia" was not open dispute but, rather, an attempt to reconsolidate the field, to defend the possibility of a depoliticized field of terrorism studies as a whole – and not primarily a matter of "boundary drawing" against experts who might be seen as fraudulent or extreme. This process of flexible boundary drawing is where we can see most clearly how terrorism studies became established as an interstitial site of knowledge production. Researchers needed to prevent their field from being completely excluded from the academic world, in order to maintain their scientific legitimacy, yet could not afford to break their ties with the political arm of the state, despite its potentially tainting influence, for this was where they saw potential for influence.[42]

---

[42] There are a number of parallels here to the constraints faced by Israeli Middle East studies experts, as observed by Gil Eyal (2002).

This manifested itself in a series of attempts to carve out a means of performing terrorism studies that was both scientific and politically unbiased and yet could maintain its ability to be heard and used by state actors.

One aspect of this struggle was waged over the question of whether it might be possible to establish a neutral, or objective, definition of terrorism. David Rapoport, in the introduction to a collection of papers from a 1979 conference, writes: "In order to strip the term of its abusive connotations, and thus make it 'objective' or 'scientific,' most academics define terrorism as illegal political violence. Though the purpose or intention is different, the definition is remarkably similar to that of governments" (Rapoport and Alexander 1982: 3). Similarly, Crenshaw (1983: 2) distinguishes analytical from normative judgments:

> The danger inherent in the normative definition is that it verges
> on the polemical. If "terrorist" is what one calls one's
> opponent…then the word is more of an epithet or a debating
> stratagem than a label that enables all who read it, whatever their
> ideological affiliation, to know what terrorism is and what it is
> not… It seems preferable to establish a neutral descriptive
> definition, general enough to be applicable to the circumstances of
> both South Africa and Northern Ireland, and only then to make
> value judgments about different cases.

Alex Schmid and Albert Jongman's handbook *Political Terrorism: A Research Guide to Concepts, Theories, Data Bases, and Literature* (first published in 1983, and updated in 1988) exemplifies this ideal of scholarly neutrality, saying (Schmid and Jongman 1988: 179):

> Ideally, the scientific literature of terrorism should be apolitical and
> amoral. The research should not take a "top-down" perspective,
> looking at the phenomenon of terrorism through the eyes of the
> power-holders; nor should the researcher look at terrorism from a
> "revolutionary" or "progressive" perspective, identifying with
> one "just cause" or another.

And Brian Jenkins, of RAND, commented (Hoffman 1984: 76–7, 83) that

> one could talk about definitions of terrorism that are strictly political, that is, for propagandistic purposes. The term "terrorism" has become, in our age, a pejorative term; an effort is made to attach the label "terrorist" to one's opponent and thereby persuade others... I would love to see someone perfect a definition that would be so precise that Menachem Begin could sit down with Yasir Arafat and reach agreement on a list of 100 randomly selected events in the world.

Two conferences held in the middle of the 1980s constituted sites of these ongoing efforts to develop a scholarly field of terrorism studies. At both these conferences, speakers repudiated not just the specific thesis of the Soviet terror network but also some of the more general popular assumptions that had come to permeate discourse on terrorism, such as the irrationality of terrorists. The attempt to produce a depoliticized field of terrorism studies often adopted some of the same critiques put forth in the "critical" literature (for example, that the field of terrorism studies focuses on insurgent terror to the exclusion of state terror). But, instead of using this to prove that the field of terrorism studies was illegitimate and hopelessly politicized, it used these as a form of internal critique in the attempt to produce a better, depoliticized field.

The first of these was a conference on "Contemporary research on terrorism," organized by Paul Wilkinson (then a professor at the University of Aberdeen, and who would go on to lead the terrorism studies center at the University of St Andrews) and held at Aberdeen from April 15 to 17, 1986 (Wilkinson and Stewart 1987). The participants were primarily academics, with some from think tanks or government institutes. They included Bonnie Cordes (RAND), Ronald Crelinsten (University of Ottawa), Bruce Hoffman (RAND), Brian Jenkins (RAND), Robert Kupperman (CSIS), Jerrold Post (George Washington University), David Rapoport (UCLA), and Fernando

Reinares (European University Institute). Paper topics included terrorism as political communication, the problem of definition, and terrorists' own writings.

Wilkinson's introduction to the conference report acknowledged that terrorism could be committed both by states and by insurgents, although the conference itself focused on sub-state actors. Further, Wilkinson writes that "terrorism is not a philosophy or a movement: it is a method of struggle," and so "there have been a number of historical cases where terrorism has been used on behalf of causes most Western liberals would regard as just" (Wilkinson and Stewart 1987: xiv). Wilkinson further reports that academic terrorism studies have constituted a relatively marginal endeavor, with a "conspicuous lack of funding for major research projects" and a position that is "small-scale, and even peripheral, in most universities and research institutes" (Wilkinson and Stewart 1987: xvii). In addition, clearly responding to accusations made against the field, Wilkinson writes that "the conference exploded the myth that terrorism research is biased in favour of Western governments and their policies, and, by the same token, incapable of rigorous critical examination of government policies and measures" (Wilkinson and Stewart 1987: xvii), taking care to note: "The Conference commenced, by an extraordinary coincidence, the morning after the US air strikes on Libya... [A]lthough there were many leading American scholars in attendance, few of them were convinced supporters of their government's action" (Wilkinson and Stewart 1987: xvii–xviii).

At this same conference, criminologist Ronald Crelinsten presented a paper on "Terrorism as political communication," noteworthy for its attempt to produce an objective/depoliticized field of terrorism studies. He writes, "While many researchers recognise and some even acknowledge that terrorism can be perpetrated by those with power or those without power, most contemporary researchers focus exclusively on terrorism perpetrated by small groups of non-state actors, i.e. non-state or anti-state terrorism" (Wilkinson and Stewart 1987: 3). He continues, "A skewed interest in insurgent forms of terrorism reflects the selective concerns of policy makers and government agencies who solicit and fund research. Governments which exercise terrorism are not really interested in funding evaluative research or basic research into the causes of state terrorism" (Wilkinson and Stewart 1987: 4). Additionally, he notes that researchers come to see terrorism as immoral and irrational, pathological, and that, as a result, "[w]hat then passes as scientific discourse is really polemics" (Wilkinson and Stewart 1987: 5).

A second conference held at around this same time, organized by Walter Reich of the US National Institute of Mental Health, and sponsored by the "International security studies program" of the Fletcher School of Law and Diplomacy at Tufts University, the Woodrow Wilson International Center for Scholars, and the National Institute of Mental Health, was later published as a book, *Origins of Terrorism: Psychologies, Identities, States of Mind* (Reich 1990). Speakers at this conference included a number of the "terrorism Mafia," including Martha Crenshaw, Jerrold Post, Konrad Kellen, Franco Ferracuti, Ehud Sprinzak, Ted Gurr, David Rapoport, and Ariel Merari. Crenshaw's paper, titled "The logic of terrorism: terrorist behavior as a product of strategic choice," confronted head-on the assertions that terrorism is irrational. Instead, Crenshaw argues that terrorism can be a rational, purposeful, and logical expression of political strategy. Walter Reich's paper, "Understanding terrorist behavior: The limits and opportunities of psychological inquiry," argues for sustained inquiry into "the psychology of the terrorists themselves: their developments, motivations, personalities, decision-making patterns, behaviors in groups, and, some would argue, psychopathologies" (Reich 1990: 261), also noting that there are some problems with psychological approaches to understanding terrorism, including "ignoring rational reasons for choosing a terrorist strategy" and "ignoring state terrorism and the destructive acts of Western governments" (Reich 1990: 273, 274).

Yet, although academically oriented terrorism researchers attempted to mark off their work as separate from the "politicized" discourse of those who put forth seemingly fantastical theories that ascribed disparate movements to the hidden hand of the Soviet Union, they were not fully successful in constructing their own work as academically legitimate. The field of terrorism studies remained an interstitial project: not quite accepted in academia, yet not quite willing to be absorbed completely into the political sphere. This must be seen as a result of not just the (relative) success of those *within* the academic disciplines who were somewhat more able to draw boundaries against "terrorism studies" as an illegitimate subject but also the continual reclamation of terrorism as a highly politically useful object of knowledge – one that could be reshaped and reformulated to fit the needs of a variety of different political and expert actors. Both these trends acted to continue to frustrate the would-be purification projects of those who would develop "terrorism" as an object to be scientifically known through politically neutral methods.

6   Loose can(n)ons: from "small wars" to the "new terrorism"

The dominance of the Soviet theory presented significant challenges to the intellectual direction and autonomy of the "terrorism mafia" in the 1980s, but the rising tide of attention to the problem had also brought an increased flow of resources and attention. With the fall of the Berlin Wall, the breakup of the Soviet Union, and the end of the Cold War, however, external demand and funding for terrorism expertise dried up, making the early 1990s a period of relative quiet. Only eight conferences were held between 1990 and 1995, while previously it had not been uncommon for there to be eight terrorism conferences to be held in a single year. Figure 6.1 highlights this trend.

By the early 1990s even RAND was having difficulty finding sufficient funding for terrorism research. In 1994 there was even talk of the RAND terrorism database being scrapped. Ultimately, Bruce Hoffman, RAND's new head of terrorism research, moved to the University of St Andrews in Scotland, taking the RAND terrorism

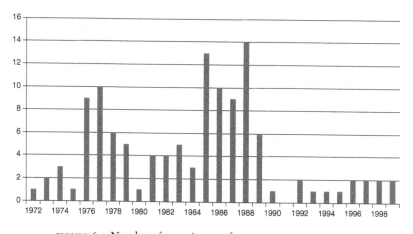

FIGURE 6.1 Number of terrorism conferences per year, 1972–2000

database with him to the newly established Centre for the Study of Terrorism and Political Violence there.[1] As Hoffman told me, "One of the reasons I left RAND in 1994 is that everybody was telling me there was no funding for terrorism research. Everybody was telling me that, with the end of the Cold War and the demise of the Soviet Union, terrorism was going to end."[2]

This chapter tells the story of how a number of new threat discourses, key among them those centered around "Islamic terrorism," "right-wing terrorism," "small wars," and "weapons of mass destruction," emerged in the 1990s and would ultimately coalesce under the framework of the "new terrorism." The "new terrorism" discourse put forth the idea that terrorism in the 1990s was being committed by a new type of terrorist, extraordinarily irrational in both goals and actions, and prone to committing unprecedented levels of violence. This discourse would lay some of the intellectual groundwork for the way in which the attacks of 9/11 2001 would be understood, and the "war on terror" that would emerge in response. And the emergence of these new threat discourses would occur in concert with the realignment of the field of terrorism expertise. Each of the new threat discourses was put forth by a new group of experts, who drew upon events to bolster their view of the problem. And, as these new sets of experts took shape, the alliances of expertise that had formed in the 1970s and 1980s also realigned, with different factions of the old "terrorism mafia" joining with new entrants into the field.

"THE MUSLIMS ARE COMING! THE MUSLIMS ARE COMING!" (PIPES 1990)

The first of the new sets of experts to rise to prominence consisted of those who argued that "Islamic terrorism" was becoming the core threat to be reckoned with. Focusing on the role of religion, and

---

[1] St Andrews' stewardship of the database ended four years later in 1998, and the database was subsequently reincarnated in cooperation with the Oklahoma City Memorial Institute for the Prevention of Terrorism.

[2] Interview with Bruce Hoffman, November 7, 2006.

sometimes claiming that Islam was an inherently violent and aggressive tradition, these experts echoed many of the themes identified by Edward Said as central to the "Orientalist" discourse about the Middle East (Said 1978, 1997). Framing Islam as the new "civilizational" threat, much as the Soviet Union had been cast as an existential threat to "the West" throughout the 1980s, these experts sought to identify the new number one national enemy. This translation of the civilizational threat discourse from the Soviet Union to the Islamic world is also evident insofar as some of the core proponents of the Soviet terror network theory began to shift their attention to the "Islamic terror" threat in the 1990s.

Concerns about "Islamic" terrorism had first begun to appear in the United States in the late 1970s, following the Iranian revolution. And congressional hearings focusing on the problem of "Islamic" terrorism were held in the 1980s, but the experts at these hearings were not concerted advocates of Islamist terror as a new threat. Rather, they tended to be academic researchers with determinedly measured views, such as John Esposito, who in 1992 would publish *The Islamic Threat: Myth or Reality?* (Esposito 1999), which took a skeptical view of many of the claims being put forth. It was not until the end of the Cold War that fears about Islam and terrorism would take center stage in the public eye. And the hearings on Islamic terrorism in the 1980s can be sharply contrasted with the 1993 report of the Task Force on Terrorism and Unconventional Warfare of the House Republican Research Committee, titled *The New Islamist International*, which would declare that "there has been a significant increase in Islamist terrorism, subversion and violence...the escalation of an Islamic Jihad against the 'Judeo-Christian world order.'" The task force was headed by Yossef Bodansky, a controversial figure[3] who would claim that "there is

---

[3] Peter Bergen, who has the distinction of being one of the few journalists to have interviewed Osama bin Laden, singled out Bodansky as a source of "misinformation" (Bergen 2002: 34).

no longer much doubt that bin Laden has succeeded in his quest for nuclear suicide bombs" (Bodansky 2001: 330).

One of the first pieces to develop the emphasis on an Islamic terror threat fully was Bernard Lewis's (1990) "The roots of Muslim rage," published in *The Atlantic Monthly*. Writing that "there is a surge of hatred that distresses, alarms, and above all baffles Americans," and that this hatred "goes beyond hostility to specific interests or actions or policies or even countries and becomes a rejection of Western civilizations as such," Lewis presents "Muslim rage" as neither truly rational nor founded in sensible grievances, but "no less than a clash of civilizations" (Lewis 1990: 48, 60). In 1993 *Foreign Affairs* published the article "The challenge of radical Islam" by *New York Times* reporter Judith Miller (who would later gain notoriety for her role in publicizing discredited claims that Iraq had "weapons of mass destruction"). Miller's article reproduces some of the most prominent voices asserting that Islam was a dire threat, such as Martin Kramer's claim that "militant Islamic groups, by nature, cannot be democratic, pluralistic, egalitarian, or pro-Western" (Miller 1993: 50). The same year *Foreign Affairs* also published political scientist Samuel Huntington's seminal article "The clash of civilizations?," which argues that world politics is entering a new phase, in which the primary causes of conflict would be not economic or ideological, but civilizational (Huntington 1993), and *Commentary* published Martin Kramer's "Islam vs. democracy," which naturalizes an essential clash between Islam and democratic society in its very title (1993).

A key theme in the discourse on the Islamist threat was the suggestion that it had taken the place of the (now diminished) Soviet threat. In a 1995 article titled "There are no moderates," Daniel Pipes likened fundamentalist Islam to fascism and communism, even comparing Islamic fundamentalists to Hitler. Writing that fundamentalist Islam was "by nature anti-democratic, anti-Semitic and anti-Western," he attacked advisors who would downplay the threat of radical Islam and especially "the usual suspect: academic specialists"

(Pipes 1995). A 1996 piece in *The New York Times* made this linkage even more explicit, in a piece entitled "The red menace is gone. But here's Islam," observing: "The end of the cold war sparked a kind of intellectual contest to identify the biggest and most credible new enemy" (Sciolino 1996).

As I argued earlier in this book, it was the combination of incidents, experts, and methods of knowledge that produced the problem of "terrorism" as we now know it. And it was the way in which experts integrated these incidents into evolving threat narratives that led them to have a lasting effect on the evolving understandings of terrorism as a problem. Advocates of the "Islamist terror" threat mobilized current events as proof of this new form of terrorism that was irrational, that broke from predictable routines, and that held the potential for mass violence.

On February 26, 1993, the World Trade Center in New York City was attacked. This attack, via bombs set off in the basement garage, killed five people and injured over 1,000, and was, according to terrorism expert Brian Jenkins, "the largest-scale bombing on US soil in modern history" (Jehl 1993a). The 1993 World Trade Center attack was an important turning point for the problematization of terrorism, not only because of the number of casualties and the prominence of its target but also on account of the seemingly puzzling behavior of its perpetrators. As a *New York Times* headline put it, officials were "baffled" by the "lack of definitive claim" for the attack (Jehl 1993b). As that article indicated, the "main goal of terrorism" (according to the current paradigm) was "attention" for a cause or organization (Jehl 1993b). What, then, could be the rationale behind an anonymous attack? This lack of any group claiming authorship led some to question as to whether this even qualified as terrorism.

The 1993 World Trade Center bombing introduced a new mode of attack, one that disrupted the expected "script" of claims-making, publicity, and stated demands. Although a suspect, Mohammed A. Salameh (who was subsequently linked to an extremist Islamic group), was identified several days later when he attempted to recover the deposit he had put down on the rental van used in the bombing, and a letter claiming responsibility, sent to *The New York Times* shortly after the attack, was discovered several weeks later, commentary on the attack centered on the mysteries of attribution and motive. This case continued to be seen as signaling a break from an earlier paradigm in which terrorists would make clear their motives and demands. As a *New York Times* article put it several days later, the "puzzle" in this case was that "no one can yet say why it was done" (Jehl 1993c: 1). And, several weeks into the investigation, the questions law enforcement were still seeking answers to were: "Why was the trade center bombed? What was the statement being made? And who abroad or at home was making it?" (Blumenthal 1993). The apparent change in terrorist strategy brought new attention to the already complicated thinking about whether or not terrorism was rational, as illustrated by the headline "Americans feel terror's senseless logic" (Jehl 1993c). A number of terrorism experts attempted to counter the assumption that this event – or terrorism more generally – was "senseless." For example, Noel Koch, a counterterrorism official in the Reagan administration, noted that a lack of attribution could heighten anxiety, Robert Kupperman, then at CSIS, commented that avoiding attribution also meant avoiding possible retaliation, and Brian Jenkins declared that "there are rarely senseless terrorists" (Jehl 1993c: 3). But the framework of irrationality nonetheless provided the framework within which discussion of the event proceeded.

A second important development boosting claims of an Islamic terror threat, and particularly arguments that the new threat was an irrational one, was the spread of suicide bombing, as heralded by Hamas's adoption of suicide bombings in Israel. Hamas did not originate the use of suicide bombings. Previously the tactic had been most strongly associated with Hezbollah, which had used suicide bombings in Lebanon in the 1980s. Hamas, founded in 1987, during the first intifada, had originally focused on military targets in the occupied territories. But after the Oslo accords of 1993 it switched tactics, targeting both civilian and military targets within Israel.

Hamas sponsored its first suicide attack on April 6, 1994, following Jewish settler Baruch Goldstein's massacre of Palestinians at a mosque in Hebron, and committed its most deadly attack later that year – a bus bombing in Tel Aviv that killed twenty-three people.

The rise of suicide bombing in particular enlivened claims as to the irrationality of terrorism. How could it be rational, so many asked, knowingly to sacrifice one's life? While the use of more violent tactics and methods, and incidents such as the 1995 Tokyo subway bombing and the 1993 World Trade Center bombing, which seemed aimed at producing large numbers of casualties (even if these were less success-ful than their perpetrators might have hoped), along with the rise of religiously oriented terrorist groups, seemed to support the claims that terrorist groups were increasingly irrational, it was the tactic of suicide bombing, above all, that appeared to be the trump card in this argument. This claim of irrationality was widely reproduced, and spread widely, even as others pointed out that suicide bombings could in some circumstances be seen as a clearly rational action (Carr 2006: 258; Pape 2005: 66).

The third incident to become important in the emergence of an expert discourse on "Islamic terror" was the April 19, 1995, bombing of the Alfred P. Murrah Federal Building in Oklahoma City. This attack killed 168 people and injured more than 800, in what was then the deadliest terrorist attack within the United States. Initial com-mentary, led, most prominently, by Steve Emerson, attributed the attacks to Arab or Muslim terrorists. Emerson was a journalist and the author of several books, including (jointly with Brian Duffy) *The Fall of Pan Am 103* (Emerson and Duffy 1990), which argues that Iran was behind the bombing of that flight, and (jointly with Cristina Del Cesto) *Terrorist* (Emerson and Del Cesto 1991), which argues that Iraq was supporting a network of terrorism, and had come most promin-ently into the public eye with a documentary aired on PBS in 1994 entitled *Terrorists among Us: Jihad in America*, copies of which were distributed to every member of the House of Representatives the following year by Representatives Bill McCollum and Gary

Ackerman. Although law enforcement shortly determined that the perpetrators were in fact a trio of home-grown Americans, this revelation did not discredit broader claims to the rise of an Islamic terror threat.

Claims of a rising Islamist threat did not go unchallenged. According to an article in *The New York Times*, the debate over "political Islam has become one of the hottest, nastiest debates in academic circles today" (Sciolino 1996). Olivier Roy's *The Failure of Political Islam* (1999), first published in 1994, was written largely in response to this discourse of fear, and John Esposito's *The Islamic Threat: Myth or Reality?* (1999), was even more explicit in debunking what it saw as exaggerated threats, suggesting that "[a]t times it seems that the West's attitude toward communism is being transferred to or replicated in the elevation of a new threat, 'Islamic fundamentalism'" (Esposito 1999: 218). Yet the Islamist threat discourse was perhaps the most influential new approach to emerge during this period, and would form a core part of the "new terrorism" theory that would soon arise.

"RIGHT-WING TERRORISM"

A second group vying for influence on the study of terrorism at this time consisted of experts on right-wing extremism and hate groups. The socially constructed nature of the categories of "right wing violence" and "Islamic terrorism" is evident in the fact that these were addressed by two separate groups of experts. Although the loosely assembled set of experts who concentrated on "right-wing" violence often focused on white, Christian groups, many of them also included Jewish, Islamic, and other organizations in their analyses. But the experts who put forth the "Islamic terror" threat tended to see it as an essentialist category in and of itself. In other words, the categories of "Islamic terror" and "right-wing terror" did not reflect essential distinctions in the world but differences in experts and the way they approached their subject matter.

The threat of "right-wing terrorism" attracted increased attention as a result of the 1995 Oklahoma City bombing in America's "heartland," together with the identification of the perpetrators as white, Christian, native-born Americans. The bombing also highlighted concerns about so-called "lone wolf"[4] terrorists and the rise of religious, right-wing terrorist movements. Perpetrators Timothy McVeigh, Terry Nichols, and Michael Fortier were linked to right-wing anti-government militia organizations, bringing greater attention to the phenomenon of terror "from the right." And the Oklahoma City bombings not only brought attention to right-wing violence but also (briefly, it would turn out) legitimated the incorporation of such activities into the broader sphere of "terrorism studies." A 2000 review article on "Freedom, hate, and violence on the American right" observed that, "[p]articularly since the 19 April 1995 bombing of the Murrah Building in Oklahoma City, there has been a spate of coverage in books, articles, and other media of the extreme right in the United States" (Cameron 2000).

Many of these experts on right-wing violence were not drawn from terrorism studies networks, in part because these groups that they worked on – particularly when the members of such groups were overwhelmingly white and Christian – were often not thought of as "terrorists." But experts on right-wing violence and hate crimes, some of whom had been trying to shift the definition of terrorism to include these sorts of events for years, were able to mobilize the Oklahoma City bombing to bring attention to right-wing violence. This group includes both those who had previously defined their work on right-wing groups as within the scope of "terrorism studies," such as Peter Merkl and Leonard Weinberg, editors of *The Revival of Right-Wing Extremism in the Nineties* (1997), who had both written on terrorism and been active in the terrorism studies community since the 1980s, and researchers who had previously defined their object of study simply as "right-wing social movements" or "hate groups" but

---

[4] RAND's preferred terminology for this type of individual was the "flaming banana."

who now were brought into the orbit of "terrorism," such as Chip Berlet (author with Matthew Lyons of *Right-Wing Populism in America*, 2000) of Political Research Associates, a "progressive think tank devoted to supporting movements that are building a more just and inclusive democratic society" that aims to "expose movements, institutions, and ideologies that undermine human rights."[5]

For a time it seemed that right-wing domestic violence would become more central to terrorism studies. This shift brought to light a tension that had been underlying the field for some time: while public and political discussions of terrorism tended to exclude right-wing movements, the more scholarly apparatus of journals and conferences, as well as books edited by experts inclining more towards the academic side, had often incorporated, in substance or in passing, studies of right-wing groups. And, perhaps not surprisingly, although the existence of right-wing domestic terrorism came to light for a short while, it would once again be eclipsed and marginalized within the broader discourse on terrorism as the decade advanced.

"LOW-INTENSITY CONFLICT"

A third new threat discourse that emerged during the 1990s focused on terrorism as a form of "low-intensity conflict" (LIC). The end of the Cold War occasioned a paradigm shift for the American defense apparatus, with threats from non-state actors, variously conceptualized as terrorism, "low-intensity conflict" or the "gray area phenomenon" (Manwaring 1993), taking on increased importance as the military sought to reconfigure itself for the post-Cold-War era. The term "low-intensity conflict" has been used to specify anything short of all-out war, but most often to refer to guerrilla warfare, rebellions, and terrorism. This approach was not new, and in fact had been an important mode of fighting wars in the Reagan era (Klare and Kornbluh 1988; McClintock 1992). But defense intellectuals took an increased interest in "low-intensity conflict" and "small wars" with

---

[5] See www.publiceye.org/about.html (last accessed June 12, 2008).

the decline of the Cold War. What was new at this time is that LIC became divorced from the Cold War context, bringing to the fore concerns about potential threats from "rogue states" and non-state actors, including terrorists. As a 1990 *Washington Post* article suggested, there were both intellectual and career-based motives for defense analysts to expand their scope of expertise (Dionne 1990):

> Suddenly, the chief premise of their work – the notion of a world organized around the US–Soviet conflict – is falling apart. As a result, the defense intellectuals are scrambling to figure out what to do next... "There is a terrible danger that defense intellectuals will have to go whoring," said Jeremy Azrael, a Soviet specialist at the RAND Corp,.... "looking for threats out there."

Defense intellectuals from four main institutional locations began to turn their attention to terrorism in the 1990s. These included policy experts in the academic sector, particularly the John F. Kennedy School of Government at Harvard University (for example, Carter, Deutch, and Zelikow 1998; Falkenrath, Newman, and Thayer 1998); intelligence analysts within the government (especially the CIA and the DOD); executive branch advisors in the Clinton administration (for example, Benjamin and Simon 2002; Clarke 2004; Simon and Benjamin 2000); and analysts at RAND (for example, Arquilla and Ronfeldt 1996; Lesser et al. 1999). Although RAND had been one of the earliest institutional locations for the development of terrorism expertise, now, for the first time, not just the relatively small terrorism research group but experts from the broader defense policy realm began to incorporate terrorism into the heart of their analyses.

The "small wars" approach to terrorism had already begun to take shape in the 1980s. Several conferences on terrorism during the 1980s centered their discussions on this "small wars" approach. A conference at RAND, sponsored by the US Department of Energy, the Department of State, and the Department of Justice, took on the theme "Terrorism and low-level conflict" (Jenkins 1982). With over

140 participants, including seventy-seven government officials, this was one of the largest conferences of the early 1980s.

A 1985 symposium on international terrorism sponsored by the Defense Academic Research Support Program (DARSP) brought together military experts with members of the "terrorism mafia," such as Martha Crenshaw, Alex Schmid, Brian Jenkins, Michael Stohl, and Paul Wilkinson. This conference sought to establish a rational method of understanding terrorism that avoided overly ideological approaches (Slater and Stohl 1988; US Defense Intelligence Agency 1985). As the introduction to the published conference report declares, they were seeking "a rational policy for dealing with and responding to international terrorism." In the words of Slater and Stohl (1988: 4–5), "Terrorism is purposeful. A consensus appears to be emerging that abandons the more traditional view of terrorism as predominantly irrational behavior." And a 1992 conference incorporated terrorism into a broader framework of "low-intensity conflict," defining it as part of the "gray area phenomenon" composed of conflicts ranging from "acts of terrorism, insurgencies, and illegal drug trafficking to warlordism, militant fundamentalism, ethnic cleansing, and civil war to other transnational threats and consequences of instability" (Manwaring 1993: x). Positioning terrorism and other "low-intensity" conflicts as the successor to the Cold War, speakers described "a potential disorder of nations and peoples in which the definition of 'bad guys' has become much more elusive and power more diffuse" (Manwaring 1993: 34).

The event that most bolstered the case of the advocates of viewing terrorism as a new form of "small war" was the simultaneous bombing, on August 7, 1998, of two US embassies, in Dar es Salaam, Tanzania, and Nairobi, Kenya. Over 250 people were killed in the attacks, and more than 5,000 wounded. The bombings were traced to Osama bin Laden, bolstering some experts' predictions of growing threats from Islamic fundamentalist terrorism – from "networked" terrorism – of "low-intensity conflict" targeting of the official US presence around the world. In response, the United

States bombed sites in Sudan and Afghanistan that had allegedly served as terrorist training camps.

FEARS OF "WEAPONS OF MASS DESTRUCTION"
The fourth new threat discourse to become important during this period focused on concerns about WMDs, and was put forth largely by new entrants into terrorism expertise, many coming from the sciences. The end of the Cold War had triggered a shift of attention from states to terrorists as potential agents of biological warfare. In 1990 and 1991 the Congressional Office of Technology produced two reports on the bioterrorism threat. The contractor for this study was Yonah Alexander, with the advisory panel for the reports including L. Paul Bremer, Robert Kupperman, and biologist Joshua Lederberg (who would become one of the foremost proponents of the bioterrorism threat) (Wright 2007).

When the Clinton administration took office, in 1993, a number of proponents of the rising threat of bioterrorism entered the government, including microbiologist Frank Young, director of the Office of Emergency Preparedness in the Public Health Service from 1993 to 1996, who organized the first civilian bioterrorism training exercise in 1993; Richard Clarke, who chaired the Counterterrorism Security Group; and Richard Danzig, undersecretary of the navy (Wright 2007). President Clinton took a personal interest in the bioterrorist threat, reportedly influenced by Richard Preston's novel *The Cobra Event*, which describes terrorists who attacked New York City by spreading smallpox in the subway. He asked intelligence agents to evaluate the credibility of the threats described in the book, and Preston even appeared before the Senate as an expert on bioterrorism (Carr 2006: 279–80). Clinton subsequently requested $94 million to provide funding "to build up a civilian stockpile of medicines in the event of chemical or biological attack" (Carr 2006: 280).

On March 20, 1995, members of Aum Shinrikyo, a Japanese religious cult, released the nerve agent sarin gas into the Tokyo subway. While only twelve individuals were killed in the attack, the group's use of sarin, deemed a chemical weapon and thus a potential "weapon of mass destruction," was seen as heralding a potential move into a new, deadlier age of terrorism. For many observers, the Aum Shinrikyo attacks highlighted the seeming incomprehensibility of motives and the lack of "rationality" of emerging new groups.

Following the Aum Shinrikyo and Oklahoma City attacks, the Office of Emergency Preparedness of the US Public Health Service held a seminar on the theme "Responding to consequences of chemical and biological terrorism," at which the organizers attempted to persuade others of the imminence of the bioterror threat. The Aum Shinrikyo attack was seen as an "index case" for bioterrorism, and as the passing of a "threshold" (Wright 2007: 73). In other words, what had earlier been seen as only a possibility was now seen as having passed into the realm of the actual. By the end of the decade, within the government, it "was now taken for granted that the Aum attack was emblematic of the new terrorism threat" (Wright 2007: 95). Counterterrorism funding, and funding for bioterrorism in particular, increased, along with the growth of new experts and research centers (Wright 2007: 96).

THE "NEW TERRORISM" SYNTHESIS

While each of the four new threat discourses reshaped the terrorist threat, it was a new synthesis, combining elements of each, that would have the most powerful effect. This was the framework of the "new terrorism," which posited the emergence of new types of terrorists, terrorist organizations, and terrorist attacks in the 1990s, all characterized in opposition to (what was then reframed as) "old" or "traditional" terrorism. New terrorism proponents described contemporary terrorists as less rational than earlier groups, both in means and ends. The new terrorists were described as driven by religious, millennial, or even nihilistic motivations, as opposed to the "political" nationalist or Marxist motivations of "traditional" terrorists. Their motivations were seen as less concrete, less understandable, and perhaps absent altogether. The new terrorists, experts suggested, might

Table 6.1 *Characteristics attributed to "new" and "old" terrorism*

	"Traditional" terrorism	*"New" terrorism*
Terrorists' goals/ motivation	Tangible/political	Inscrutable/ religious/ nihilistic
Organizational characteristics	Hierarchical, focused	Networked, dispersed
Are terrorists likely to use WMDs?	No/unlikely	Yes/possibly
Possible to predict nature of future terrorism on the basis of past events?	Yes/somewhat	No
Appropriate mode of governance	Punishment (via criminal justice or military)/ event management	Precaution/ pre-emption/ preparedness

even be motivated by a desire to incur destruction for its own sake (rather than as a means to an end), thus making them both more likely to use "weapons of mass destruction" and less subject to the logic of deterrence, which had guided US defense strategy throughout the Cold War and which had informed earlier counterterrorism policy. The "new terrorists" were also portrayed as having distinct organizational forms, characterized by decentralized and "networked" – as opposed to hierarchical – structures. In the "new terrorism" discourse, elements of each of the four approaches came together with the dramatic attacks in the middle of the 1990s to appear as a harbinger of a new era – one in which terrorists were less understandable, more unpredictable, and more dangerous than ever before.

A handful of texts emerged as key sources of the new terrorism synthesis, including Bruce Hoffman's (1998) *Inside Terrorism*, Walter Laqueur's (1999) *The New Terrorism*, Mark Juergensmeyer's (2003) *Terror in the Mind of God*, Ian Lesser et al.'s (1999) *Countering the New Terrorism*, and Daniel Benjamin and Steven Simon's (2003) *The*

Age of Sacred Terror. Walter Laqueur was one of the originating voices in terrorism studies, author of multiple books and articles on the subject, and an affiliate of Georgetown University and the Center for Strategic and International Studies, and his career trajectory closely tracks a number of shifts in the terrorism discourse – from his early work on guerrillas to his latest work on the "new terrorism." In *The New Terrorism: Fanaticism and the Arms of Mass Destruction*, Laqueur argues that, while terrorism "has been with us for centuries,... there has been a radical transformation, if not a revolution, in the character of terrorism" (Laqueur 1999: 3–4). He further writes that "[t]hese new fanatical terrorists may not be subject to deterrence, as they are characterized by blind aggression...rage... suicidal impulses...sheer madness" (Laqueur 1999: 5). The book lays out what might be considered a canonical case for the "new terrorism." The back cover blurb proclaims that the book "traces the chilling trend away from terrorist acts committed by groups of oppressed nationalists and radicals seeking political change to those perpetrated by small clusters of fanatics bent on vengeance and simple destruction." Laqueur contrasts "traditional terrorism," which "had political and social aims," with the "new terrorism," which, he writes, "is different in character, aiming not at clearly defined political demands but at the destruction of society and the elimination of large sections of the population" (Laqueur 1999: 81). Furthermore, "the coincidence of this new fanaticism with the development of weapons of mass destruction creates a threat unprecedented in the history of mankind" (Laqueur 1999: 79). And, in an essay published shortly after 9/11, Laqueur would reiterate these points, proclaiming that contemporary terrorism is caused by frustration, fanaticism, and madness, concluding that "the world is now entering a new phase in its history, more dangerous than any before" (Laqueur 2001: 82).

Another core text for advocates of the new terrorism hypothesis was *Terror in the Mind of God* by Mark Juergensmeyer (2003), a professor of sociology and religious studies at the University of California at Santa Barbara. A relatively recent entrant to terrorism studies, Juergensmeyer was an academic, and intellectually aligned with core members of the "terrorism mafia," as indicated by the book's acknowledgments, in which he thanks Martha Crenshaw, Ehud Sprinzak, Bruce Hoffman, Ariel Merari, Jerrold Post, David Rapoport, and Paul Wilkinson (Juergensmeyer 2003: xv). With a cover featuring the faces of Timothy McVeigh, Osama bin Laden, and Shoko Asahara of Aum Shinrikyo, and featuring chapters on Jewish, Christian, Muslim, Buddhist, and Sikh terrorists, this is a book that highlights the role of religion in political violence from an ecumenical approach. And, although the book became central to discussions of religious terrorism, and the role of religion in the "new terrorism," Juergensmeyer was himself relatively skeptical about the connotations of the "terrorism" concept, and the term "new terrorism" does not even appear in the text. As he writes (Juergensmeyer 2003: 7–8),

> [T]he term "terrorist" is problematic. For one thing, the term makes no clear distinction between the organizers of an attack, those who carry it out, and the many who support it both directly and indirectly. Are they all terrorists, or just some of them – and if the latter, which ones? Another problem with the word is that it can be taken to single out a certain limited species of people called "terrorists" who are committed to violent acts... This logic concludes that terrorism exists because terrorists exist, and if we just got rid of them the world would be a more pleasant place.

But while Juergensmeyer himself was skeptical about the concept of "terrorism," his work would be adopted and celebrated by advocates of the "new terrorism."

On the opposite end of the spectrum, Daniel Benjamin and Steven Simon were purposeful agents in the construction of the new terrorism synthesis. In their book *The Age of Sacred Terror* (2003), as well as in several articles published before 9/11, they warned that a new, more dangerous and unpredictable form of terrorism was threatening the United States. Both had served in the Clinton administration, Simon as senior director for transnational threats and Benjamin as director for transnational threats. In 2000, after both had moved to positions at think tanks (Simon at the International Institute for Strategic Studies, Benjamin at the United States Institute of Peace), they authored a widely influential article titled "America and the new terrorism" (Simon and Benjamin 2000). Declaring that: "the old paradigm of predominantly state-sponsored terrorism has been joined by a new, religiously motivated terrorism that neither relies on the support of sovereign states nor is constrained by the limits on violence that state sponsors have observed themselves or placed on their proxies," and citing the 1993 World Trade Center bombing, Oklahoma City, the Aum Shinrikyo subway attack, and the 1998 east Africa bombings as harbingers of the new terrorism, they write, presciently, that "the face of the phenomenon belongs to Osama bin Laden" (Simon and Benjamin 2000: 59). Summing up the threat, they write that the key development in terrorism in the 1990s was the emergence of a "new, more dangerous brand," characterized by "the emergence of religion as the predominant impetus for terrorist attacks; the increasing lethality of attacks; the increasing techno-logical and operational competence of terrorists; and the demon-strated desire of these terrorists to obtain weapons of mass destruction" (Simon and Benjamin 2000: 66).

Another key text on the "new terrorism" was Jessica Stern's (1999) *The Ultimate Terrorists*. A faculty member at Harvard's John F. Kennedy School of Government, Stern had previously been a member of President Clinton's national security staff as an expert on the WMD threat. The book's first chapter opens with the question "What if terrorists exploded a homemade nuclear bomb at the Empire State Building in New York City?" (Stern 1999: 1). Stern suggests that "[f]ive interrelated developments have increased the risk that terrorists will use nuclear, chemical, or biological weapons against civilian targets." These are, first, that terrorists now may have different goals from terrorists in the past, including "to conjure a sense of divine retribution, to display scientific prowess, to kill large numbers of people, to invoke dread, or to retaliate against states that have used these weapons in the past"; second, that terrorist motivations may be different, and these new motivations, particularly religious motivations, may make terrorists more likely to use "extreme violence"; third, that the breakup of the Soviet Union increases the potential for nuclear weapons to become available; fourth, that there is a general proliferation of chemical and biological weapons; and, fifth, that broad technological changes make WMD terrorism more likely (Stern 1999: 8). As these excerpts show, Stern's approach closely aligned with the themes of the "new terrorism" discourse.

Finally, the works of Bruce Hoffman (previously head of terrorism studies at RAND and the Center for the Study of Terrorism and Political Violence at the University of St Andrews) were also central to the emergence of the new terrorism discourse. Although his book *Inside Terrorism* (Hoffman 1998) doesn't even use the phrase, the book, with substantive discussions of suicide terrorism and the connections between religion and terrorism, became central to the "new terrorism" approach, and a revised and expanded second edition (Hoffman 2006) includes an entire chapter on suicide terrorism. And, although Hoffman insists that terrorists are largely rational, his diagnosis concludes that terrorism in the 1990s was moving in a more dangerous direction, with an increased likelihood that terrorists would make the use of weapons of mass destruction fit right in with the larger new terrorism discourse (Hoffman 1998). And, in his contribution to a collection of RAND reports entitled *Countering the new terrorism*, Hoffman writes that, whereas previously, terrorism "had a clear command and control apparatus and a defined set of political, social, or economic objectives... However disagreeable or distasteful their aims and motivations may have been, their ideology and intentions were at least comprehensible," in the late 1990s these more "traditional and familiar" types of terrorist groups were "joined by a variety of organizations with less-comprehensible nationalist or ideological motivations" (Lesser et al. 1999: 8).

REIMAGINING TERRORISM AND TERRORISM EXPERTISE

At this point, an attentive reader might note some apparent inconsistencies between the narrative presented within the new terrorism framework and the history of terrorism expertise as presented in the preceding chapters. This presentation of "traditional" terrorism as fully rational actually entailed a rewriting of the pasts of both terrorism and terrorism expertise. Despite the contrast presented in the writings on the "new terrorism," it is not at all clear that, prior to this point, there actually had been a consensus that terrorism was "rational" in this way. However, through this reframing process, the earlier terrorists of the 1960s, 1970s, and 1980s, now reclassified as examples of "old" or "traditional" terrorism, were retrospectively cast as rational, goal-oriented, and understandable.

While proponents of the new terrorism presumed a clear contrast with the past in the "new" terrorism of the 1990s, many of the characteristics they point to as new were evident in earlier analyses of terrorism as well. A number of the very characteristics presented as central to the "new" terrorism had plainly been ascribed to terrorism in the past, or points of contestation through which the meaning of "terrorism" was hammered out. For example, Walter Laqueur himself had earlier written, in his 1974 article "Guerrillas and terrorists," that terrorists aim at "the destruction of a whole society," and that, while "[i]t is sometimes argued that terrorism is bound to decrease once society becomes less repressive," "[s]uch an assessment rests on an overly optimistic view of the rationality of human behavior" (Laqueur 1974: 46, 48). The role played by the concepts of rationality and irrationality in the new terrorism discourse thus entailed a reimagining of both the history of terrorism and the field of terrorism studies itself. Although the "new terrorism" presumed that the irrationality of terrorists was something *new*, often explicitly comparing the "new" terrorism of the 1990s to the earlier, seemingly more rational terrorism of the 1970s, if we look back to the sorts of contemporaneous discourse on terrorism at that time it is clear that the rationality of terrorists and terrorism was certainly not assumed or assured, but was problematic even then.

Framing the "new terrorists" of the 1990s as the ultimate irrational actors was accomplished by theoretically rehabilitating the older terrorist groups of the 1970s and 1980s in retrospect. Although the rationality of these groups' means and motives had been fiercely debated in earlier years, these "traditional" terrorist groups were now reconceived as a more rational, understandable foil to the current threat of the "new" terrorism. Furthermore, the process of introducing a new framework into the discourse on terrorism entailed not just a reformulation of understandings of what terrorism is and was but also a reworking of the field's understanding of its own past – a type of collective memory work (Olick and Robbins 1998: 111), and a recasting of the very history of terrorism expertise itself. The construction of the new terrorism framework required a reinterpretation of the role of ideas about rationality, categories, and boundaries in thinking about terrorism. The super-irrationality of the "new terrorists" thus entails a reimagining of not just the history of terrorism but the history of terrorism studies itself as well. This inconsistency did not pass unnoticed. A number of other experts, for the most part those coming from the most academic end of the spectrum, treated the claims of "new terrorism" quite skeptically (Copeland 2001; Crenshaw 2009; Duyvesteyn 2004; Zimmerman 2004).

CRITICS AND SKEPTICS

As the idea of the new terrorism spread, there was also a degree of skepticism voiced towards its claims. Some of these responses dismissed the new terrorism as simply self-interested behavior on the part of would-be experts. Others focused on a lack of respect for established work on terrorism. For example, Karen Colvard, program officer at the Harry Frank Guggenheim Foundation, which focuses on funding research into the causes of violence and aggression, and had funded a number of academic terrorism researchers throughout the 1980s and 1990s, including J. Bowyer Bell, Martha Crenshaw, Ehud Sprinzak,

Jerrold Post, Donatella della Porta, and Scott Atran, wrote in 1996 that "some of the insights produced by earlier research are in danger of being left behind." Speaking critically of the rush to frame recent events as "new," Colvard (1996: 3) observed, from her viewpoint as a funder and facilitator of research, that earlier research was being overlooked:

> Applications to the foundation to study small-group political violence dropped off, to be replaced by applications from, in most cases, wholly different scholars to study activists from the radical right and then anti-immigrant violence.

Ehud Sprinzak, professor of political science at the Hebrew University of Jerusalem, and later dean of the Lauder School of Government, Policy, and Diplomacy at the Interdisciplinary Center, Herzliya (Israel), presented a skeptical view of the new terrorism in several articles in *Foreign Policy*. In a 1998 piece titled "The great superterrorism scare," he writes, "Three recent events seem to have convinced the policymaking elite and the general public that a disaster is imminent" (Sprinzak 1998: 110). Judging this to be an overreaction, he asserts (Sprinzak 1998: 113):

> Thirty years of field research have taught observers of terrorism a most important lesson: Terrorists wish to convince us that they are capable of striking from anywhere at anytime, but there really is no chaos. In fact, terrorism involves predictable behavior, and the vast majority of terrorist organizations can be identified well in advance.

In this piece, Sprinzak highlights the importance of experience in the field of terrorism studies, and warns against newcomers who fail to pay attention to the history of work in the field, asserting that terrorism is still subject to rational analysis as terrorists generally "possess political objectives" and are "[n]either crazy nor stupid" (Sprinzak 1998). Similarly, in a 2000 piece titled "Rational fanatics," Sprinzak writes that terrorists are not "undeterrable fanatics" but "cold, rational killers who employ violence to achieve specific political objectives" (Sprinzak 2000: 73).

More recently, political scientist Martha Crenshaw has critiqued the new terrorism discourse in "The debate over 'new' vs. 'old' terrorism," which expresses the frustration that some of the more established scholarly experts have felt with purveyors of the new terrorism (Crenshaw 2009):

> Knowledge of the "old" or traditional terrorism is sometimes considered irrelevant at best, and obsolete and anachronistic, even harmful, at worst. Some of those who argue for the appearance of a "new" terrorism think that the old paradigms should be discarded entirely and replaced with a new understanding.

Arguing for a continuation of the sort of historical, contextualized work that she had fostered in her earlier work (for example, Crenshaw 1995, 1983)), Crenshaw writes that "analysis of what is new about terrorism needs to be based on systematic empirical research that compares a wide range of cases over extended time periods" (Crenshaw 2009: 135). The "new terrorism model" is based on "simple assumptions," however, that permit the "top-down processing of information," which prevents policymakers from grasping the "contradictory and confusing reality" of terrorism (Crenshaw 2009: 134). This framework may be appealing to "terrorism "experts," she writes, especially "newcomers to the field," who "might find it convenient not to have to take the time to study the long and complicated history of the terrorist phenomenon" (Crenshaw 2009: 134). Yet, despite these skeptical evaluations from many of the most long-standing experts in the field, the new terrorism approach would be highly influential, going on to serve as the basis for a new logic of risk that would come to underlie counterterrorism in the post-9/11 era.

THE NEW LOGIC OF RISK

Each of the primary characteristics identified with the "new terrorism" can be seen as expressing a conflict over the perceived "rationality" of terrorism in the three dimensions laid out by Max Weber (1978 [1922]). These are, most centrally, the claimed shifts from tangible/political goals to inscrutable/irrational goals (rationality of ends), from limited tactics to potential unlimited destruction and use of WMDs (rationality of means), and from hierarchical organizations to networked/dispersed organizations (rationality of organization). Each of these also parallels one of Weber's (1978 [1922]) types of rationality: rationality of motive (substantive rationality), rationality of method (means/end rationality), and rationality of organization (bureaucracy/hierarchy rationality). Together, these culminated in a shifting judgment as to whether "terrorism" could be subject to rational analysis, and, if so, of what sort. Is it possible to predict the nature and likelihood of future terrorism on the basis of past events? What tends to follow from this are propositions that the new terrorism's different relation to rationality requires a transformation of rationality on "our" part, in response.

What did this reimagining of the terrorism canon mean for governance? The governance of terrorism in the 1990s continued to be dominated by a logic of retaliation, along with a new emphasis on precautionary techniques, especially as related to potential threats of biological, chemical, or nuclear attack. A precautionary logic is one in which actions are taken that aim to avoid or prevent risks. In the case of WMD terrorism, this would include practices such as the increased regulation of biological and nuclear materials. Louise Amoore and Marieke de Goede (2008: 11) write:

> Precautionary risk practices exceed the logic of (statistical)
> calculability and involve, instead, imaginative or "visionary"
> techniques such as stress testing, scenario planning and
> disaster rehearsal... Such imaginative new ways of dealing
> with uncertainty continue to deploy the language of risk, while
> outstripping, in practice, established technologies of risk
> calculation.

Stephen Collier and Andrew Lakoff (Collier and Lakoff 2008; Collier, Lakoff, and Rabinow 2004) draw upon and extend François Ewald's (2002) notion of the "precautionary principle," which counsels the avoidance of actions with potentially unknown consequences in the face of new risks, to theorize a shift from a logic of "normal" risk to one of "catastrophic risk" in contemporary society. According to Lakoff, the logics of preparedness and precaution both apply to "events whose regular occurrence cannot be mapped through actuarial knowledge and whose probability therefore cannot be calculated" (Lakoff 2007: 253). While precaution seeks to avoid unpredictable disaster by proscribing actions with unknown consequences, preparedness assumes that disasters are both unpredictable and inevitable, and acts to transform "potentially catastrophic threats into vulnerabilities to be mitigated" (Lakoff 2007: 253).

The new terrorism discourse entailed both a logic of preparedness, which focuses on the domestic sector (and which had been a part of the practices of managing terrorism since the 1970s), and also a new logic of "pre-emption," which is focused outward upon the "enemy," aiming to prevent terrorist attacks before they happen. The management of the new terrorism would not stop with techniques associated with the logics of preparation or precaution, although these were important to the governance of terrorism in the 1990s. The threat of bioterrorism, in particular, was managed through techniques associated with preparation (including the use of scenario exercises such as "Dark winter," which portrayed a smallpox attack on the United States, and in which participants role-played emergency response possibilities), and precaution (such as attempts to regulate substances, such as viruses, and even knowledge (Fischman 2012), that were deemed dangerous). Yet the threat of the new terrorism, which portrayed terrorists as evil, irrational, unpredictable actors, potentially with access to WMDs, led to a threat conceptualization that exceeded both the logics of preparation and precaution, because terrorism – unlike other potentially catastrophic threats, such as tornados or bird flu – was perpetrated by intelligent agents who could seek to evade any preparations or precautions put forth in anticipation of possible attacks. Some at the time consequently began to argue that the only solution was a preventive defense: to prevent any new terrorist attacks before they happened (Carter and Perry 1999).

As Walter Laqueur would write after 9/11, "[I]n an age of weapons of mass destruction...even one attack can be overwhelmingly devastating," and so, consequently, society should "take the offensive" (Laqueur 2001: 81). While the logic of pre-emption, whose practices would come to include assassination, pre-emptive war, torture, and the imprisonment of individuals who might engage in terrorist activity in the future, would not come to fruition until after 9/11, the logic that underlies them was already encapsulated in the "new terrorism" discourse.[6]

---

[6] Some would even argue that a pre-emptive logic was already taking hold more generally in American society at this time (Ericson 2008: 57).

7   The road to pre-emption

In our society we have no major crimes...but we do have a detention camp full of would-be criminals.[1]

On September 11, 2001, teams of men armed with box cutters hijacked four transcontinental flights, turning the planes into guided missiles with which to attack the World Trade Center and the Pentagon. This was the first time the United States had dealt with multiple simultaneous hijackings, and the first time that the country had faced hijackings that did not follow the usual sequence of seizure, demands, and release of passengers. Almost 3,000 people were killed, making this the largest terrorist attack ever on American soil.

The attacks dominated the media, with practically every television channel replaying the footage of the planes hitting the World Trade Center on a seemingly endless loop. The coverage continued in an unbroken stream for days, with the banners of news stations announcing the "Attack on America." Many viewers observed that the footage seemed like a movie, echoing the simulated destruction of American cities they had previously seen in films such as *Independence Day*. Adding to the trauma of that day was the initial uncertainty as to what exactly had happened, and the number of those killed and injured, as well as the question of whether or not additional attacks were on their way.

That evening President George W. Bush declared the United States at war, proclaiming that "we will make no distinction between the terrorists who committed these acts and those who harbor them" (National Commission on Terrorist Attacks 2004: 326). And this was to be not just any war, but a "monumental struggle between good and

[1] Philip K. Dick (2002 [1953]: 3).

evil."[2] The president's address that first evening was brief, emphasizing the country's strength and resilience. On the causes of the attacks, which he named "evil, despicable acts of terror," Bush proclaimed only that "America was targeted for attack because we're the brightest beacon for freedom and opportunity in the world."[3] This language of "evil" would become a dominant theme of Bush's rhetoric in response to the attacks. On September 16 Bush made a short statement to the press that referred to "evil" or "evildoers" seven times (Woodward 2002: 94). According to one tally, Bush used the word "evil" well over 1,000 times in his speeches between his inauguration and June 16, 2003, and, what is more, he used the word as a noun, a thing unto itself, many more (914) times than as an adjective (182).[4]

On September 14, Congress formally authorized President Bush (Suskind 2006: 17)

> to use all necessary and appropriate force against those nations, organizations, or persons he determines planned, authorized, committed, or aided the terrorist attacks that occurred on Sept. 11, 2001, or harbored such organizations or persons, in order to prevent any future acts of international terrorism against the United States by such nations, organizations, or persons.

The next week, in a speech before a joint session of Congress, Bush reiterated that the attacks were "an act of war" committed by "enemies of freedom."[5] As for the reasons behind the attacks, this speech framed the question, in language that would reverberate throughout the country for the length of the war on terror, as "Why

---

[2] President Bush, statement to the press, September 12, 2001, quoted by Woodward (2002: 45).
[3] President Bush, address to the nation, September 11, 2001; source: White House online, September 12, 2001, www.whitehouse.gov.
[4] Peter Singer, *The President of Good and Evil: The Ethics of George W. Bush*, cited by Khan (2006: 69).
[5] President Bush, address to Congress and the nation on terrorism, September 20, 2001; source: White House online, September 21, 2001.

do they hate us?" The answer supplied was that the terrorists held an irrational hatred for the very essence of American values and practices: "They hate what we see right here in this chamber – a democratically elected government... They hate our freedoms – our freedom of religion, our freedom of speech, our freedom to vote and assemble and disagree with each other." Such an absolutist enemy could be neither reasoned with nor understood. Likening al Qaeda to "fascism, and Nazism, and totalitarianism," President Bush set up the fight as one in defense of civilization as a whole: "This is the world's fight. This is civilization's fight. This is the fight of all who believe in progress and pluralism, tolerance and freedom."[6] Subsequently, he declared: "Every nation, in every region, now has a decision to make: Either you are with us, or you are with the terrorists" (National Commission on Terrorist Attacks 2004: 337).

The enemy in this new war was not simply Osama Bin Laden, al Qaeda, or even Islamist terrorism writ large, but was extended to include "every terrorist group of global reach" (National Commission on Terrorist Attacks 2004: 337). On October 7 the president announced to the nation: "On my orders, the United States military has begun strikes against al Qaeda terrorist training camps and military installations of the Taliban regime in Afghanistan."[7] Over the next several years this war on terror would come to encompass full-fledged wars in Iraq and Afghanistan, as well as a number of smaller military interventions. It would also incorporate practices such as assassinations, torture, and a system of detention that would ensnare some 2,000 young men with Arab and Muslim backgrounds (Suskind 2006: 152) both within the United States and at prisons worldwide, including the notorious centers at Guantanamo Bay and Abu Ghraib, as well as "extraordinary rendition" to third countries and secret prisons abroad known as "black sites."

---

[6] President Bush, address to Congress and the nation on terrorism, September 20, 2001.
[7] President Bush, address to the nation, October 7, 2001; source: White House online, October 14, 2001.

This chapter argues that many of the seemingly disparate practices that composed the "war on terror" were united by a logic of pre-emption, in which the slightest possibility of attack could warrant any degree of preventive action. Although alternative approaches to managing the terrorist threat, such as crisis management, criminal justice, and limited retaliatory warfare, would persist alongside the more radical alternatives, the war on terror quickly came to be characterized by the more expansive pre-emptive approach.

The logic of pre-emption was not just about justifying pre-emptive war in Iraq. It also underpinned a number of other crucial practices comprising the war on terror, including extraordinary rendition and the indefinite detention, frequently coupled with torture, of "enemy combatants" abroad, and of Muslims within the United States. What all these practices have in common is that they make no sense within a logic of punishment, in which groups, individuals, and states are subjected to retaliation, nor via a logic of response, which focuses on our techniques for managing crises, nor even through a logic of precaution, in which the focus is on regulating potentially hazardous materials and situations. Rather, they make sense within a logic of pre-emption, which relies upon a notion of imminent threats that must be prevented from coming to fruition at any cost. As in the parable of the "ticking time bomb," which justifies torture so as to induce a terrorist to reveal the location of a "ticking bomb," the logic of pre-emption entails action *before* the event, and relies upon an imaginary of extreme threats, which justify otherwise unthinkable actions.

It is not that these practices were unknown before September 11, 2011. At the height of the Cold War, game theorists had pondered pre-emptive nuclear strikes (Ghamari-Tabrizi 2005). American advisors trained Latin American militaries in the use of torture in the 1980s (Klare and Kornbluh 1988), and assassinations were carried out during the Vietnam War through the infamous Phoenix program. During the 1980s and 1990s the CIA organized "snatches" of wanted individuals abroad (Clarke 2004: 143–5; Mayer 2008: 108). But, whereas previously these tactics had been used sparingly, secretly, and exceptionally, in the war on terror these practices came to be used regularly and openly.

The explicit legal authorization of torture, extraordinary rendition (the extrajudicial seizure and transport of a person to another state), and indefinite detention moved these practices from the realm of the sub rosa to the center of governance. The transformation of extraordinary rendition illustrates this change particularly well. The practice had begun in the 1980s, but was used sparingly until after 9/11. The total number of renditions carried out by the CIA prior to 9/11, according to CIA director George Tenet, was around seventy (Mayer 2008: 108). But, in the period from 9/11 to the end of 2007, it has been estimated that between 100 and several thousand individuals were renditioned (Mayer 2008: 108). As Jane Mayer (2008: 108) recounts, renditions

> were originally used on an extremely limited basis and for a different purpose... What began as a program aimed as a small, discrete set of suspects – people against whom there were outstanding foreign arrest warrants – came to include the wide and ill-defined population that the administration termed "illegal enemy combatants"... Before September 11, the program was aimed at rendering criminal suspects to justice but afterward it was used to render suspects outside the reach of the law... Rendition thus became an enforcement mechanism for the Bush Administration's preemptive criminal model, disrupting and punishing suspects before they were probably guilty.

Together, these practices became the core of a new mode of governance.

How did we get to a position that it made sense to adopt such a radical mode of governance? While the attacks of 9/11 were a shock, it was not simply the force of the events of that day that conditioned the nature of the subsequent response. Rather, the logic of pre-emption can be understood as the successor to a series of other forms of governance applied to terrorism over the years, one that was thinkable only because it built upon a history of a problem that had exceeded and surpassed all attempts to contain it within the bounds of rational management. This chapter will show, first, how the discourse of "terrorism" enabled the post-9/11 "war on terror" and, second, how the process and conflicts through which the war on terror took shape echo previous knowledge controversies.

"WE DON'T WANT THE SMOKING GUN TO BE A MUSHROOM CLOUD"[8]

There have been a number of good accounts of the emergence of the war on terror (for example, Bergen 2011; Clarke 2004; Hersh 2004; Mann 2004; Mayer 2008; Suskind 2006; Woodward 2002). Most of these have focused either on the precipitating role of the attacks themselves or on the personal actions and intentions of President Bush and his advisors, however. The conflicts and disagreements that came to light as the war on terror took shape have most often been understood as reflecting clashes between members of the Bush administration, who pushed a radical new agenda, and bureaucratic actors representing more "mainstream conservative" viewpoints. Further, many of these accounts have focused on the role of a neoconservative "cabal" in the Bush administration, and organizations such as the Project for the New American Century in pushing through a radical new approach (for example, Hersh 2004; Mann 2004). This chapter does not dispute these accounts but adds a further dimension to the analysis, asking how it was that the "neoconservative cabal" was able to push through its agenda. The neoconservative actors and ideas did not come out of nowhere but had their origins in some of the earlier conflicts over terrorist expertise recounted in this book. And they were successful in enacting the pre-emptive war on terror not simply

[8] Condoleezza Rice, Secretary of State, speaking on CNN, September 8, 2002, quoted by Hersh (2004: 231). The "mushroom cloud" here refers to the threat of nuclear terrorism, and the "smoking gun" to evidence that Saddam Hussein was seeking nuclear weapons.

through brute force, or due only to the shock of the events of 9/11. The pre-emptive logic built upon the pre-existing rhetoric of terrorism, and fit with extant practices of counterterrorism, in ways that aided its adoption. The question to be explained here is not simply why the Bush administration responded to the 9/11 attacks with a pre-emptive war on terror but why the American people consented to it.

Traces of a pre-emptive logic were present from the start in the rhetoric of the Bush administration, whose members often explicitly contrasted their approach to earlier logics. As Bob Woodward (2002: 42) recounts of a meeting of the National Security Council on September 12:

> FBI Director Mueller began to describe the investigation under way to identify the hijackers. He said it was essential not to taint any evidence so that if accomplices were arrested, they could be convicted. Attorney General John D. Ashcroft interrupted. Let's stop the discussion right here, he said. The chief mission of US law enforcement, he added, is to stop another attack and apprehend any accomplices or terrorists before they hit us again. If we can't bring them to trial, so be it... [T]he focus of the FBI and the Justice Department should change from prosecution to prevention, a radical shift in priorities.

And by November 2001 what Ron Suskind would label the "Cheney doctrine," or the "one percent doctrine," had taken shape: "Even if there's just a one percent chance of the unimaginable coming due, act as if it is a certainty" (Suskind 2006: 62).

Members of the Bush administration quickly began to link terrorism and fears of "weapons of mass destruction," presenting the potential convergence of the two as an undeniable justification for pre-emptive warfare. As early as November 2001 Bush administration officials began to publicly focus on the possibility that terrorists might obtain WMDs, with Donald Rumsfeld, the secretary of defense, proclaiming on television that it could reasonably be assumed that bin Laden could obtain chemical and biological weapons, while Bush told the UN General Assembly that terrorists were "searching for weapons of mass destruction, the tools to turn their hatred into holocaust'" (Mann 2004: 317). As the war on terror developed, President Bush made increasing reference to the threat of weapons of mass destruction,[9] and to supposed links between terrorists and state sponsors. Bush's first state of the union address, on January 29, 2002, not only famously proclaimed Iran, Iraq, and North Korea an "axis of evil" but also emphasized the necessity of preventing terrorists and states alike from gaining access to WMDs.[10]

It was in his June 2002 graduation speech at the United States Military Academy at West Point, however, that the president first and most clearly laid out the emerging doctrine of pre-emption. As a number of observers have noted, a graduation was an unusual setting for such a groundbreaking speech. But this talk is widely noted as one of the most significant of President Bush's career, or even "one of the most significant presidential foreign policy addresses of all time" (Goodnight 2005: 97). In this speech, Bush declared that "new threats...require new thinking." The logic of deterrence, which underlay the Cold War, "means nothing against shadowy terrorist networks with no nation or citizens to defend," and could therefore no longer be relied upon.[11] The alternative he proposed was that of pre-emption, for "[i]f we wait for threats to fully materialize we will have waited too long." Instead, he proclaimed, "[w]e must take the battle to the enemy, disrupt his plans and confront the worst threats before they emerge." In sum, the nation had to "be ready for pre-emptive action," putting the name "pre-emption" to the emerging logic for the first time.[12]

---

[9] At this point we should also keep in mind that the concept of WMDs was itself a contested construct, which conflated a number of qualitatively quite different threats.

[10] President Bush, address to the nation, October 7, 2001.

[11] President Bush, commencement address at the United States Military Academy, West Point, reprinted by *The New York Times*, June 1, 2002; accessed online April 29, 2012.

[12] According to *The Weekly Standard*, this speech was the first time that Bush used the term "pre-emption," which was "both a word the president had never used

The doctrine of pre-emption would be formally enshrined in the September 2002 national security strategy (NSS) of the United States, which quoted liberally from the West Point speech. The NSS named the enemy as "rogue states and terrorists" (with the clarification that the "enemy is not a single political regime or person or religion or ideology" but, rather, "terrorism" itself) who, it was especially feared, might use weapons of mass destruction (Bush 2002: 5). The very nature of this new enemy, the NSS declared, enjoined a new strategy:

> Traditional concepts of deterrence will not work against a terrorist enemy whose avowed tactics are wanton destruction and the targeting of innocents; whose so-called soldiers seek martyrdom in death and whose most potent protection is statelessness... To forestall or prevent such hostile acts by our adversaries, the United States will, if necessary, act preemptively.[13]

The same month Donald Rumsfeld told reporters that "this isn't punishment. We've got the wrong model in our minds if we're thinking about punishment. We're not. This isn't retaliation or retribution" (Hersh 2004: 267). Indeed, this was not intended as punishment, or retribution. Rather, it was a preventive strategy – intended to take action before attacks could be made.

A key aspect of this discourse of pre-emption was its ambiguous relation to the similar concept of prevention. Traditionally, *pre-emption* had been used to refer to action taken against an imminent threat, while *prevention* was generally used to refer to action taken against a looming but less immediate problem. But the Bush administration's use of the term appeared to blur the distinction deliberately. As Suskind (2006: 150) observes, "The carefully chosen word was 'preemptive' – a parlance generally understood to be driven by evidence, by evidence of both

---

before and a strategic concept he hadn't fully articulated." Barnes (2002); accessed online April 29, 2012.

[13] Bush (2002: 15). This was Bush's first national security strategy, and the first issued since 9/11. The issuing of such statements each year was a requirement instituted by the Goldwater–Nichols Act of 1986.

means and desire... But many of those who heard the speech felt it danced close to a much broader concept – prevention."[14]

The 2003 invasion of Iraq, justified as necessary to prevent a "rogue" regime from attaining weapons of mass destruction, can be seen as the culmination of this logic of pre-emption. According to former counterterrorism czar Richard Clarke, there was an emphasis on the possible role of Iraq in the earliest meetings after 9/11 (Clarke 2004: 30), and later that year the argument for invading Iraq went public with a "surge of articles and columns" (Hersh 2004: 169). On November 14, 2001, Bush advisor Richard Perle gave a speech in which he asked whether the United States should "take some pre-emptive action" against Saddam Hussein, the Iraqi president (Hersh 2004: 214). President Bush's January 2002 state of the union address highlighted the role of Iraq as part of an "axis of evil," and that spring he openly called for regime change in Iraq, and spoke of the possibility of pre-emptive warfare (Woodward 2002: 330). In a television interview in September, when asked about the situation in Iraq, Condoleezza Rice declared, referring to the nuclear threat, "We don't want the smoking gun to be a mushroom cloud." Bush adopted this language as well, declaring in an October 7 speech: "Facing clear evidence of peril, we cannot wait for the final proof – the smoking gun – that could come in the form of a mushroom cloud" (Hersh 2004: 231). The message was clear: when faced with (potential) threats of a devastating nature, the United States could not afford to wait for proof, but had to act. On October 10 and 11, 2003, the House and Senate voted to give President Bush authority to attack Iraq.

This discourse of terrorism, whose history I have traced in the first six chapters of this book, acted as a cultural toolkit (Swidler 1986) that both enabled and constrained those who constructed the response to the 9/11 attacks. The discourse did not predetermine the nation's response to the 9/11 attacks, but it did enable certain forms of response and make others less likely. And, further, once the

---

[14] On this point, see also Goodnight (2005: 97) and Holloway (2008: 46).

administration had determined to enact the pre-emptive war on terror, this history made it more likely that the administration's framing would "stick," and that the American people would accept it. The way in which "terrorism" had come to be constructed as a problem laid the groundwork for the post-9/11 war on terror.

Prior modes of governance had conceptualized terrorism as a problem to be responded to, punished, managed, predicted, or even disrupted. But it was only after 9/11 that pre-emption, or preventing the possibility of acts of terror before they could happen, came to dominate American counterterrorism policy. The emergence of the war on terror can be explained only by paying attention to the inter-actions between political actors (within and outside the Bush admin-istration) and the pre-existing foundation of rhetoric about "terrorism" and the logics of managing the problem that had emerged over the past decades. The world that began to emerge on September 11, 2001, did not erase, but, rather, built upon the three decades of counterterrorism knowledge and practices that had preceded it.

THE "CABAL"

The "neoconservative cabal," which consisted of the initiators of much of the war on terror, built directly on prior rhetoric on terror-ism, as well as on specific individual experts who had been involved in forming the terrorism problem and on specific practices of knowledge used to develop authority and "truth" in the past. Where did the architects of the war on terror, often referred to collectively as neo-conservatives, or "neocons,"[15] come from? These individuals are

---

[15] The origins of the "neocons" derive from a break from the Democratic Party in the 1970s by former liberals who identified themselves as strongly anti-communist and generally hawkish on foreign policy. Some of the original prominent neoconservatives included Daniel Patrick Moynihan, Norman Podhoretz, Jeanne Kirkpatrick, and Irving Kristol. The group came to power as part of the Reagan administration in 1981, but then lost influence during Reagan's second term, and the administration of George H. W. Bush, and was out of power during the Clinton years, but it experienced a resurgence during the George W. Bush administration. Key organizational centers of the neoconservative movement include the American Enterprise Institute, the Jewish Institute for National Security Affairs, and the

most often considered to have been the core members of the neocon-servative "clique" in the Bush administration: Paul Wolfowitz, the deputy secretary of defense; Douglas Feith, number three at the Penta-gon; Lewis "Scooter" Libby, chief of staff for Dick Cheney, the vice president; John R. Bolton, at the Department of State; Elliott Abrams, head of Middle East policy at the National Security Council; David Frum, who served as a special assistant to the president: and Richard Perle, as chairman of the Defense Policy Board; most of them had been appointed to their positions by Vice President Cheney.

The history of the neoconservatives is entangled with the his-tory of terrorism expertise in a number of ways. Some of the key connections were made during the episodes traced in Chapter 5, when a new interpretive framework that situated the problem of terrorism within a broader, more world-historical set of narratives, claiming that the Soviet Union was behind the epidemic of international ter-rorism, linked terrorism to the Cold War, organized around a series of moral oppositions pitting "terrorism" against the trifecta of civiliza-tion, democracy, and "the West." Some of the same individuals who had championed this "Soviet theory" in the 1980s, such as Michael Ledeen, reemerged as key advisors to the Bush administration. Ledeen holds a PhD in history from the University of Wisconsin, but was denied tenure at Washington University in St Louis with questions about the quality of his scholarship and possible plagiarism (Babcock 1987). In 1977 he joined the CSIS, home to fellow terrorism experts Yonah Alexander and Ray Cline, and subsequently took a position at the American Enterprise Institute. Ledeen came to national promin-ence in the 1980s as a proponent of the "Soviet theory" of inter-national terrorism, testifying in the Senate subcommittee hearings on Soviet support for terrorism, and acting as an advisor to Secretary

Project for the New American Century, which had called for an invasion of Iraq throughout the 1990s. Core ideological tenets included a belief in the importance and rightness of US power, a belief in internationalism, and a generally hawkish foreign policy characterized by support for "democracy promotion," capitalism and free markets, a fierce anti-communism, and strong support for Israel.

of State Alexander Haig. Ledeen came back into national prominence after the 9/11 attacks as a central proponent of the links between Saddam Hussein and international terrorism.

A second expert championed by the "cabal" was Laurie Mylroie, a writer who had been promoting the idea that there were links between Saddam Hussein and international terrorism since the 1990s. Mylroie first came to prominence after claiming that Iraq was behind the 1993 World Trade Center bombing, and she develops this argument in greater detail in her book *Study of Revenge: Saddam Hussein's Unfinished War against America* (Mylroie 2000), published by the AEI, where Mylroie was a fellow together with Richard Perle and David Frum. *Study of Revenge* featured a blurb from Richard Perle that calls it "splendid and wholly convincing," while a revised edition published in 2001 featured a blurb from Paul Wolfowitz, who calls it "provocative and disturbing." And, in an even more expansive version of her theory, Mylroie would argue that Saddam Hussein was behind not only the 1993 World Trade Center bombing but also a number of other attacks, including the Oklahoma City bombing and the 1998 bombings of US embassies in Kenya and Tanzania.[16]

Mylroie testified before the National Commission on Terrorist Attacks upon the United States (often called the 9/11 Commission) in 2003, when she was a key witness in support of the link between al Qaeda and Iraq. Thomas Kean and Lee Hamilton, the chairs, wrote (Kean and Hamilton 2006: 127):

> One of our witnesses, Laurie Mylroie, was a leading supporter of the theory that Saddam Hussein had ties to al Qaeda, and possibly the 9/11 attacks. She argued, among other things, that Khalid Sheikh Mohammed, the mastermind of 9/11, was an operative of Iraqi intelligence. This sparked disagreement.

[16] These linkages were put forward by Mylroie in an interview published in the November 19, 2001, issue of *Insight on the News* magazine.

"Disagreement" was a diplomatic way of putting it. Mylroie's testimony sparked criticism from other experts, including Daniel Benjamin (Benjamin and Simon 2005: 145) and Peter Bergen, who has called her a "crackpot," quoting several CIA analysts who dismissed her work (Bergen 2003) in a way reminiscent of the debate over Claire Sterling's work in the 1980s.

In addition to these linkages of specific individuals tying together the "neocon cabal" with earlier episodes in the history of terrorism expertise, there were also connections with the knowledge practices deployed in the war on terror and earlier episodes. These include deploying the rhetoric of "objectivity" against the CIA, which had traditionally relied on it to bolster its credibility, and bringing in outside experts to bolster their preferred theories. The way in which this happened during the lead-up to the Iraq war of 2003 echoed previous controversies over knowledge and intelligence, especially those associated with the "team B" events of the 1970s, and the controversy over the work of Claire Sterling in the 1980s. "Team B" refers to a "competitive intelligence" exercise that took place in the 1970s, wherein a panel of outside experts were commissioned by the CIA (who would comprise the putative "team A") to carry out a threat analysis of the Soviet Union. The origins of the exercise lay with a number of individuals, including Cold War theorist Albert Wohlstetter, Paul Wolfowitz, and the then secretary of defense, Donald Rumsfeld, all of whom were concerned that the CIA was underestimating the Soviet nuclear threat. The conclusion of the outside panel – that the CIA had indeed underestimated the Soviet threat – was commonly understood as a politicized attack upon the authority of the intelligence community.

The attacks on the expertise of the professional intelligence community in the lead-up to the Iraq war of 2003 echoed these earlier events. Seymour Hersh reports: "By the fall of 2002, Rumsfeld was in a public fight with the CIA over the agency's inability to document significant direct ties between Al Qaeda and Iraq" (Hersh 2004: 210), and: "One internal Pentagon memorandum, from December 2001, went so far as to suggest that terrorism experts in the government and outside it had deliberately 'downplayed or sought to disprove' the link between Al Qaeda and Iraq" (Hersh 2004: 211). After analysts failed to find a connection between bin Laden and Saddam Hussein, Frum and Perle (2003: 47) directly attacked the objectivity of the intelligence core. Given the resistance of the professional intelligence community to affirm the connection between Iraq and al Qaeda, the solution adopted by the "neocon cabal" was to create its own "Iraqi intelligence cell" within the Pentagon, the Policy Counterterrorism Evaluation Group (PCTEG), which "was tasked to study policy implications of connections between terrorist organizations" (Mitchell and Newman 2006: 81). The PCTEG criticized the work of CIA analysts, arguing that the CIA had downplayed the connection between Iraq and terrorism (Mitchell and Newman 2006: 81). Just as the original "Team B" had "turned a lack of intelligence data" into proof of the vastness of the Soviet threat, post-9/11 critiques of the CIA turned an apparent lack of data on the connections between Iraq and terrorism into proof of the very nefariousness of the threat, and the need for pre-emptive action to forestall it (Mitchell and Newman 2006: 83). In the next section, I show how the pre-emptive war on terror was built upon several specific aspects of the "terrorism" problem as it had taken shape from the 1970s onward. These were, first, the conceptualization of the terrorist as evil, irrational, and immune to both rational explanation, and, second, the emergence of terrorism as a problem that resists rational techniques of management and governance.

"WE ARE DEALING HERE WITH EVIL PEOPLE WHO DWELL IN THE SHADOWS, PLANNING UNIMAGINABLE VIOLENCE AND DESTRUCTION"[17]

As the problem of terrorism took shape over the course of the 1970s, 1980s, and 1990s, it came to be understood as rooted to a terrorist *identity*, rather than as a tactic that any group might adopt. This led to the proposition that terrorists commit terrorism *because* they are

[17] Dick Cheney (2011: 343).

terrorists. The identity contains its own explanation: "terrorists" are evil, irrational actors whose action is driven not by normal interests or political motives but, instead, by their very nature as terrorists. According to this framework, terrorists did not necessarily commit acts of violence for any rational political purpose (as they claimed) but, rather, because of their inherently evil nature.

This view of terrorism as absolute evil, not subject to rational understanding, is central to the book *An End to Evil: How to Win the War on Terror*, published in 2003 by Bush advisors Richard Perle and David Frum. Terrorism, they write, is "the great evil of our time, and the war against this evil, our generation's great cause" (Frum and Perle 2003: 9). There is "no middle way" in fighting this potentially "genocidal" foe: "It is victory or holocaust" (Frum and Perle 2003: 9). As for the terrorists themselves, Frum and Perle present them as unstoppable, and their goals as inexplicable. They are driven by "an apocalyptic vision... They cannot be deterred. They cannot be appeased. The terrorists kill and will accept death for a cause with which no accommodation is possible" (Frum and Perle 2003: 41). And, while the terrorists may have different identities on the surface ("[r]eligious extremists and secular militants; Sunnis and Shiites; communists and fascists"), their true motives all stem from "the same enormous target of combustible rage" (Frum and Perle 2003: 59–60).

This denial of the possibility of rational causes, and the attribution of terrorism to pure evil, are key constraints shaping what can be said about terrorism. The two world views – that terrorism is evil and inexplicable, or that terrorism is rational and subject to understanding – are generally framed as incompatible opposites. And, although the equation of terrorism with "evil," and the exclusion of rational causes, are usually presented by advocates of this position as straightforward facts (despite the continual rolling in of evidence that many terrorists do, in fact, seem to have political motives and goals), it is rare to encounter anyone who faces this contradiction head-on.

One exception is Alan Dershowitz, who in his 2002 book *Why Terrorism Works* is remarkably straightforward about his approach to this contradiction (Dershowitz 2002). For him is it not a contradiction at all, but an intentional and explicit political move. Terrorists, he writes, clearly have political goals, and, what is more, terrorism often helps them *achieve* those goals. For Dershowitz, the key goal of political terrorists is to draw attention and understanding for their cause, and, therefore, the key to fighting them is to deny them that attention and understanding (Dershowitz 2002: 24–5; emphasis in original):

> The current mantra of those opposed to a military response to terrorism is a plea to understand and eliminate the root causes of terrorism. There are several reasons why this is exactly the wrong approach... The reason terrorism works – and will persist unless there are significant changes in the responses to it – is precisely because its perpetrators believe that by murdering innocent civilians they will succeed in attracting the attention of the world to their perceived grievances and their demand that the world "understand them" and "eliminate their root causes"... We must take precisely the opposite approach to terrorism. We must commit ourselves *never to try to understand or eliminate its alleged root causes*, but rather to place it beyond the pale of dialogue and negotiation.

And yet, by taking this stance, Dershowitz exposes the feint of those who deny the meaning of terrorism, thus standing apart both from those who seek to explain terrorism and from those who deny that understanding is possible.

The language of "evil" was perhaps the most striking constant in President Bush's speeches throughout the war on terror. The repetition of this trope of terrorists as "evil" was, as reading Dershowitz suggests, not without purpose or targets. It was addressed, in part, towards a growing discourse that highlighted the ways in which terrorism was a response to American interventions abroad. Among the popular books that "situated 9/11 as a retaliatory attack on US imperialism in Asia and the Middle East" (Holloway 2008: 17) were

Imperial Hubris by "Anonymous" (Michael Scheuer, a senior CIA official who had been head of the bin Laden unit in the 1990s), Chalmers Johnson's *Blowback*, Noam Chomsky's *Hegemony or Survival*, William Blum's *Rogue State*, and Ziauddin Sardar and Merryl Wyn Davies' *Why Do People Hate America?*.

This formulation of terrorism as inexplicable evil culminated in the March 2006 national security strategy (Bush 2006). In this document, terrorism is explicable only as a "murderous ideology" unto itself, with a denial of any possible link to rational political grievances. Straightforwardly, the text declares (Bush 2006: 9–10):

> [W]e must be clear-eyed about what does and does not give rise to terrorism... Terrorism is not the inevitable by-product of poverty... Terrorism is not simply a result of hostility to US policy in Iraq... Terrorism is not simply a result of Israeli-Palestinian issues... Terrorism is not simply a response to our efforts to prevent terror attacks.

What, then, *are* the causes of terrorism? The 2006 NSS offers forth "failures...blamed on others," "perceived injustices," "sub-cultures of conspiracy and misinformation," and "an ideology that excuses or even glorifies the deliberate killing of innocents" (Bush 2006: 10). What is specifically excluded is any reference to concrete social and political conflicts.

EXCEEDING RATIONALIZATION

As I have discussed throughout this book, the problem of terrorism has been governed through a number of distinct logics since its emergence in the 1970s. Table 7.1 illustrates the core features of each of these logics of governance. The earliest attempts at dealing with the terrorism problem can be characterized as attempts at a rationalization of the problem. These modes of governance entailed attempts to subject the problem of terrorism to rational methods of knowledge production and governance, through techniques such as legal analysis, quantification, and simulation. Not one of these approaches was able

Table 7.1 Changing logics of governing terrorism

Logic of governance	Key time period	Archetypal knowledge technique	Corresponding techniques of management	Associated experts	Key actors	Object of governance
Legal/crime and punishment	Early/middle 1970s	Legal analysis	International law/diplomacy; extradition; use of national and international courts	Lawyers; diplomats; criminologists; law enforcement	States and the international system	Terrorist actors and organizations; the international system
Crisis management	1970s	Simulation	Routine procedures for managing (crisis) events	Emergency responders; terrorism experts, police	Emergency responders: police, doctors, etc.	Events/incidents
Risk management	1970s	Databases	Forecasting; insurance; precautionary behaviors	RAND; statisticians; CIA/intelligence agencies; analysts	Insurance/security organizations (public or private)	Risk (possible events)
Warfare (retributive/limited)	1980s	Narratives/"intelligence," tracing connections between terrorism and states	Retributive strikes against terrorist groups/sites	Journalists; think tanks; military	States (military)	Terrorist groups (and, implicitly, the Cold War balance of power)
Precaution	1990s	Scenarios – fantastic; extrapolating future possibilities	Regulation of WMDs; tracing and preventing spread of nuclear, chemical, biological materials	Scientists, experts in science policy and re WMDs	State and international regulatory agencies	Circulation of nuclear, biological, and chemical weapons
Disruption	2001–present	Network modeling; data mining	Financial interventions; no-fly lists; border control	Network analysts; economists; software engineers	State/international system (bureaucratic/regulatory side)	Terrorist networks and ability to act
Pre-emption	2001–present	Intelligence; law	Pre-emptive warfare; rendition; "enhanced interrogations"	Lawyers	State (executive/military/intelligence/secret agencies)	Pre-emption of terrorist actions

to capture fully the management of the terrorism problem, however. The attempt to govern terrorism via diplomacy and international law was largely abandoned by the United States after the 1970s. Quantification and risk management persisted, but would play a relatively subordinate role after the 1970s. And the routinization/crisis management policy has also persisted, though it has formed only a partial component of the response to terrorism since the 1970s.

In the 1980s these prior approaches to the governance of terrorism were largely displaced by the new framework of terrorism as war. New experts wove narratives that situated terrorism within the broader strategic framework of the Cold War, positing connections between international terrorism and the Soviet Union. Under the Reagan administration the United States began to treat terrorism as a problem of war, rather than one to be governed through frameworks of crime and punishment, and retributive military actions against terrorist groups became the new norm. The first "war on terror" differed from the current one in a number of ways, however. Military action against terrorists in the 1980s was driven by rationales of punishment, retaliation, and deterrence, not a logic of pre-emption. And, although assassinations and renditions were undertaken, in general the CIA and the military operated under much tighter legal and political controls during this period when compared to the current era.

With the end of the Cold War, the overriding narrative behind the first war on terror deflated. And, while the practice of retaliatory strikes against terrorist groups would continue into the Clinton administration, the overall level of attention given to the problem of terrorism declined in the early 1990s. The rise of the "new terrorism" and, in particular, concerns with the possibility that terrorists might use "weapons of mass destruction" reanimated attention to the terrorism problem in the middle of the decade. Two prominent notions about terrorism in the 1990s – the idea that we were now facing a new form of terrorist that was more irrational and more dangerous than those who had come beforehand, and the fear that terrorists might obtain and use WMDs – made terrorism seem a more potent threat.

And these same two animating shifts can also be seen as important precursors to the rise of the logic of pre-emption after 9/11. The "new terrorism" of the 1990s was, in practice, mostly governed through a logic of precaution, however, which sought to limit the access of terrorists and others to dangerous materials, and the overall scope of the concern was quite limited in comparison to the current day.

The next chapter connects this inability to capture the problem back to the problem of expertise in the war on terror and beyond. How and why were experts influential after 9/11? And how and why was their influence severely limited? Is the field of terrorism studies becoming, as some have suggested, a legitimate discipline? And, if so, what might the effect of this be upon the power and influence of terrorism experts?

8   The politics of (anti-)knowledge: disciplining terrorism after 9/11

*I asked these two [advisers to a government counterterrorism expert],
"How did you get your jobs?" and they say, "Oh, we had the only
qualification this person wanted... [W]e knew nothing about terrorism."*[1]

The only thing I know certain about him is that he's evil.[2]

"Why do they hate us?" The question became inescapable in the days
and weeks after the 9/11 attacks. *"They hate us for our values."*
Public discussion of the 9/11 attacks swiftly came to be dominated
by the language of "evil." The explanation that dominated the air-
waves was that the hijackers had attacked the United States because
of an inexplicable hatred for America and its values. Alternative
answers, especially those that sought to connect the attacks to US
foreign policy, were marginalized. In one of the most well-known
such incidents, when Susan Sontag wrote in *The New Yorker*, just
weeks after the attacks, that "this was not a 'cowardly' attack on
'civilization' or 'liberty' or 'humanity' or 'the free world' but an attack
on the world's self-proclaimed superpower, undertaken as a conse-
quence of specific American alliances and actions" (Sontag 2001), she
was called "deranged," an "ally of evil," and "morally obtuse," and
accused of hating "America and the West and freedom and democratic
goodness."[3] Judith Butler writes in the preface to *Precarious Life* (Butler
2010: xiii) about "the rise of censorship and anti-intellectualism that

---

[1] Interview with a terrorism expert, 2006.
[2] President George W. Bush, press conference with President Pervez Musharraf of
Pakistan, New York, November 10, 2001.
[3] "Deranged" and "ally of evil": Andrew Sullivan of the *New Republic*; "moral
idiocy": John Podhoretz in the *New York Post*; "hating America": Jay Nordlinger of
the *National Review*; all quoted by Faludi (2007). "Morally obtuse": Charles
Krauthammer in *Time* magazine, cited at the blog of the Society for US Intellectual
History, http://us-intellectual-history.blogspot.com/2011/09/susan-sontag-and-911-
haze.html).

took hold in the fall of 2001 when anyone who sought to understand the 'reasons' for the attack on the United States was regarded as someone who sought to 'exonerate' those who conducted that attack." Attempts to seek reasons for the attacks were heard as justifications. The slippage between reason, reasons and justifiable reasons led to a situation in which explanation itself became suspect.

And it was not just overtly critical or leftist voices that faced this backlash. Even "mainstream" terrorism experts, especially those who endeavored to situate the attacks in a context of broader knowledge about terrorism and its causes, were open to criticism. Academic experts who sought explanations for the attacks and highlighted the need to understand the motivations of terrorists were viewed with suspicion, as illustrated by Martha Crenshaw's recollection that "[p]eople [in the government] would feel mostly indignant, they would get upset when we said you have to understand the motivations of terrorists" (Crenshaw, quoted by Easton 2001). Explanation itself came to be seen by some as profane, as in this recent debate over the construction of a 9/11 museum (Cohen 2012):

> Explaining the terrorists' motivations aroused similar concerns. To some families of victims, asking what caused Sept. 11 "is literally a profane question," said Rabbi Irwin Kula, president of the National Jewish Center for Learning and Leadership and a participant in the conversation series. "It is like blaming the victim."

And, although these sorts of reactions have commonly been attributed to the shock and trauma of the 9/11 attacks, this book has shown that the attribution of terrorism to "evil," and the subsequent resistance to discussion of broader causes, have been defining features of terrorism discourse since the 1970s.

This chapter argues that both expert and popular discourse about terrorism in the wake of 9/11 were characterized by a politics of *anti-knowledge*, an active refusal of explanation itself. Like James Ferguson's (1994) "*anti-politics*," the concept of anti-knowledge suggests that a problem has been removed from the realm of (some types of) political debate. In this case, though, the mechanism is not the capture of a problem by experts professing technological solutions; in fact, it is quite the opposite, as the most frequent complaint of terrorism experts after 9/11 was that their views were marginalized and ignored.[4] The distance between the views of experts and those of policymakers is illustrated by the results of a survey of terrorism experts undertaken in 2006 by *Foreign Policy* magazine and the liberal think tank the Center for American Progress. When asked to choose the two most important factors motivating "global terrorists," the most popular choices of terrorism experts from across the political spectrum were "extremist religious beliefs" (chosen by 51 percent of respondents), "governments and rulers of Middle Eastern countries," "opposition to US government policies in the Israeli-Palestinian conflict," and "opposition to US government policies in Iraq." Among the least popular choices were "rejection of American democratic values" (chosen by 4 percent of respondents) and "they are evil" (chosen by 1 percent) (Center for American Progress 2006).

Interviews with experts, conducted several years after 9/11, frequently elicited the opinion that terrorism experts' views had been ignored, and the expert community alienated from policymakers. For example, Brian Jenkins declared that, while he had "no doubts in [his] mind that the terrorists are the bad guys," the post-9/11 debate on terrorism had become a kind of "theological debate" without "empirical evidence," and that "if you put it in too stark terms of good versus evil it becomes anti-analytical." Continuing, he observed:

> I see this particularly in terms of understanding our terrorist foes. This is not to mitigate the savagery of their acts, but [we need to] understand... them, in the way that we devoted time to

---

[4] Kanishka Jayasuriya (2002) has argued that the American reaction to 9/11 was dominated by a form of "anti-politics" – the displacement of political conflict by techniques of "risk management and control." But I argue that it was not that rational practices of risk management displaced political debate, but that certain forms of political discourse and intellectual inquiry were marginalized by a political language of "evil."

understanding Soviet behavior during the Cold War, or German military leadership during World War II. Patton said, "Rommel, you magnificent bastard, I read your book!" But that's the point: you read the book.[5]

But, in the situation of anti-knowledge, knowledge and inquiry that entail knowing the terrorist are proscribed. It is as though the language of evil creates a "black box" around the terrorist, which creates its own explanation: terrorists commit terrorism because they are evil. Any further attempt to pursue alternative explanations, thereby seeking to break the black box of "evil," is seen as a profanation, even a sacrilege. The root of the politics of anti-knowledge is hence that, if terrorists are evil and irrational, then one cannot – and, indeed, *should not* – know them.

How can we account for the politics of anti-knowledge? Like the "war on terror," it is neither a straightforward outcome of the phenomena that we have come to know as terrorism nor a simple reaction to the massive shock of the 9/11 attacks. Instead, it should be seen as the outcome of the construction of both "terrorism" and "terrorists" as evil and irrational, together with the relatively weak position of advocates of "terrorism studies" to discipline either "terrorism" as an object of knowledge or the broader arena of terrorism expertise. Insofar as terrorists are understood to be inherently evil, it follows both that "evil" is the explanation for terrorism and that we ought not to seek to know terrorists, for such knowledge is potentially contaminating. And, further, insofar as terrorism is understood to be irrational, the very possibility of understanding it can be called into question.

President Bush's framing of the 9/11 attacks was dominated by the language of evil, frequently pointing to "evil" as the sole cause of the attacks, and disavowing any alternative explanations. On September 25, 2001, he proclaimed at a meeting, "These are evildoers. They

---

[5] Interview with Brian Jenkins, June 26, 2007.

have no justification for their actions. There's no religious justification, there's no political justification. The only motivation is evil." A month later, on November 2, he declared, "I don't accept the excuse that poverty promotes evil. That's like saying poor people are evil people. I disagree with that. Osama bin Laden is an evil man... [W]e are fighting evil, and we will continue to fight evil, and we will not stop until we defeat evil." And in a meeting with Muslim community leaders at the White House on September 26, after declaring, "I consider bin Laden an evil man... This is a man who hates freedom. This is an evil man," he was asked "But does he have political goals?," to which Bush could only reply: "He has got evil goals. And it's hard to think in conventional terms about a man so dominated by evil."[6]

The conceptualization of terrorists as evil was paired with an understanding of terrorism as irrational. The claim was subject to pushback from experts, who expressed frustration at its resilience, and its logical implication, that there was not much that terrorism experts could usefully explain. As Brian Jenkins has written recently (Jenkins 2006: 53):

> We are likewise inclined to see terrorists as fiends, wild-eyed expressions of evil, diabolical but two-dimensional, somehow alien – in a word, inhuman. Government officials routinely denounce terrorists as mindless fanatics, savage barbarians, or, more recently, "evildoers" – words that dismiss any intellectual content... [and] imped[e] efforts to understand the enemy.

And Andrew Silke has identified the heart of the difficulty when he writes (Silke 2004a: 19),

> [T]here is a tendency to regard the perpetrators as psychologically abnormal and deviant... To attempt comprehension in any other terms can...be seen to imply a level of sympathy and acceptance of what has been done and of who has done it.

---

[6] All the above quotes are available at https://en.wikiquote.org/wiki/Wikiquote: Transwiki/Terrorism_disambiguation/Evil_Doers (accessed July 10, 2012).

The construction of terrorism as inherently evil constrained those who would speak out as experts. In order to maintain their credibility and authority, experts needed to maintain a certain distance from their very object of expertise. This made certain forms of knowledge about terrorists taboo: attempts to explain would be taken as justification, and attempts to understand would be elided with sympathy. And the construction of terrorism as irrational meant that attempts at rational explanation could be dismissed, on the grounds that terrorism was not subject to rational understanding. Research in the sociology of science has often argued that the moral character of scientists has been used as a basis for establishing and evaluating their credibility (Hilgartner 2000; Shapin 1994; Stark 2012). But what is distinctive here is that the credibility of experts on terrorism is dependent upon their taking a moral stand against the very object they study, and maintaining a suitable distance from it.[7]

Enforcement of the taboo has taken a number of forms. Experts have been accused of "sympathizing" with their research subjects. At times even the notion of causation altogether came to seem suspect. A 2006 article in *International Affairs* accused British terrorism experts of perpetuating "discourse failure" by critiquing the government and identifying actions on the part of the government that were linked to terrorist attacks. Experts and the media, the authors claim, have led to "moral confusion" and a "murky" response to terrorism by "promulgating the view that terrorism must possess 'root causes'" (Jones and Smith 2006: 1107). By focusing on "root causes," they write, the work of such experts both "reduces the significance" of terrorism and "explains it away" (Jones and Smith 2006: 1109). Similarly, Martin Kramer's *Ivory Towers on Sand*, published shortly after 9/11 by the right-wing Washington Institute for Near East Policy, broadly attacks the academic field of Middle East studies for what he

---

[7] It is worth noting that the field of terrorism studies is not the only area in which this occurs, however; similar dynamics take place in other studies of "deviant" behavior, and in sexuality studies.

sees as an overly sympathetic approach to the Arab world, and a failure to foresee the rise of Islamic terrorism, arguing that this led the public to "write off academic 'expertise' on political Islam" (Kramer 2001: 57).

Experts have acknowledged the taboo and its effects on their work. Joseba Zulaika (2012) suggests that there is a "cordon sanitaire" around terrorism preventing researchers from interviewing or otherwise getting too close to understanding the mind frame and world view of terrorists. Gaetano Joe Ilardi writes that "the atmosphere that prevailed after the attacks left little room for pluralism or diversity of thought and opinion" (Ilardi 2004: 216), specifying (Ilardi 2004: 217):

> Efforts to understand the terrorists' grievances, including their historical roots and the function of US foreign policy in shaping these grievances, were paid scant attention. To demonstrate any degree of empathy, regardless of how slight, was to place one's credibility in harm's way.

According to Joseba Zulaika and William Douglass (1996: x), "It is one of the tenets of counterterrorism that any interaction with the terrorist 'Other' is a violation of a taboo," for "it is a discourse grounded in the very prohibition of discourse" (Zulaika and Douglass 1996: 182). Terrorism experts, they write, are "forbidden" from interacting with terrorists, for "there must be no common ground between terrorist Unreason and political Reason" (Zulaika and Douglass 1996: 180).

And this taboo is not limited to those who might conceivably be considered sympathetic to the terrorists, but can be turned upon anyone who seeks to understand them. Rita Katz, head of the SITE (Search for International Terrorist Entities) Institute,[8] a private intelligence firm that monitors "Jihadi" websites, reports that her work has "met with institutional resistance" from officials in Washington: "They said, 'Oh, Rita, I'm not sure you should even be communicating

---

[8] The SITE Institute reportedly ceased operations in 2008, to be replaced by the SITE Intelligence Group, set up by some of the members of the former institute.

with them – you might be providing material support!'" (Katz, quoted by Wallace-Wells 2006). And Katz is about as far from "sympathetic" as one might get. She believes that radical Islamic terrorism poses a dire threat to the United States, and that "the war against radical Islam is likely to last for decades, and that the outcome is far from clear." But she also argues (Wallace-Wells 2006) that

> it is wrong to assert, as President Bush does, that terrorists are motivated by hatred for our freedoms rather than by our policies in the Middle East or those of their own governments... Her project is, in large measure, to convince Americans of the seriousness of the threat by building a direct conduit to the terrorist mind.

One of the main effects of the taboo has been the paucity of experts who have had direct contact with terrorists. Bruce Hoffman (2004: xviii) notes:

> Brian Jenkins, a doyen of the field, if not one of its "founding fathers", once compared terrorism analysts to Africa's Victorian-era cartographers. Just as the cartographers a century ago mapped from a distance a vast and impenetrable continent few of them had ever seen, most contemporary terrorism research is conducted far removed from, and therefore with little direct knowledge of, the actual terrorists themselves.

We can also observe assertions from experts *against* the taboos, assertions of disagreement that make sense only if we understand that the context is a broad denial of precisely what they feel the need to assert. Louise Richardson, author of *What Terrorists Want* (2006b), writes, "When I consider a terrorist atrocity, I do not think of the perpetrators as evil monsters" (Richardson, quoted by Wolfe 2011: 146).

The 2005 Club de Madrid "International summit on democracy, terrorism and security" sought to investigate the roots of terrorism. Bringing together some of the most well-respected researchers in terrorism studies, including Ted Gurr, Mark Juergensmeyer, Jerrold Post, Michael Stohl, Leonard Weinberg, Scott Atran, Ariel Merari,

Marc Sageman, Alex Schmid, Martha Crenshaw, and Jessica Stern, this conference was a serious endeavor. Yet the book of papers from the conference opens on a highly defensive note, with the forward noting: "Looking at the root causes of terrorism, however, is not as uncontroversial as it seems. Some dismiss it as simplistic; others even believe it is an effort to justify terrorism" (Richardson 2006a: xvi). Louise Richardson opens the book's introduction by noting (Richardson 2006a: 1):

> In June 2005, White House advisor Karl Rove criticized what he described as the effort of liberals after the attacks of September 11, 2001, to understand the terrorists...reflecting a common predilection to equate understanding terrorism with sympathy for terrorists.

If even the organizers of such a successful a conference as this one, attended by some of the most high-status academic terrorism researchers, felt the need to be pre-emptive in staving off criticism that sought to delegitimize their very purpose and existence, then the taboo must be strong indeed.

The key to explaining the politics of anti-knowledge is the central role of evil and irrationality in our understanding of the problem of terrorism. But, as the previous chapters of this book have made clear, the problem of "terrorism" did not take shape in an uncontested way. Although evil and irrationality have been central tropes in the discourse of terrorism since the 1970s, there have always been significant factions of experts who have contested both the assumption that terrorists are irrational and the conclusion that terrorism can be attributed to "evil." Such experts have not been in a position to overturn the politics of anti-knowledge, however.

Part of the reason why the politics of anti-knowledge holds such power is the "undisciplined" nature of not just terrorism studies as a field but "terrorism" as an object of knowledge. As I traced the emergence of the field of terrorism expertise, a central aspect of the story was that terrorism studies did not take shape as an ideal-typical discipline or intellectual field. The terrorism studies field remains a relatively weak, "undisciplined" one, and "terrorism" itself remains an unstable, "undisciplined" object of knowledge. This does not mean that experts cannot, and do not, attempt to develop rational knowledge that explores terrorists' motives, only that they are in a relatively weak position when they do so. Because terrorism studies never developed into a mature "discipline," experts were prevented from using many of the typical ways in which professions exercise power and influence over the production of knowledge and expertise, whether through certification, through legal regulation, or through a monopoly on certain forms of technical knowledge. Terrorism experts have failed to gain control over either the boundaries of the field or the production and certification of experts. There is little regulation of who may become an expert, and, emblematically, experts have themselves complained that the field is filled with "self-proclaimed experts." From the academic perspective, rather than developing into an independent discipline or subfield, the terrorism studies field has tended to occupy the fringes of more established academic fields. Psychologist Ariel Merari has observed that the study of terrorism "falls between the chairs" (Merari 1991), while the author of a recent overview of the field concludes that "the science of terror has been conducted in the cracks and crevices which lie between the large academic disciplines" (Silke 2004b: 1–2).

This relative marginality of terrorism studies within academia was a common theme in interviews that I conducted. According to one researcher, "For many years, terrorism was an 'untouchable' issue, a topic that despite its practical impact was isolated from the field of scholarly research" (Wieviorka 1995: 597). One interviewee told me that "you still can't get a job in history in this country if you're studying counter-terrorism," while another told me that "it wasn't a respectable academic subject" when he started out, and a third said that, before 9/11, terrorism was considered to be an "unimportant" subject and even "the kiss of death" for untenured scholars.

Given the attention I place on the undisciplined nature of terrorism and terrorism studies, it is fair to ask whether this situation has changed with the influx of money, attention, and researchers into the field since 2001. Is the terrorism studies field becoming institutionalized? Has "terrorism" been disciplined? These are questions that experts themselves have raised often, with varying opinions. Some commentaries indicate an assumption that progression towards a disciplinary form was the natural and expected direction. In 2007 Paul Wilkinson asked how to "explain the long delay in the emergence of terrorism studies as a viable branch of multi-disciplinary research in international studies, political science and other branches of learning" (Wilkinson 2007: 318). Alex Schmid (2011) asks whether the terrorism studies field has become a "major stand-alone" academic discipline, and does not give a definitive answer, but declares that the field "has matured" and that "a fairly solid body of consolidated knowledge has emerged" (Schmid 2011: 470). Israeli chronicler of the field Avishag Gordon (2010) has argued that the field is indeed becoming an autonomous discipline, citing as evidence increasing collaboration among terrorism researchers, an increase in the number of conferences, new journals, and an increase in sub-specialties. Andrew Silke, in his 2004 overview of the field, writes: "The increased attention, interest, money and activity are taken by many as an indication that the terrorism research world is on the threshold of becoming an academic discipline in its own right," but also asserts that "many experienced commentators are doubtful that the study of terrorism can (or should) emerge as a distinct discipline" (Silke 2004a: 26).

The field of terrorism expertise has been a site of tremendous growth since 2001. Quite a few reports have found that the number of articles on terrorism skyrocketed after 2001. Cynthia Lum, Leslie Kennedy and Alison Sherley (2006) find that 54 percent of all scholarly articles on terrorism published from 1972 to 2002 were published in 2001 and 2002. Another survey finds that 2,281 nonfiction books with "terrorism" in the title were published between September 2001 and September 2008, while only 1,310 similar titles had been released before September 2001 (Silke 2009). Jackson (2009) writes: "Terrorism studies is one of the fastest-growing areas of social-scientific research in the English-speaking world," with "literally thousands" of books, articles and reports published each year. And, according to Yonah Alexander, more than 150 books on terrorism were published in the first year after the 9/11 attacks (Alexander, quoted by Silke 2004a: 25).

The availability of funding for terrorism research has also increased exponentially. Ian Lustick writes that the war on terror created opportunities for "every group, every company, every sector of society, and every lobbyist" (Lustick 2006: 71). In the four years after 2001 the National Science Foundation (NSF) awarded 135 grants, totaling $47.7 million, for research on terrorism, as compared to just eight grants, totaling $1.5 million, in the four preceding years (Lustick 2006: 91). And this is just a fraction of the funding for research available from the federal government, the majority of which comes not through the NSF but through agencies such as the Department of Defense, much of it going to consulting firms, think tanks, and private research institutes. Moreover, since 9/11 the Department of Homeland Security has funded twelve university-based "centers of excellence" for research into terrorism and the security of the United States.[9]

Course offerings and degree programs in terrorism studies have also increased in number, and, although there are as yet no freestanding "terrorism studies" departments, the first MA degree in terrorism opened its doors in 2002 (Silke 2004a: 25). A 2004 article in *The New Statesman* declared that graduate programs in terrorism studies were "springing up like an intifada across the western world" (Toolis 2004). A more recent survey of the field found over 100 "credible" and "professional" terrorism research centers in operation worldwide, with sixty-three of these in the United States (Freedman 2010). These included both university research centers, focused on terrorism, and private institutes and think tanks with terrorism research programs. Another (2012) overview found that the majority of US colleges and universities surveyed offered at least one course on terrorism (Sheehan 2012). In 2007 the American Political Science Association

---

[9] See www.dhs.gov/files/programs/editorial_0498.shtm.

released a report of recommendations for curricula on terrorism in political violence.[10] And the "Summer workshop on teaching about terrorism" (SWOTT) brought together faculty members for several years after 9/11 to "introduce professors and graduate students to new and innovative techniques utilized to teach terrorism and research terrorism," "strengthen the community of terrorism scholars," and "provide access to high-level officials working in the intelligence and counter-terrorism fields."[11]

Even as the study of terrorism moves towards academic legitimacy, however, it seems unlikely that "terrorism studies" will be able to gain control over the problem of "terrorism." The aim of disciplining terrorism studies has usually been paired with attempts to stabilize the definition of terrorism (Stampnitzky 2011). But the problem of definition persists as a key feature of terrorism expertise, and as a core problem for those experts seeking to stabilize the field. The extent of the problem is borne out by Alex Schmid's survey of 109 definitions of "terrorism," in which he separated out twenty-two distinct elements, not one of which was shared by all the definitions. The most common element, "violence/force," was present in only 83.5 percent of the definitions, and the next most common element, "political," was present in only 65 percent of the definitions (Schmid 2011).[12] Further illustrating the ongoing nature of this problem, a 2007 paper (Bogatyrenko 2007: 2, quoted by Schmid 2011: 90) notes that "over 77% of scholars in leading political science journals who focus on terrorism fail to define it, and many of the remaining 23% offer definitions of their own without paying due consideration to the implications of their conceptual choices."

Studies of science and expertise usually expect experts to try to purify, or rationalize, the concepts they work upon. In the case of

---

[10] See www.apsanet.org/content_15710.cfm.

[11] See www.start.umd.edu/start/announcements/announcement.asp?id=60.

[12] Schmid is referring to his 1984 data here, but he concludes that the problem of definition is still ongoing, and one of his main goals here, in fact, is to establish a revised "academic consensus definition of terrorism" (Schmid 2011: 87).

terrorism studies, those experts who tend to align themselves with the ideals and institutions of academia have often, as we might expect, focused on the need to come up with a stable, non-partisan, non-polemical definition for the sake of scientific progress and legitimacy (Sproat 1996; Stampnitzky 2011). In response to a survey of terrorism experts, the majority of respondents to the question "Do you find that endeavors to come to a commonly agreed-upon definition in the field of political violence in general and terrorism in particular are (a) a waste of time; (b) a necessary precondition for cumulative research; or (c) other?" chose the response: "a necessary precondition for cumulative research" (Schmid and Jongman 1988: 27). And a recurrent stated goal among terrorism studies experts has been to arrive at a neutral definition of terrorism – one not predicated upon moral/political judgments, as when one expert expressed the hope that analysts might develop a definition of terrorism that would be acceptable to both Israel and the PLO (Brian Jenkins, quoted by Hoffman 1984).

Yet most experts, even those invested in stabilization, engage in strategic ambiguity (Eisenberg 1984: 230). Strategic ambiguity enables experts to bridge between the academic, public, and policy worlds, and experts may also engage in ambiguity as a protective mechanism, against those who would try to attack their credibility. This ambiguity often takes the form of a vagueness of definition, or even an elision of the problem of definition altogether. As one informant told me,[13]

> I basically define what I did as going after the far enemy. Because I didn't really define terrorism in my book...I'm interested in studying those people that I'm studying, and I know who I'm interested in...the people who did 9/11 and the other guys like them.

Another academic told me that he doesn't define terrorism at all, considering this unproblematic for his work:[14]

---

[13] Interview with Marc Sageman, November 14, 2006.
[14] Interview with Jacob Shapiro, December 14, 2007.

So I don't define terrorism or not. Particular acts are not terrorist or not for me. Terrorist organizations are organizations whose modal use of violence for me violates the standards of distinction in proportionality under the law of armed conflict. So it's basically organizations that mostly make inappropriate uses of violence.

The concept of terrorism must be understood as a moving target: those who wish to stabilize it, even momentarily, find that they are up against a constantly changing set of counter-pressures, reproduced both from within and from without.

Where does this leave the politics of anti-knowledge? As academics seek to stabilize terrorism, it is likely either that they will become irrelevant to broader understandings of "terrorism" in the world, or that they will continue on with a hybrid concept that holds within it both purified and politicized meanings. So, while it is possible that we might see the development of an academically more or less purified terrorism concept as an object of knowledge, as long as terrorism "in the world" retains the meaning of illegitimate violence and irrational evil, terrorism as an object of political and public discourse, and as a site of governance, will remain a moving target. And, although terrorism studies may become a more legitimate subject within the academy, as long as terrorism experts within academia do not have the power to regulate who is treated as an expert in the broader world, and as long as experts on terrorism are still "disciplined" by the taboo on "understanding," they will have difficulty bringing rational explanation to bear on how Americans think about the problem. In the concluding chapter, I address this study's implications for thinking about the relation between expert knowledge and democratic decision-making, and for future studies of expertise.

9 Conclusion: the trouble with experts

Analyses of "terrorism" and the war on terror have tended to assume that experts possess, and wield, a significant amount of power (for example, Bartosiewicz 2008; Burnett and Whyte 2005; Miller and Mills 2009; Mueller 2006). For instance, Richard Jackson, the founding editor of the journal *Critical Studies on Terrorism*, has written in a recent article that "processes of knowledge subjugation function to stabilise meanings, discipline boundaries and maintain hierarchical knowledge-power structures within the broader social structure," and that, consequently, "discourse stabilisation allows the field to perform its key legitimizing role in maintaining state hegemony (Jackson 2012). In other words, he argues that a core group of terrorism experts is dominant, and that it is able to subjugate and exclude other sorts of knowledges, thus maintaining control over the terrorism discourse, which, in turn, legitimizes state power. Jackson argues that terrorism expertise is a hierarchical field, that terrorism experts are able to control both the production of terrorism expertise and the production of expert discourse. Further, he suggests that the discourse on terrorism is stable, and that this is a key reason why it has such power and, moreover, why it is so problematic.

Whereas Jackson and other critics see a hierarchical field of experts enforcing a rigid discourse, this book has shown that the terrorism discourse and the field of terrorism expertise are both highly fluid. As the analysis in the book has revealed, the case of terrorism is one in which experts assuredly do not control the production of knowledge. Rather, "terrorism" has taken shape, often against experts' explicit wishes, as a flexible, unstable site of meaning. Critiques that focus on "terrorism experts" as the producers of politicized meanings tend to elide the fact that terrorism experts are themselves significantly constrained by what I have called the politics of anti-knowledge.

Jackson's approach, and the broader "critical terrorism studies" movement, not only represent an influential approach to terrorism discourse and expertise but also reflect a number of common assumptions in the broader scholarly literature on expertise. The study of expertise has commonly been framed around tensions between expert knowledge and popular decision-making in democratic societies (for example, Brint 1994; Chomsky 2002; Derber, Schwartz, and Magrass 1990; Schudson 2006; Smith 1991), with the key problem generally assumed to be that experts have too much power and control.[1] In accordance with this assumption, studies of knowledge and expertise within sociology have tended to focus on the processes that lead to the production of stable and effective knowledge and expertise. Consequently, many recent empirical studies of the role of experts in politics (for example, Evans 2002; Fourcade 2009; Gilman 2003) have focused on cases in which rationalizing experts have in fact had the power to define agendas and shape decisions. Even studies that have focused on challenges to the authority of experts, such as Steven Epstein's (1996) work on the emergence of "lay expertise" in the AIDS movement, often focus on challenges to the *monopolization* of expert knowledge rather than on the displacement of rational/scientific expertise altogether.

But the case of terrorism is not simply an outlier. Recent work on other areas has observed a similar dispossession of rational/professional expertise, in areas from schooling (Mehta forthcoming) to crime and punishment (Garland 2001). This does not mean that knowledge and expertise no longer matter, but that to analyze their effects we need to look beyond "the claim to intervene in the public sphere in the name of abstract knowledge and universal values," and

---

[1] Occasionally the reverse is also true (Schudson 2006).

pay attention to "a multiplicity of truth-producing practices and modes of intervention" (Eyal and Bucholtz 2010: 123).

Research into the history of the social sciences has frequently pointed out that expertise and policy developed symbiotically in the nineteenth century (Burchell, Gordon, and Miller 1991; Foucault 1970 [1966], 1979 [1975]; Hacking 1999). This relation between expertise and the state has generally been conceived as one that took place by *rationalizing* government and social policy, or even by producing *new* rationalities through techniques such as statistics and mathematical modeling (Desroieres 2002; Porter 1995). Michel Foucault, in his theory of disciplinary power (1979 [1975]), argues that governance in the modern era is based on the creation of knowledge about problematic (and ordinary) populations, in minute detail, and the emergence of associated bodies of experts, who would collect data and create such knowledge. Similarly, James Scott (1998) analyzes how modern states govern territories and populations by making them legible.

Yet the case of terrorism and terrorism expertise, as presented in this book, is one in which the opposite appears to be true. Counter-terrorism in recent years has not relied upon governing the problem by making it legible. Rather than rely upon the creation of knowledge about terrorism, the dominant approach has rejected the very possibility of knowing terrorists. The conceptualization of "terrorism," whose contentious history this book has traced, contains within it a political and moral "truth": that terrorism is *illegitimate* violence. As a result, debates on terrorism invariably develop into contests of judgment as to whether particular acts, and actors, are, or are not, terrorist. But, once an event, an individual, or an organization has been placed into this category, it is easy to assert – as President Bush frequently did – that all we need to know about them is that they are evil.

Where, then, does this leave terrorism experts? As long as "ter-rorism" remains the dominant framework through which Americans make sense of the nexus of power, politics, morality, and violence, those who would create rational knowledge about the problem are on a terrain they cannot control. The discourse of "terrorism" may appear inevitable from our contemporary vantage point, but, as this book has shown, it was not "as necessary as all that" (Foucault 1987: 97). And, while formations of knowledge and practice, once enacted, can be resistant to change, they are not immutable.

References

Abbott, Andrew. 1988. *The System of Professions: An Essay on the Division of Expert Labor*. University of Chicago Press.

Abella, Alex. 2008. *Soldiers of Reason: The RAND Corporation and the Rise of the American Empire*. Orlando, FL: Harcourt.

Ahmad, Eqbal. 2006 [1971]. "Counterinsurgency," in Carollee Bengelsdorf, Margaret Cerullo, and Yogesh Chandrani (eds.), *The Selected Writings of Eqbal Ahmad*, 36–64. New York: Columbia University Press.

Alexander, Yonah, David Carlton, and Paul Wilkinson (eds.). 1979. *Terrorism: Theory and Practice*. Boulder, CO: Westview.

Amoore, Louise, and Marieke de Goede (eds.). 2008. *Risk and the War on Terror*. Abingdon: Routledge.

Arblaster, Anthony. 1977. "Terrorism: myths, meanings, and morals," *Political Studies* **25**: 413–24.

Arquilla, John, and David Ronfeldt. 1996. "The advent of netwar," RAND Corporation, Santa Monica, CA.

Avishai, Bernard. 1979. "In cold blood," *New York Review of Books*, March 8: 41–4.

Babcock, Charles R. 1987. "Ledeen seems to relish Iran insider's role," *Washington Post*, February 2: A1 (available at https://en.wikipedia.org/wiki/Michael_Ledeen).

Barnes, Fred. 2002. "Bush's big speech: it was the one at West Point, not the one on homeland security," *Weekly Standard* **7**: 12–14.

Barron, John. 1983. *KGB Today: The Hidden Hand*. New York: Reader's Digest Association.

Bartosiewicz, Petra. 2008. "Experts in terror," *The Nation*, February 4: 18–22.

Bassiouni, M. Cherif. 1975. *International Terrorism and Political Crimes*. Springfield, IL: Thomas.

Becker, Howard. 1982. *Art Worlds*. Berkeley: University of California Press.

Becker, Jillian. 1985. *The Soviet Connection: State Sponsorship of Terrorism*. London: Alliance Publishers.

Bell, J. Bowyer. 1977. "Trends on terror: the analysis of political violence," *World Politics* **29**: 476–88.

Bell, J. Bowyer. 1978. *A Time of Terror: How Democratic Societies Respond to Revolutionary Violence*. New York: Basic Books.

Benjamin, Daniel, and Steven Simon. 2002. *The Age of Sacred Terror: Radical Islam's War against America.* New York: Random House.

Benjamin, Daniel, and Steven Simon. 2005. *The Next Attack: The Failure of the War on Terror and a Strategy for Getting It Right.* New York: Times Books.

Bergen, Peter. 2003. "Armchair provocateur: Laurie Mylroie: the neocons' favorite conspiracy theorist," *Washington Monthly* **35**: 27–31.

Bergen, Peter. 2011. *The Longest War: The Enduring Conflict between America and al-Qaeda.* New York: Free Press.

Bergen, Peter L. 2002. *Holy War, Inc.: Inside the Secret World of Osama Bin Laden.* New York: Simon & Schuster.

Berlet, Chip, and Matthew N. Lyons. 2000. *Right-Wing Populism in America: Too Close for Comfort.* New York: Guilford Press.

Birtle, Andrew J. 2006. *US Army Counterinsurgency and Contingency Operations Doctrine 1942–1976.* Washington, DC: Center of Military History.

Bliss, Catherine. 2012. *Race Decoded: The Genomic Fight for Social Justice.* Palo Alto, CA: Stanford University Press.

Bloomfield, Lincoln P., and Cornelius J. Gearin. 1973. "Games foreign policy experts play: the political exercise comes of age," *Orbis* **16**: 1012–13.

Blum, William. 2000. *Rogue State: A Guide to the World's Only Superpower.* Monroe, ME: Common Courage Press.

Blumenthal, Ralph. 1993. "Trade Center inquiry: a web of clues," *New York Times*, March 21: 1.

Blumstein, Alfred, and Jesse Orlansky. 1965. *Behavioral, Political, and Operational Research Programs on Counterinsurgency Supported by the Department of Defense.* Alexandria, VA: IDA.

Bodansky, Yossef. 2001. *Bin Laden: The Man Who Declared War on America,* 2nd edn. New York: Random House.

Bogatyrenko, Olga. 2007. "Definitional analysis of terrorism: constructing concepts and populations for social science research," paper presented at 48th annual convention of the International Studies Association, Chicago, February 28.

Borgatti, Steven P., Martin G. Everett, and Lin C. Freeman. 2002. *UCINET 6.0 for Windows: Software for Social Network Analysis: User's Guide.* Harvard, MA: Analytic Technologies.

Boston, Guy D. 1977. *Terrorism: A Selected Bibliography: Supplement to the Second Edition,* US Department of Justice, Rockville, MD.

Boston, Guy D., Marvin Marcus, and Robert J. Wheaton. 1976. *Terrorism: A Selected Bibliography.* Washington, DC: US Department of Justice.

Bourdieu, Pierre. 1988 [1984]. *Homo Academicus* (trans. Peter Collier). Palo Alto, CA: Stanford University Press.

Bourdieu, Pierre. 1993 [1983]. *The Field of Cultural Production: Essays on Art and Literature* (trans. Claud DuVerlie). New York: Columbia University Press.

Bourdieu, Pierre. 1996 [1992]. *The Rules of Art: Genesis and Structure of the Literary Field* (trans. Susan Emanuel). Cambridge: Polity Press.

Bourdieu, Pierre. 2005. "The political field, the social science field, and the journalistic field," in Rodney Benson and Erik Neveu (eds.), *Bourdieu and the Journalistic Field*, 29–47. Cambridge: Polity Press.

Bourdieu, Pierre, and Loïc J. D. Wacquant. 1992. *An Invitation to Reflexive Sociology*. University of Chicago Press.

Bowker, Geoffrey C., and Susan Leigh Star. 1999. *Sorting Things Out: Classification and Its Consequences*. Cambridge, MA: MIT Press.

Brannan, David W., Philip F. Esler, and N. T. Anders Strindberg. 2001. "Talking to 'terrorists': towards an independent analytical framework for the study of violent substate activism," *Studies in Conflict and Terrorism* **24**: 3–24.

Braungart, Richard G., and Margaret M. Braungart. 1981. "Survey essay: international terrorism: background and responses," *Journal of Political and Military Sociology* **9**: 263–88.

Brewer, Garry D. 1974. "Gaming: prospective for forecasting," RAND Corporation, Santa Monica, CA.

Brint, Steven. 1994. *In an Age of Experts: The Changing Role of Professionals in Politics and Public Life*. Princeton University Press.

Burchell, Graham, Colin Gordon, and Peter Miller. 1991. *The Foucault Effect: Studies in Governmentality*. University of Chicago Press.

Burnett, Jonny, and Dave Whyte. 2005. "Embedded expertise and the new terrorism," *Journal for Crime, Conflict and the Media* **1**: 1–18.

Bush, George W. 2002. *The National Security Strategy of the United States of America: September 2002*. New York: Morgan James Publishing.

Bush, George W. 2006. *The National Security Strategy of the United States of America: March 2006*. New York: Morgan James Publishing.

Butler, Judith. 2010. *Precarious Life: The Powers of Mourning and Violence*. New York: Verso.

Callon, Michel. 1986. "Some elements of a sociology of translation: domestication of the scallops and the fishermen of St Brieuc Bay," in John Law (ed.), *Power, Action, and Belief: A New Sociology of Knowledge?*, 196–223. Abingdon: Routledge.

Cameron, Gavin. 2000. "Freedom, hate, and violence on the American right," *Studies in Conflict and Terrorism* **23**: 197–204.

Carr, Matthew. 2006. *The Infernal Machine: A History of Terrorism*. New York: New Press.

Carter, Ashton B., John Deutch, and Philip Zelikow. 1998. "Catastrophic terrorism: tackling the new danger," *Foreign Affairs* **77**: 80–94.

Carter, Ashton B., and William B. Perry. 1999. *Preventive Defense: A New Security Strategy for America*. Washington, DC: Brookings Institution Press.

Center for American Progress. 2006. *The Terrorism Index: A Survey of US National Security Experts on the War on Terror*. Washington, DC: Center for American Progress.

Cheney, Dick. 2011. *In My Time: A Personal and Political Memoir*. New York: Simon & Schuster.

Chomsky, Noam. 1986. *Pirates and Emperors: International Terrorism in the Real World*. New York: Claremont Research and Publications.

Chomsky, Noam. 2001. "Middle East terrorism and the American ideological system," in Edward W. Said and Christopher Hitchens (eds.), *Blaming the Victims: Spurious Scholarship and the Palestinian Question*, 2nd edn, 97–146. New York: Verso.

Chomsky, Noam. 2002. *American Power and the New Mandarins*, 2nd edn. New York: The New Press.

Chomsky, Noam. 2003. *Hegemony or Survival: America's Quest for Global Dominance*. London: Hamish Hamilton.

Chomsky, Noam, and Edward S. Herman. 1979. *The Political Economy of Human Rights*. Nottingham: Spokesman Books.

Clarke, Richard A. 2004. *Against All Enemies: Inside America's War on Terror*. New York: Free Press.

Cline, Ray S., and Yonah Alexander. 1984. *Terrorism: The Soviet Connection*. New York: Crane Russak.

Cline, Ray S., and Yonah Alexander. 1986. *Terrorism as State-Sponsored Covert Warfare: What the Free World Must Do to Protect Itself*. Fairfax, VA: Hero Books.

Clutterbuck, Richard. 1977. *Guerrillas and Terrorists*. London: Faber & Faber.

Cohen, Patricia. 2012. "At museum on 9/11, talking through an identity crisis," *New York Times*, June 3: A1.

Collier, Stephen J., and Andrew Lakoff. 2008. "The vulnerability of vital systems: how 'critical infrastructure' became a security problem," in Myriam Dunn Cavelty and Kristian Søby Kristensen (eds.), *Securing the Homeland: Critical Infrastructure, Risk, and (In)Security*, 17–39. Abingdon: Routledge.

Collier, Stephen J., Andrew Lakoff, and Paul Rabinow. 2004. "Biosecurity: towards an anthropology of the contemporary," *Anthropology Today* **20**: 3–7.

Colvard, Karen. 1996. "The politics of violence," *HFG Review* **1**: 3–8.

Cooper, Melinda. 2010. "Turbulence: between financial and environmental crisis," *Theory, Culture, and Society* **27**: 1–24.

Copeland, Thomas. 2001. "Is the 'new terrorism' really new? An analysis of the new paradigm for terrorism," *Journal of Conflict Studies* **21** : 7–27.

Coxe, Betsy. 1977. "Terrorism." US Air Force Academy, Colorado Springs.

Crane, Diana. 1976. "Reward systems in art, science, and religion," *American Behavioral Scientist* **6**: 719–34.

Crelinsten, Ronald D. (ed.). 1977. *Final Report on Research Strategies for the Study of International Political Terrorism*. Montreal: International Centre for Comparative Criminology, University of Montreal.

Crelinsten, Ronald D. 1989a. "Images of terrorism in the media: 1966–1985," *Terrorism* **12**: 167–98.

Crelinsten, Ronald D. 1989b. "Terrorism, counter-terrorism and democracy: the assessment of national security threats," *Terrorism and Political Violence* **1**: 242–69.

Crelinsten, Ronald D., Danielle Laberge-Altmejd, and Denis Szabo. 1976. *Final Report on Management Training Seminar: Hostage Taking: Problems of Prevention and Control*. Montreal: International Centre for Comparative Criminology, University of Montreal.

Crelinsten, Ronald D., and Alex P. Schmid. 1993. "Western responses to terrorism: a twenty-five year balance sheet," in Alex P. Schmid and Ronald D. Crelinsten (eds.), *Western Responses to Terrorism*, 307–40. London: Frank Cass.

Crenshaw, Martha. 1983. *Terrorism, Legitimacy, and Power: The Consequences of Political Violence*. Middletown, CT: Wesleyan University Press.

Crenshaw, Martha. 1995. *Terrorism in Context*. University Park: Pennsylvania State University Press.

Crenshaw, Martha. 1996. "Review of *Fighting Terrorism: How Democracies Can Defeat Terrorism*," *Terrorism and Political Violence* **8**: 177–9.

Crenshaw, Martha. 2009. "The debate over 'new' vs. 'old' terrorism," in Ibrahim A. Karawan, Wayne McCormack, and Stephen E. Reynolds (eds.), *Values and Violence: Intangible Aspects of Terrorism*, 117–36. Dordrecht, Netherlands: Springer.

Crozier, Brian. 1959. "Anatomy of terrorism," *The Nation* **188**: 250–2.

Crozier, Brian. 1960. *The Rebels: A Study of Post-War Insurrections*. Boston: Beacon Press.

DeLeon, Peter. 1973. "Scenario designs: an overview." RAND Corporation, Santa Monica, CA.

Derber, Charles, William A. Schwartz, and Yale Magrass. 1990. *Power in the Highest Degree: Professionals and the Rise of a New Mandarin Order*. New York: Oxford University Press.

Dershowitz, Alan M. 2002. *Why Terrorism Works: Understanding the Threat, Responding to the Challenge*. New Haven, CT: Yale University Press.

Desroieres, Alain. 2002. *The Politics of Large Numbers: A History of Statistical Reasoning*. Cambridge, MA: Harvard University Press.

Dick, Philip K. 2002 [1953]. *Minority Report*. London: Orion Books.

Dionne, Eugene J., Jr. 1990. "'Defense intellectuals' in a new world order; RAND analysts rethink the study of conflict," *Washington Post*, May 29: A10.

Douglass, William A., and Joseba Zulaika. 1990. "On the interpretation of terrorist violence: ETA and the Basque political process," *Comparative Studies in Society and History* **32**: 238–57.

Duyvesteyn, Isabelle. 2004. "How new is the new terrorism?," *Studies in Conflict and Terrorism* **27**: 439–54.

Easson, Joseph J., and Alex P. Schmid. 2011. "Appendix 2.1: 250-plus academic, governmental, and intergovernmental definitions of terrorism," in Alex P. Schmid (ed.), *The Routledge Handbook of Terrorism Research*, 98–144. Abingdon: Routledge.

Easton, Nina J. 2001. "Putting theory into practice: those once-obscure terrorism experts are now trying to answer the tough questions – as the world watches," *Los Angeles Times*, November 18: E1.

Eckstein, Harry (ed.). 1964. *Internal War: Problems and Approaches*. New York: Free Press of Glencoe.

Edelman, Murray. 1988. *Constructing the Political Spectacle*. University of Chicago Press.

Eisenberg, Eric M. 1984. "Ambiguity as strategy in organizational communication," *Communication Monographs* **51**: 227–42.

Emerson, Steven, and Cristina Del Cesto. 1991. *Terrorist: The Inside Story of the Highest-Ranking Iraqi Terrorist Ever to Defect to the West*. New York: Villard Books.

Emerson, Steven, and Brian Duffy. 1990. *The Fall of Pan Am 103: Inside the Lockerbie Investigation*. London: Penguin Books.

Epstein, Steven. 1996. *Impure Science: AIDS, Activism, and the Politics of Knowledge*. Berkeley: University of California Press.

Ericson, Richard V. 2008. "The state of preemption: managing terrorism through counter law," in Louise Amoore and Marieke de Goede (eds.), *Risk and the War on Terror*, 57–76. Abingdon: Routledge.

Espeland, Wendy Nelson, and Mitchell L. Stevens. 1998. "Commensuration as a social process," *Annual Review of Sociology* **24**: 313–43.

Espeland, Wendy Nelson, and Mitchell L. Stevens. 2008. "A sociology of quantification," *European Journal of Sociology* **49**: 401–36.

Esposito, John. 1999. *The Islamic Threat: Myth or Reality?*, 3rd edn. Oxford University Press.

Evans, Alona, and John F. Murphy. 1978. *Legal Aspects of International Terrorism*. Lexington, MA: D. C. Heath.

Evans, John. 2002. *Playing God? Human Genetic Engineering and the Rationalization of Public Bioethical Debate*. University of Chicago Press.

Ewald, François. 2002. "The return of Descartes's malicious demon: an outline of a philosophy of precaution" (trans. Stephen Utz), in Tom Baker and Jonathan Simon (eds.), *Embracing Risk: The Changing Culture of Insurance and Responsibility*, 273–301. University of Chicago Press.

Eyal, Gil. 2002. "Dangerous liaisons between military intelligence and Middle Eastern studies in Israel," *Theory and Society* **31**: 653–93.

Eyal, Gil. 2006. *The Disenchantment of the Orient: Expertise in Arab Affairs and the Israeli State*. Palo Alto, CA: Stanford University Press.

Eyal, Gil, and Larissa Bucholtz. 2010. "From the sociology of intellectuals to the sociology of interventions," *Annual Review of Sociology* **36**: 117–37.

Fairbairn, Geoffrey. 1974. *Revolutionary Guerrilla Warfare: The Countryside Version*: London: Penguin Books.

Falkenrath, Richard A., Robert D. Newman, and Bradley A. Thayer. 1998. *America's Achilles Heel: Nuclear, Biological, and Chemical Terrorism and Covert Action*. Cambridge, MA: MIT Press.

Faludi, Susan. 2007. *The Terror Dream: Myth and Misogyny in an Insecure America*. New York: Picador.

Farrell, William Regis. 1982. *The US Government Response to Terrorism: In Search of an Effective Strategy*. Boulder, CO: Westview Press.

Ferguson, James. 1994. *The Anti-Politics Machine: "Development," Depoliticization, and Bureaucratic Power in Lesotho*. Minneapolis: University of Minnesota Press.

Fine, Gary Alan. 1999. "John Brown's body: elites, heroic embodiment, and the legitimation of political violence," *Social Problems* **46**: 225–49.

Fischman, Josh. 2012. "Bird-flu papers, recently deemed too dangerous, are freed for publication," *Chronicle of Higher Education*, March 30, http://chronicle.com/article/Bird-Flu-Papers-Recently/131412.

Fligstein, Neil. 2001. "Social skill and the theory of fields," *Sociological Theory* **19**: 105–25.

Fligstein, Neil, and Doug McAdam. 2012. *A Theory of Fields*. Oxford University Press.

Foucault, Michel. 1970 [1966]. *The Order of Things: An Archaeology of the Human Sciences* (trans. Robert Hurley). New York: Random House.

Foucault, Michel. 1979 [1975]. *Discipline and Punish: The Birth of the Prison* (trans. Alan Sheridan). New York: Vintage Books.

Foucault, Michel. 1987. "Questions of method: an interview with Michel Foucault," in Kenneth Baynes, James Bohman, and Thomas McCarthy (eds.), *After Philosophy: End or Transformation?*, 95–117. Boston: MIT Press.

Foucault, Michel. 1991. "Politics and the study of discourse," in Graham Burchell, Colin Gordon, and Peter Miller (eds.), *The Foucault Effect: Studies in Governmentality*, 53–72. University of Chicago Press.

Foucault, Michel. 2003. "Questions of method," in Paul Rabinow and Nikolas Rose (eds.), *The Essential Foucault*, 246–58. New York: New Press.

Fourcade, Marion. 2009. *Economists and Societies: Discipline and Profession in the United States, Britain, and France, 1890s to 1990s*. Princeton University Press.

Fowler, William W. 1980. "An agenda for quantitative research on terrorism," RAND Corporation, Santa Monica, CA.

Fowler, William W. 1981. "Terrorism data bases: a comparison of missions, methods, and systems," RAND Corporation, Santa Monica, CA.

Freedman, Benjamin. 2010. "Terrorism research centres: 100 institutes, programs, and organisations in the field of terrorism, counter-terrorism, radicalisation and asymmetric warfare studies," *Perspectives on Terrorism* **4**: 48–56.

Frickel, Scott. 2004. "Building an interdiscipline: collective action framing and the rise of genetic toxicology," *Social Problems* **51**: 269–87.

Frickel, Scott, and Neil Gross. 2005. "A general theory of scientific/intellectual movements," *American Sociological Review* **70**: 204–32.

Frost, Gerald. 1985. "Preface," in Jillian Becker, *The Soviet Connection: State Sponsorship of Terrorism*, 5–7. London: Alliance Publishers.

Frum, David, and Richard Perle. 2003. *An End to Evil: How to Win the War on Terror*. New York: Random House.

Galula, David. 1964. *Counter-Insurgency Warfare: Theory and Practice*. New York: Praeger.

Garland, David. 2001. *The Culture of Control: Crime and Social Order in Contemporary Society*. Oxford University Press.

Gendzier, Irene. 1998. "Play it again Sam: the practice and apology of development," in Christopher Simpson (ed.), *Universities and Empire: Money and Politics in the Social Sciences during the Cold War*, 57–96. New York: New Press.

Ghamari-Tabrizi, Sharon. 2005. *The Worlds of Herman Kahn: The Intuitive Science of Thermonuclear War*. Cambridge, MA: Harvard University Press.

Gieryn, Thomas. 1983. "Boundary work and the demarcation of science from non-science: strains and interests in professional ideologies of scientists," *American Sociological Review* **48**: 781–95.

Gilman, Nils. 2003. *Mandarins of the Future: Modernization Theory in Cold War America*. Baltimore: Johns Hopkins University Press.

Gold-Biss, Michael. 1994. *The Discourse on Terrorism: Political Violence and the Subcommittee on Security and Terrorism, 1981–1986*. New York: Peter Lang.

Goldhamer, Herbert, and Hans Speier. 1959. "Some observations on political gaming," *World Politics* **12**: 71–83.

Gonzales, Roberto J. 2009. *American Counterinsurgency: Human Science and the Human Terrain*. Chicago: Prickly Paradigm Press.

Goodnight, G. Thomas. 2005. "Strategic doctrine, public debate, and the terror war," in William W. Keller and Gordon R. Mitchell (eds.), *Hitting First: Preventive Force in US Security Strategy*, 93–114. University of Pittsburgh Press.

Goren, Roberta. 1984. *The Soviet Union and Terrorism*. New York: HarperCollins.

Gordon, Avishag. 1995. "Terrorism and computerized databases: an examination of multidisciplinary coverage," *Terrorism and Political Violence* **7**: 171–7.

Gordon, Avishag. 1996. "Terrorism and science, technology and medicine databases: new concepts and terminology," *Terrorism and Political Violence* **8**: 167–73.

Gordon, Avishag. 1997. "Terrorism on the internet: discovering the unsought," *Terrorism and Political Violence* **9**: 159–65.

Gordon, Avishag. 1998. "The spread of terrorism publications: a database analysis," *Terrorism and Political Violence* **10**: 190–3.

Gordon, Avishag. 2001. "Terrorism and the scholarly communication system," *Terrorism and Political Violence* **13**: 116–24.

Gordon, Avishag. 2004a. "The effect of database and website inconstancy on the terrorism field's delineation," *Studies in Conflict and Terrorism* **27**: 79–88.

Gordon, Avishag. 2004b. "Terrorism and knowledge growth: a databases and internet analysis," in Andrew Silke (ed.), *Research on Terrorism: Trends, Achievements and Failures*, 104–18. London: Frank Cass.

Gordon, Avishag. 2005. "Terrorism as an academic subject after 9/11: searching the internet reveals a Stockholm syndrome trend," *Studies in Conflict and Terrorism* **28**: 45–9.

Gordon, Avishag. 2010. "Can terrorism become a scientific discipline? A diagnostic study," *Critical Studies on Terrorism* **3**: 437–58.

Guelke, Adrian B. 1995. *The Age of Terrorism and the International Political System*. London: I. B. Tauris.

Gusfield, Joseph. 1981. *The Culture of Public Problems: Drinking-Driving and the Symbolic Order*. University of Chicago Press.

Hacking, Ian. 1999. *The Social Construction of What?*. Cambridge, MA: Harvard University Press.

Herman, Edward S. 1982. *The Real Terror Network: Terrorism in Fact and Propaganda*. Boston: South End Press.

Herman, Edward S., and Gerry O'Sullivan. 1989. *The "Terrorism" Industry: The Experts and Institutions that Shape Our View of Terror*. New York: Pantheon Books.

Herman, Ellen. 1998. "Project Camelot and the career of cold war psychology," in Christopher Simpson (ed.), *Universities and Empire: Money and Politics in the Social Sciences during the Cold War*, 97–133. New York: New Press.

Hersh, Seymour M. 2004. *Chain of Command: The Road from 9/11 to Abu Ghraib*. New York: HarperCollins.

Hilgartner, Stephen. 2000. *Science on Stage: Expert Advice as Public Drama*. Palo Alto, CA: Stanford University Press.

Hitchens, Christopher. 1986. "Wanton acts of usage: terrorism: a cliché in search of a meaning," *Harper's*, September: 66–70.

Hocking, Jenny. 1984. "Orthodox theories of 'terrorism': the power of politicized terminology," *Politics* **19**: 103–10.

Hoffman, Bruce. 1991. "An agenda for research on terrorism and LIC in the 1990s." RAND Corporation, Santa Monica, CA.

Hoffman, Bruce. 1998. *Inside Terrorism*. New York: Columbia University Press.

Hoffman, Bruce. 2004. "Foreword," in Andrew Silke (ed.), *Research on Terrorism: Trends, Achievements and Failures*, xvii–xix. London: Frank Cass.

Hoffman, Bruce. 2006. *Inside Terrorism*, rev, expanded edn. New York: Columbia University Press.

Hoffman, Robert Paul. 1984. "Terrorism: a universal definition," MA thesis, Claremont Graduate School, CA.

Holloway, David. 2008. *9/11 and the War on Terror*. Edinburgh University Press.

Horowitz, Irving L. 1967. *The Rise and Fall of Project Camelot: Studies in the Relationship between Social Science and Practical Politics*. Cambridge, MA: MIT Press.

Horowitz, Irving L. 1973. "Political terrorism and state power," *Political and Military Sociology* **1**: 147–57.

Hosmer, Stephen T., and Sibylle O. Crane. 2006 [1963]. *Counterinsurgency: A Symposium, April 16–20, 1962*. Santa Monica, CA: RAND Publishing.

Huntington, Samuel. 1993. "The clash of civilizations?," *Foreign Affairs* **72**: 22–49.

IFPA. 1985. *Terrorism and Other "Low-Intensity" Operations: International Linkages: Fourteenth Annual Conference, Held at the Cabot Intercultural Center, Medford, Mass., April 17–19, 1985*. Cambridge, MA: IFPA.

Ilardi, Gaetano Joe. 2004. "Redefining the issues: the future of terrorism research and the search for empathy," in Andrew Silke (ed.), *Research on Terrorism: Trends, Achievements and Failures*, 214–28. London: Frank Cass.

Jackson, Richard. 2005. *Writing the War on Terrorism: Language, Politics, and Counter-Terrorism*. Manchester University Press.

Jackson, Richard. 2009. "The study of terrorism after 11 September 2001: problems, challenges and future developments," *Political Studies Review* **7**: 171–84.

Jackson, Richard. 2012. "Unknown knowns: the subjugated knowledge of terrorism studies," *Critical Studies on Terrorism* 5: 11–29.

Jacobs, Ronald N. 1996. "Civil society and crisis: culture, discourse, and the Rodney King beating," *American Journal of Sociology* 101: 1238–72.

Jayasuriya, Kanishka. 2002. "September 11, security, and the new postliberal politics of fear," in Eric Hershberg and Kevin W. Moore (eds.), *Critical Views of September 11: Analyses from Around the World*, 131–47. New York: New Press.

Jehl, Douglas. 1993a. "Car bombs: a tool of foreign terror, little known in the US," *New York Times*, February 27: 1.

Jehl, Douglas. 1993b. "A lack of definitive claim for attack baffles officials," *New York Times*, March 1: 1.

Jehl, Douglas. 1993c. "Americans feel terror's senseless logic," *New York Times*, March 7: 1–3.

Jenkins, Brian M. 1971. "The five stages of urban guerrilla warfare: challenge of the 1970s," RAND Corporation, Santa Monica, CA.

Jenkins, Brian M. 1972. "An urban strategy for guerrillas and governments," RAND Corporation, Santa Monica, CA.

Jenkins, Brian M. 1982. "Terrorism and beyond: an international conference on terrorism and low-level conflict." RAND Corporation, Santa Monica, CA.

Jenkins, Brian M. 1983. "Research in terrorism: areas of consensus, areas of ignorance," in Burr Eichelman, David A. Soskis, and William H. Reid (eds.), *Terrorism: Interdisciplinary Perspectives*, 153–77. Washington, DC: American Psychiatric Association.

Jenkins, Brian M. 2006. *Unconquerable Nation: Knowing Our Enemy, Strengthening Ourselves*. Santa Monica, CA: RAND Publishing.

Jenkins, Brian M., and Janera A. Johnson. 1975. "International terrorism: a chronology, 1968–1974," RAND Corporation, Santa Monica, CA.

Jenkins, Brian M., and Janera A. Johnson. 1976. "International terrorism: a chronology (1974 supplement)," RAND Corporation, Santa Monica, CA.

Johnson, Chalmers. 1976. "Perspectives on terrorism," University of California, Berkeley.

Johnson, Chalmers. 2000. *Blowback: The Costs and Consequences of American Empire*. New York: Henry Holt.

Jones, David Martin, and Michael L. R. Smith. 2006. "The commentariat and discourse failure: language and atrocity in cool Britannia," *International Affairs* 82: 1117–24.

Juergensmeyer, Mark. 2003. *Terror in the Mind of God: The Global Rise of Religious Violence*, 3rd edn. Berkeley: University of California Press.

Kahn, Ely Jacques, Jr. 1978. "How do we explain them?," *The New Yorker*, June 12: 37–62.

Kean, Thomas H., and Lee H. Hamilton. 2006. *Without Precedent: The Inside Story of the 9/11 Commission*. New York: Alfred A. Knopf.

Kelly, John D., Beatrice Jauregui, Sean T. Mitchell, and Jeremy Walton. 2010. *Anthropology and Global Counterinsurgency*. University of Chicago Press.

Kempe, Frederick. 1983. "Violent tactics: Soviet Union's role in global terrorism is subject of debate," *Wall Street Journal*, April 26: 1, 22.

Khan, Liaquat Ali. 2006. "The essentialist terrorist," *Washburn Law Journal* **45**: 47–88.

Kitson, Frank. 1974 [1971]. *Low Intensity Operations: Subversion, Insurgency and Peacekeeping*. Hamden, CT: Archon Books.

Klare, Michael T., and Peter Kornbluh. 1988. *Low-Intensity Warfare: Counterinsurgency, Proinsurgency, and Antiterrorism in the Eighties*. New York: Pantheon Books.

Kramer, Martin. 1993. "Islam vs. democracy," *Commentary* **95**: 35–42.

Kramer, Martin. 2001. *Ivory Towers on Sand: The Failure of Middle Eastern Studies in America*. Washington, DC: Washington Institute for Near East Policy.

Kupperman, Robert H. 1977. *Facing Tomorrow's Terrorist Incident Today*. Washington, DC: LEAA.

Lakoff, Andrew. 2007. "Preparing for the next emergency," *Public Culture* **19**: 247–71.

Lamont, Michele, and Virag Molnar. 2002. "The study of boundaries in the social sciences," *Annual Review of Sociology* **28**: 167–95.

Lampland, Martha, and Susan Leigh Star. 2009. *Standards and Their Stories: How Quantifying, Classifying, and Formalizing Practices Shape Everyday Life*. Ithaca, NY: Cornell University Press.

Laqueur, Walter. 1974. "Guerillas and terrorists," *Commentary* **58**: 40–8.

Laqueur, Walter. 1999. *The New Terrorism: Fanaticism and the Arms of Mass Destruction*. New York: Oxford University Press.

Laqueur, Walter. 2001. "Left, right, and beyond: the changing face of terror," in James F. Hoge, Jr., and Gideon Rose (eds.), *How Did This Happen?: Terrorism and the New War*, 71–82. New York: PublicAffairs.

Lardner, George, Jr. 1981. "Assault on terrorism: internal security or witch hunt?," *Washington Post*, April 20: A1, A11.

Larson, Magali Sarfatti. 1977. *The Rise of Professionalism: A Sociological Analysis*. Berkeley: University of California Press.

Latour, Bruno. 1987. *Science in Action: How to Follow Engineers and Scientists through Society* (trans. Catherine Porter). Cambridge, MA: Harvard University Press.

Latour, Bruno. 1993 [1991]. *We Have Never Been Modern* (trans. Catherine Porter). Cambridge, MA: Harvard University Press.

Latour, Bruno. 2005. *Reassembling the Social: An Introduction to Actor-Network Theory*. Oxford University Press.

Lesser, Ian O., Bruce Hoffman, John Arquilla, David Ronfeldt, Michele Zanini, and Brian M. Jenkins. 1999. *Countering the New Terrorism*. Santa Monica, CA: RAND Publishing.

Lewis, Bernard. 1990. "The roots of Muslim rage," *Atlantic Monthly*, **266**: 47–60.

Livingston, Marius H., Lee Bruce Kress, and Marie G. Wanek (eds.). 1978. *International Terrorism in the Contemporary World*. Westport, CT: Greenwood Press.

Los Angeles Times. 1972a. "World leaders voice horror, condemnation," *Los Angeles Times*, September 6: A11.

Los Angeles Times. 1972b. "Olympics tragedy seen destroying Arab cause," *Los Angeles Times*, September 7: A23.

Lum, Cynthia, Leslie W. Kennedy, and Alison J. Sherley. 2006. "The effectiveness of counter-terrorism strategies," *Journal of Experimental Criminology* 2: 489–516.

Lustick, Ian S. 2006. *Trapped in the War on Terror*. Philadelphia: University of Pennsylvania Press.

Lybrand, William (ed.). 1962. *Proceedings of the Symposium "The US Army's Limited-War Mission and Social Science Research," March 26–28, 1962*. Washington, DC: SORO.

Lyons, Gene M. 1969. *The Uneasy Partnership: Social Science and the Federal Government in the Twentieth Century*. New York: Russell Sage Foundation.

McClintock, Michael. 1992. *Instruments of Statecraft: US Guerrilla Warfare, Counterinsurgency, and Counterterrorism, 1940–1990*. New York: Pantheon Books.

McDowell, Edwin. 1980. "Behind the best sellers: Arnaud de Borchgrave and Robert Moss," *New York Times*, June 22: 8.

Maechling, Charles, Jr. 1988. "Counterinsurgency: the first ordeal by fire," in Michael T. Klare and Peter Kornbluh (eds.), *Low-Intensity Warfare: Counterinsurgency, Proinsurgency, and Antiterrorism in the Eighties*, 21–48. New York: Pantheon Books.

Mandel, Robert. 1977. "Political gaming and foreign policy making during crises," *World Politics* **29**: 610–25.

Mann, James. 2004. *Rise of the Vulcans: The History of Bush's War Cabinet*. New York: Viking Penguin.

Manwaring, Max G. 1993. *Gray Area Phenomenon: Confronting the New World Disorder*. Boulder, CO: Westview Press.

Marlowe, Ann. 2010. *David Galula: His Life and Intellectual Context*. Carlisle, PA: Strategic Studies Institute.

Martin, Aryn, and Michael Lynch. 2009. "Counting things and people: the practices and politics of counting," *Social Problems* **56**: 243–66.

Martin, John Levi. 2003. "What is field theory?," *American Journal of Sociology* **109**: 1–49.

Marx, Karl. 1994 [1852]. *The Eighteenth Brumaire of Louis Bonaparte*. New York: International Publishers.

Mayer, Jane. 2008. *The Dark Side: The Inside Story of How the War on Terror Turned into a War on American Ideals*. New York: Anchor Books.

Medvetz, Thomas. 2012. *Think Tanks in America*. University of Chicago Press.

Mehta, Jal. Forthcoming. *The Chastened Dream* (book manuscript in progress). Harvard Graduate School of Education, Cambridge, MA.

Merari, Ariel. 1991. "Academic research and government policy on terrorism," in Clark McCauley (ed.), *Terrorism Research and Public Policy*, 88–102. London: Frank Cass.

Merkl, Peter H., and Leonard Weinberg (eds.). 1997. *The Revival of Right-Wing Extremism in the Nineties*. London: Frank Cass.

Mickolus, Edward F. 1976. *Annotated Bibliography on Transnational and International Terrorism*. Washington, DC: CIA.

Mickolus, Edward F. 1980. *The Literature of Terrorism: A Selectively Annotated Bibliography*. Westport, CT: Greenwood Press.

Mickolus, Edward F. 1981. "Combating international terrorism: a quantitative analysis," PhD dissertation, Yale University, New Haven, CT.

Mickolus, Edward F., Edward S. Heyman, and James Schlotter. 1980. "Responding to terrorism: basic and applied research," in Richard H. Shultz, Jr., and Stephen Sloan (eds.), *Responding to the Terrorist Threat: Security and Crisis Management*, 174–87. New York: Pergamon.

Milbank, David L. 1976. *International and Transnational Terrorism: Diagnosis and Prognosis*. Washington, DC: CIA.

Miller, David, and Tom Mills. 2009. "The terror experts and the mainstream media: the expert nexus and its dominance in the news media," *Critical Studies on Terrorism* **2**: 414–37.

Miller, Judith. 1993. "The challenge of radical Islam," *Foreign Affairs* **72**: 43–56.

Mitchell, Gordon R., and Robert P. Newman. 2006. "By 'any measures' necessary: NSC-68 and Cold War roots of the 2002 national security strategy," in William W. Keller and Gordon R. Mitchell (eds.), *Hitting First: Preventive Force in US Security Strategy*, 70–90. University of Pittsburgh Press.

Mooney, Chris. 2005. *The Republican War on Science*. New York: Basic Books.

Moss, Robert. 1972. *Urban Guerrillas: The New Face of Political Violence*. London: Temple Smith.

Moss, Robert. 1980. "Terror: a Soviet export," *New York Times Magazine*, November 2: 42–58.

Mueller, John. 2006. *Overblown: How Politicians and the Terrorism Industry Inflate National Security Threats, and Why We Believe Them*. New York: Free Press.

Murphy, John F. 1980. *Legal Aspects of International Terrorism: Summary Report of an International Conference, December 13–15, 1978, Washington, DC*. Washington, DC: ASIL.

Mylroie, Laurie. 2000. *Study of Revenge: Saddam Hussein's Unfinished War against America*. Washington, DC: AEI Press.

Naftali, Timothy. 2005. *Blind Spot: The Secret History of American Counterterrorism*. New York: Basic Books.

National Commission on Terrorist Attacks. 2004. *The 9/11 Commission Report: Final Report of the National Commision on Terrorist Attacks upon the United States*. New York: W. W. Norton.

Nelson, Barbara J. 1984. *Making an Issue of Child Abuse: Political Agenda Setting for Social Problems*. University of Chicago Press.

Netanyahu, Benjamin (ed.). 1980. *International Terrorism: Challenge and Response: Proceedings of the Jerusalem Conference on International Terrorism (1979)*. Jerusalem: Jonathan Institute.

Netanyahu, Benjamin (ed.). 1984. *Terrorism: How the West Can Win*. New York: Farrar Straus Giroux.

Network of Concerned Anthropologists. 2009. *The Counter-Counterinsurgency Manual: Or, Notes on Demilitarizing American Society*. Chicago: Prickly Paradigm Press.

New York Times. 1961a. "Two hijack jetliner and hold it nine hours," *New York Times*, August 4: 1.

New York Times. 1961b. "The hijackers," *New York Times*, August 6: E2.

New York Times. 1961c. "US jury indicts Beardens in airliner hijacking," *New York Times*, August 8: 2.

New York Times. 1961d. "Airliner's hijacker gets life sentence," *New York Times*, November 1: 79.

New York Times. 1963. "Partial reversal is won by jet plane hijacker," *New York Times*, July 11: 43.

New York Times. 1964. "Violence is rare aboard aircraft," *New York Times*, May 9: 54.

New York Times. 1965a. "Cuban exile fails in attempt to seize airliner over Florida," *New York Times*, October 27: 21.

New York Times. 1965b. "Jet hijacking attempt laid to hate for communism," *New York Times*, November 19: 14.

New York Times. 1972a. "Murder in Munich." *New York Times*, September 6: 44.

New York Times. 1972b. "Munich, 1972," *New York Times*, September 7: 42.

New York Times. 1987. "Despite success, research centers are rebuffed by two universities," *New York Times*, November 28: 46.

Norton, Augustus R. 1981. "International terrorism: a review essay," *Armed Forces and Society* 7: 597–627.

Norton, Augustus R., and Martin H. Greenberg. 1980. *International Terrorism: An Annotated Bibliography and Research Guide.* Boulder, CO: Westview Press.

O'Brien, Conor Cruise. 1976. "Reflections on terrorism," *New York Review of Books*, September 16: 48.

Olick, Jeffrey K., and Joyce Robbins. 1998. "Social memory studies: from 'collective memory' to the historical sociology of mnemonic practices," *Annual Review of Sociology* 24: 105–40.

Paget, Julian. 1967. *Counter-Insurgency Operations: Techniques of Guerrilla Warfare.* New York: Walker.

Panofsky, Aaron L. 2006. "Fielding controversy: the genesis and structure of behavior genetics," PhD dissertation, New York University.

Pape, Robert. 2005. *Dying to Win: The Strategic Logic of Suicide Terrorism.* New York: Random House.

Paull, Philip. 1982. "International terrorism: the propaganda war," MA thesis, San Francisco State University.

Perenyi, Peter. 1972. "State Department conference on terrorism: summary of conference sponsored by the Bureau of Intelligence and Research and the Planning and Coordination Staff," External Research Study no. XR/RNAS-21. US Department of State, Washington, DC.

Persico, Joseph E. 1990. *Casey: From the OSS to the CIA.* New York: Viking.

Peterson, Richard A. 1976. "The production of culture," *American Behavioral Scientist* 19: 669–84.

Peterson, Richard A., and Naramsimhan Anand. 2004. "The production of culture perspective," *Annual Review of Sociology* 30: 311–34.

Pipes, Daniel. 1990. "The Muslims are coming! The Muslims are coming!," *The National Review*, November 19: 28–31.

Pipes, Daniel. 1995. "There are no moderates: dealing with fundamentalist Islam," *The National Interest*, 41: 48–57.

Porter, Theodore M. 1995. *Trust in Numbers: The Pursuit of Objectivity in Science and Public Life.* Princeton University Press.

Pustay, John S. 1965. *Counterinsurgency Warfare.* New York: Free Press.

Rangil, Teresa Tomás. 2010. "Rebellions across the (rice) fields: social scientists and Indochina, 1965–1976," *History of Political Economy* **42**: 105–30.

Ranstorp, Magnus. 2007. *Mapping Terrorism Research: State of the Art, Gaps and Future Direction*. Abingdon: Routledge.

Rapoport, David C., and Yonah Alexander (eds.). 1982. *The Rationalization of Terrorism*. Frederick, MD: Aletheia Books.

Reich, Walter (ed.). 1990. *Origins of Terrorism: Psychologies, Identities, States of Mind*. Cambridge University Press.

Reid, Edna F. 1983. "An analysis of terrorism literature: a bibliometric and content analysis study," PhD thesis, Faculty of the School of Library and Information Management, University of Southern California, Los Angeles.

Reid, Edna F. 1992. "Using online databases to analyze the development of a specialty: case study of terrorism," in Martha E. Williams (ed.), *The 13th National Online Meeting Proceedings – 1992*, 279–91. Medford, NJ: Learning Information.

Reid, Edna F. 1993. "Terrorism research and the diffusion of ideas," *Knowledge and Policy: International Journal of Knowledge Transfer and Utilization* **6**: 17–37.

Reid, Edna F. 1997. "Evolution of a body of knowledge: an analysis of terrorism research," *Information Processing and Management* **33**: 91–106.

Reid, Edna F., Jialun Qin, Wingyan Chung, Jennifer Xu, Yilu Zhou, Rob Schumaker, Marc Sageman, and Hsinchun Chen. 2004. "Terrorism knowledge discovery project: a knowledge discovery approach to addressing the threats of terrorism," in Hsinchun Chen, Reagan Moore, Daniel D. Zeng, and John Leavitt (eds.), *Intelligence and Security Informatics: Second Symposium on Intelligence and Security Informatics, ISI 2004, Tucson, AZ, USA, June 2004, Proceedings*, 125–45. Berlin: Springer-Verlag.

Richardson, Louise. 2006a. *The Roots of Terrorism*. Abingdon: Routledge.

Richardson, Louise. 2006b. *What Terrorists Want: Understanding the Enemy, Containing the Threat*. New York: Random House.

Ringer, Fritz. 1990. "The intellectual field, intellectual history, and the sociology of knowledge," *Theory and Society* **19**: 269–94.

Robin, Ron. 2001. *The Making of the Cold War Enemy: Culture and Politics in the Military– Intellectual Complex*. Princeton University Press.

Ross, Jeffrey Ian. 2004. "Taking stock of research methods and analysis on oppositional political terrorism," *American Sociologist* **35**: 26–37.

Roy, Olivier. 1999. *The Failure of Political Islam* (trans. Carol Volk), 2nd edn. London: I. B. Taurus.

Russell, Charles A., Leon J. Banker, Jr., and Bowman H. Miller. 1979. "Out-inventing the terrorist," in Yonah Alexander, David Carlton, and Paul Wilkinson (eds.), *Terrorism: Theory and Practice*, 3–42. Boulder, CO: Westview.

Sabetta, Anne R. 1977. "Annotated bibliography on terrorism," *Stanford Journal of International Studies* **12**: 157–64.

Said, Edward W. 1978. *Orientalism*. London: Penguin.

Said, Edward W. 1997. *Covering Islam: How the Media and the Experts Determine How We See the Rest of the World*, 2nd edn. London: Vintage.

Said, Edward W. 2001. "The essential terrorist," in Edward W. Said and Christopher Hitchens (eds.), *Blaming the Victims: Spurious Scholarship and the Palestinian Question*, 2nd edn, 147–56. New York: Verso.

Said, Edward W., and Christopher Hitchens (eds.). 2001. *Blaming the Victims: Spurious Scholarship and the Palestinian Question*, 2nd edn. New York: Verso.

Sardar, Ziauddin, and Merryl Wyn Davies. 2003. *Why Do People Hate America?*. New York: Disinformation Books.

Schlesinger, Philip, Graham Murdock, and Philip Elliot. 1983. *Televising "Terrorism": Political Violence in Popular Culture*. London: Comedia Publishing.

Schmid, Alex P. 1993. "The response problem as a definition problem," in Alex P. Schmid and Ronald D. Crelinsten (eds.), *Western Responses to Terrorism*, 7–13. London: Frank Cass.

Schmid, Alex P. 2011. *The Routledge Handbook of Terrorism Research*. Abingdon: Routledge.

Schmid, Alex P., and Albert J. Jongman. 1988. *Political Terrorism: A New Guide to Actors, Authors, Concepts, Data Bases, Theories, and Literature*. New Brunswick, NJ: Transaction Books.

Schorr, Daniel. 1981. "Tracing the thread of terrorism," *New York Times*, May 17: 2.

Schreiber, Jan. 1978. *The Ultimate Weapon: Terrorists and World Order*. New York: Morrow.

Scheuer, Michael. 2008. *Imperial Hubris: Why the West Is Losing the War on Terror*. Dulles, VA: Potomac Books.

Schudson, Michael. 2006. "The trouble with experts – and why democracies need them," *Theory and Society* **35**: 491–506.

Sciolino, Elaine. 1996. "The red menace is gone. But here's Islam," *New York Times*, January 21: E1.

Scott, James C. 1998. *Seeing Like a State: How Certain Schemes to Improve the Human Condition Have Failed*. New Haven, CT: Yale University Press.

Sewell, William H., Jr. 1996. "Historical events as transformations of structures: inventing revolution at the Bastille," *Theory and Society* **25**: 841–81.

Shafer, D. Michael. 1988. *Deadly Paradigms: The Failure of US Counterinsurgency Policy*. Princeton University Press.

Shapin, Steven. 1994. *A Social History of Truth*. University of Chicago Press.

Sheehan, Ivan Sascha. 2012. "Mapping contemporary terrorism courses at top-ranked national universities and liberal arts colleges in the United States," *Perspectives on Terrorism* **6**: 19–50.

Silke, Andrew. 2004a. "An introduction to terrorism research," in Andrew Silke (ed.), *Research on Terrorism: Trends, Achievements and Failures*, 1–29. London: Frank Cass.

Silke, Andrew. (ed.) 2004b. *Research on Terrorism: Trends, Achievements and Failures*. London: Frank Cass.

Silke, Andrew. 2009. "Contemporary terrorism studies: issues in research," in Richard Jackson, Marie Breen Smyth, and Jeroen Gunning (eds.), *Critical Terrorism Studies: A New Research Agenda*, 34–48. Abingdon: Routledge.

Simon, Jeffrey D., and Daniel Benjamin. 2000. "America and the new terrorism," *Survival* **42**: 59–75.

Slann, Martin, and Bernard Schechterman (eds.). 1987. *Multidimensional Terrorism*. Boulder, CO: Lynne Rienner Publishers.

Slater, Robert O., and Michael Stohl (eds.). 1988. *Current Perspectives on International Terrorism*. New York: St Martin's Press.

Sloan, Stephen, Richard Kearney, and Charles Wise. 1978. "Learning about terrorism: analysis, simulations, and future directions," *Terrorism: An International Journal* **1**: 315–29.

Smith, James A. 1991. *The Idea Brokers: Think Tanks and the Rise of the New Policy Elite*. New York: Free Press.

Solovey, Mark. 2001. "Project Camelot and the 1960s epistemological revolution: rethinking the politics–patronage–social science nexus," *Social Studies of Science* **31**: 171–206.

Sontag, Susan. 2001. "Talk of the town," *The New Yorker*, September 24: 32; available at www.newyorker.com/archive/2001/09/24/010924ta_talk_wtc#ixzz20H3NsbWx (accessed July 10, 2012).

Spjut, R. J. 1978. "A review of counter-insurgency theorists," *Political Quarterly* **49**: 54–64.

Sprinzak, Ehud. 1998. "The great superterrorism scare," *Foreign Policy* **112**: 110–24.

Sprinzak, Ehud. 2000. "Rational fanatics," *Foreign Policy* **120**: 66–73.

Sproat, Peter Alan. 1996. "The quantitative results of a questionnaire on state terrorism," *Terrorism and Political Violence* **8**: 64–86.

Stampnitzky, Lisa. 2011. "Disciplining an unruly field: terrorism studies and theories of scientific/intellectual production," *Qualitative Sociology* **34**: 1–19.

Stark, Laura. 2012. *Behind Closed Doors: IRBs and the Making of Ethical Research*. University of Chicago Press.

Sterling, Claire. 1981a. "Terrorism: tracing the international network," *New York Times Magazine*, March 1: 16–19, 24, 54–6, 58–60.

Sterling, Claire. 1981b. *The Terror Network: The Secret War of International Terrorism*. New York: Holt, Rinehart & Winston.

Stern, Jessica. 1999. *The Ultimate Terrorists*. Cambridge, MA: Harvard University Press.

Suskind, Ron. 2004. "Without a doubt," *New York Times Magazine*, October 17: 44–52.

Suskind, Ron. 2006. *The One Percent Doctrine: Deep Inside America's Pursuit of Its Enemies since 9/11*. New York: Simon & Schuster.

Swidler, Ann. 1986. "Culture in action: symbols and strategies," *American Sociological Review* 51: 273–86.

Szulc, Tad. 1972a. "Nixon tightens security in US against 'outlaws,'" *New York Times*, September 6: 1.

Szulc, Tad. 1972b. "US moves for world campaign to counter political terrorists," *New York Times*, September 7: 1.

Thayer, Charles W. 1963. *Guerrilla*. New York: Harper & Row.

Thomas, William I., and Dorothy Swaine Thomas. 1929. *The Child in America: Behavior Problems and Programs*. New York: Alfred A. Knopf.

Thompson, Robert. 1966. *Defeating Communist Insurgency: The Lessons of Malaya and Vietnam*. New York: Praeger.

Thornton, Thomas. 1964. "Terror as a weapon of political agitation," in Harry Eckstein (ed.), *Internal War: Problems and Approaches*, 71–99. New York: Free Press of Glencoe.

Tilly, Charles. 2004. "Terror, terrorism, terrorists," *Sociological Theory* **22**: 5–13.

Timmermans, Stefan, and Steven Epstein. 2010. "A world of standards but not a standard world: toward a sociology of standards and standardization," *Annual Review of Sociology* 36: 69–89.

Toolis, Kevin. 2004. "Rise of the terrorist professors," *New Statesman*, June 14: 26–7.

Trinquier, Roger. 2006 [1961]. *Modern Warfare: A French View of Counterinsurgency* (trans. Daniel Lee). Westport, CT: Praeger Security International.

Tucker, David. 1997. *Skirmishes at the Edge of Empire: The United States and International Terrorism*. Westport, CT: Praeger.

US Army. 1975. "Annotated bibliography on transnational terrorism," presented at 7th Security Analysis Symposium of the Foreign Area Officer Course, US Army Institute for Military Assistance, Fort Bragg, NC.

US Department of Justice. 1975. "Terrorist activities: bibliography," FBI Academy, Quantico, VA.

US Department of State. 1976. "Unclassified bibliography on terrorism," Department of State, Washington, DC.

US Defense Intelligence Agency. 1985. *Symposium on International Terrorism, 2–3 December 1985, Defense Intelligence Agency, Washington, DC*. Washington, DC: DIA.

Vitas, Robert A., and John Allen Williams. 1996. *US National Security Policy and Strategy, 1987–1994*. Westport, CT: Greenwood Press.

Wagner-Pacifici, Robin. 1986. *The Moro Morality Play: Terrorism as Social Drama*. University of Chicago Press.

Wagner-Pacifici, Robin. 1995. *Discourse and Destruction: The City of Philadelphia versus MOVE*. University of Chicago Press.

Wallace-Wells, Benjamin. 2006. "Private jihad: how Rita Katz got into the spying business," *The New Yorker*, May 29: 28–41.

Walter, Eugene V. 1964. "Violence and the process of terror," *American Sociological Review* **29**: 248–57.

Weaver, R. Kent. 1989. "The changing world of think tanks," *PS: Political Science and Politics* **22**: 563–78.

Weber, Max. 1978 [1922]. *Economy and Society: An Outline of Interpretive Sociology* (trans. Guenther Roth and Claus Wittich). Berkeley: University of California Press.

Weinberger, Casper W., and US Department of Defense. 1986. *Proceedings of the Low-Intensity Warfare Conference, 14–15 January 1986*. Washington, DC: Department of Defense.

Wicker, Tom. 1981. "In the nation: the great terrorist hunt," *New York Times*, May 5: A23.

Wieviorka, Michel. 1995. "Terrorism in the context of academic research," in Martha Crenshaw (ed.), *Terrorism in Context*, 597–606. University Park: Pennsylvania State University Press.

Wilkinson, Paul. 1974. *Political Terrorism*. London: Macmillan.

Wilkinson, Paul. 2007. "Research into terrorism studies: achievements and failures," in Magnus Ranstorp (ed.), *Mapping Terrorism Research: State of the Art, Gaps and Future Direction*, 316–28. Abingdon: Routledge.

Wilkinson, Paul, and Alasdair M. Stewart (eds.). 1987. *Contemporary Research on Terrorism*. Aberdeen University Press.

Wilson, James Q. 1981. "Thinking about terrorism," *Commentary*, July: 34–9.

Wolfe, Alan. 2011. *Political Evil: What It Is and How to Combat It*. New York: Alfred A. Knopf.

Woodward, Bob. 1987. *Veil: The Secret Wars of the CIA 1981–1987*. New York: Simon & Schuster.

Woodward, Bob. 2002. *Bush at War*. New York: Simon & Schuster.

Worthington, Roger. 1981. "Training for terror: the Soviet connection," *Chicago Tribune*, May 11: 2.

Wright, Susan. 2007. "Terrorists and biological weapons: forging the linkage in the Clinton administration," *Politics and the Life Sciences* **25**: 57–115.

Zelizer, Viviana. 2006. "Why and how to read *Why?*," *Qualitative Sociology* **29**: 531–4.

Zimmerman, Doron. 2004. "Terrorism transformed: the 'new terrorism,' impact scalability, and the dynamic of reciprocal threat perception," *Quarterly Journal* **3**: 19–39.

Zulaika, Joseba. 2012. "Drones, witches and other flying objects: the force of fantasy in US counterterrorism," *Critical Studies on Terrorism* **5**: 51–68.

Zulaika, Joseba, and William A. Douglass. 1996. *Terror and Taboo: The Follies, Fables and Faces of Terrorism*. New York: Routledge.

Index

CPSIA information can be obtained at www.ICGtesting.com
Printed in the USA
BVOW08s0254070814

361954BV00006B/111/P

390